ABORTION
&
COMMON SENSE

ABORTION

&

COMMON SENSE

Ruth Dixon-Mueller, Ph.D.
Paul K.B. Dagg, M.D.

This book was printed in the United States of America.

To order additional copies of this book, contact:
Xlibris Corporation
1-888-795-4274
www.Xlibris.com
Orders@Xlibris.com
15400

CONTENTS

INTRODUCTION

"Abortion is a subject that is embroiled in fierce debate . . . .
The heat of the conflict tends to melt boundaries between
medicine and philosophy, between church and state,
between demonstrated fact and personal belief. The
legislative and judicial outcome of this debate may
profoundly affect both the physical and psychological health
of the population as well as the practice of medicine." Nada
L. Stotland, *Journal of the American Medical Association*

Abortion. Is there another word these days that, when uttered
in public, elicits stronger emotions, more deeply held
convictions, more divisive debate? Yet abortion, like sex, is a fact of
life. Despite people's best efforts at trying to avoid unwanted
conceptions (or because they didn't use anything at all), an estimated
38 percent of all known pregnancies worldwide happen
unintentionally. And when a woman gets pregnant without
intending or wanting to—whether outside of marriage, or as the
result of violence, or when she and her husband already have all
the children they want or are able to care for, or when her health is
at risk—the pressures to interrupt the pregnancy can be intense.

About half of all unintended pregnancies in the world end in
induced abortion. Of the estimated forty-six million women who
terminate an unwanted pregnancy every year, almost four-fifths
live in developing countries. Some terminate their pregnancies safely
and legally, others are forced to do so clandestinely and often

dangerously. Many girls and women die or suffer terribly at the hands of unskilled practitioners or from their attempts to self-induce. The World Health Organization estimates that eighty thousand women lose their lives unnecessarily every year and uncounted numbers are infected or injured from the complications of botched procedures.

Women who are desperate to terminate an unwanted pregnancy often face strong moral or religious condemnations of their actions. But like the fear of physical harm, the threat of social condemnation must also be endured. As we shall see in this book, religious and moral values are one thing, practicalities another. It can be easy and costless to get (someone) pregnant, difficult and costly to raise a child. Faced with the birth of a child she does not want, or wants but cannot care for, a woman will often choose practicalities over moralities. "I had to do it," she will say. "I had no other choice."

This is a book about the practicalities of abortion. At a time when the rhetoric is highly charged with emotion and the terrain is littered with unscientific statements, ethical accusations, and sometimes violently held opinions, we hope to introduce a fact-based, *common sense* account of how and why women have abortions and what can be done to make them safe. We are not seeking to stake out some elusive common ground in this contentious terrain, for there is probably none. Rather, we want to counter myth with reality, fiction with fact. We want to describe the concrete dilemmas confronting women who have unwanted pregnancies in our own society and in all parts of the world and to consider, pragmatically, how these dilemmas can be resolved through sound social and medical policies.

The facts about abortion are often startling. But what to make of these facts is not always obvious. A common-sense approach to abortion must raise questions about the consequences to women's and men's lives, to children and families, and to society as a whole of certain laws, public policies, and widely held opinions. Thus, in addition to the medical, safety, legal, and personal issues, we look closely at what it means when people say they believe in a qualified right to abortion that would limit the reasons allowed for legal terminations or set restrictions on those who are seeking safe services. We ask what happens when a government will not fund the full range of reproductive health care services for girls and women who cannot afford to pay. We examine the consequences of the refusal on the part of some doctors and health facilities to refer women to safe providers in countries where abortion has been established as a woman's legal right. We explore the results of US foreign policy on women's access to family planning in developing countries. And, in the midst of the war of words over the right to liberty of the pregnant woman versus the right to life of the fetus, we raise the question of the rights of the living child to be wanted and nurtured by its parents.

As scientists (one social, one medical), we believe that it is not only possible but also necessary to find workable solutions to the common problem of what to do when a woman—adolescent or adult, married or not—finds herself unintentionally pregnant and does not want to, or is not able to, have the child. In Part One, "Private Lives," we explore a variety of personal, social, economic, and health issues affecting women and couples in their efforts to regulate their fertility and the role that safe and unsafe abortion plays in this endeavor. In Part Two, "Public Settings," we look at the legal, medical, and political institutions that shape the environment in which abortion occurs. How responsive are these institutions to the needs of women and families? How do their ideologies and practices affect women's access to reproductive health care?

While the primary focus of the book is on Canada and the United States, we have placed the North American experience in a broader historical and geographical context. In doing so, we can see that abortion means quite different things in different cultures; that it has not always been condemned even in Western societies; that it was widely practiced in the United States (and probably Canada) in the nineteenth and early twentieth centuries when it was a criminal offense; that religious interpretations of whether the early interruption of pregnancy is a sin are by no means uniform or consistent; and that indigenous methods of "bringing down" the menstrual period or inducing miscarriage have been part of the fertility-regulating repertoire of human beings in virtually all cultures since the beginnings of recorded history. We can also see how the legal situation in Canada and the United States, and the proportions of pregnancies that end in abortion, compare with European countries and with the developing countries of the world.

Evidence suggests that regardless of the moral, religious, legal, medical, and social impediments placed in its way, abortion has always been with us and it always will be. Because no group of people anywhere practices universally effective contraception, and because individuals and couples increasingly want to have children only if and when they plan to, unwanted conceptions are bound to occur. And because so many of these unwanted conceptions are profoundly distressing to those who experience them, some women will decide, alone or with their partners, not to carry the pregnancy to term. In our view, then, the key question is not how to *prevent* women from having an early, safe abortion (in which case they will have a late or unsafe one, or bear an unwanted child against their will). Rather, it is how to ensure that those abortions that do occur are performed correctly, legally, and humanely. In this light, safe abortion can be understood as a normal part of good medical care and of a sane and compassionate social policy.

Ruth Dixon-Mueller, Ph.D.
Paul K. B. Dagg, M.D.

QUICK QUIZ:
TEST YOURSELF

True or false? Read these statements about abortion and circle the answer that you think applies. Then check the answers below. (You may be surprised!)

1. The practice of induced abortion is quite a recent phenomenon, historically speaking. It was unknown in the ancient world. T/F

2. The major professional associations of obstetricians and gynecologists agree that a pregnancy begins at the moment of conception. T/F

3. The highest probability of getting pregnant occurs when a woman has sexual intercourse on the day that she ovulates. T/F

4. After a woman has a baby she is not at risk of getting pregnant again until after she resumes menstruation. T/F

5. The most popular (widely used) method of contraception in the United States today is the pill. T/F

6. Once fertilization takes place, the fertilized ovum implants itself almost immediately in the uterus and starts to grow. T/F

7. The "morning after pill" (emergency contraception) has to be taken within 24 hours of having unprotected sex. If not, it doesn't work. T/F

8. Despite improvements in surgical abortion techniques, it's still more dangerous to have an abortion than to have a baby. T/F

9. Before abortion was legalized in the United States by the Supreme Court in 1973, there were far fewer abortions than there are now. T/F

10. The Roman Catholic Church has always been absolutely opposed to abortion at whatever stage of gestation because it has always held the position that the fetus acquires a soul the moment it is conceived. T/F

11. Abortion is a complicated procedure that requires extensive training and can be performed only by a qualified medical doctor. T/F

12. In Canada, none of the provincial health insurance plans covers the costs of elective abortions, whether performed in clinics or hospitals. T/F

13. In the United States, the federal Medicaid program reimburses states for abortions for low-income women who are eligible for medical assistance. T/F

14. Every year in the United States the rate of teenage pregnancies is going up because more adolescents are having unprotected sex, and at younger ages. T/F

15. In general, abortion rates are much lower in Catholic countries

than they are in non-Catholic countries throughout the world. T/F

16. Research shows that most women suffer intense feelings of guilt, depression, or regret following an abortion. T/F

17. One problem with having even a safe abortion is that the woman may have trouble conceiving again or carrying a pregnancy to term. T/F

18. At least eight or nine of every ten Canadian and American women will never have an induced abortion. T/F

19. The so-called abortion drug RU 486 (mifepristone) has not yet been adequately tested for safety and effectiveness in large populations. T/F

20. The technique of early vacuum aspiration ("menstrual regulation") requires complicated equipment that is too costly for most health systems in developing countries. T/F

21. For medical students graduating from residency programs in obstetrics and gynecology in the United States and Canada, training in the routine performance of early abortions is a requirement for certification. T/F

22. The danger from antiabortion protesters to clinic providers and staff has been exaggerated. Although there have been some incidents of violence, these are limited to a small number of clinics in a few states. T/F

23. The American public is very divided on the question of whether the government should fund contraceptive services for poor women as part of their overall health care. T/F

24. The idea that life begins at conception and must be protected from that point forward represents the majority opininion in the United States. T/F

25. Prolife groups in the United States who want to make abortion illegal all agree that an exception should be made for saving the woman's life. T/F

ALL OF THESE STATEMENTS ARE FALSE. If you marked five or more as true, you really need to read this book!

PART I:
PRIVATE LIVES

CHAPTER ONE

Regulating Our Fertility:
Ancient Customs, Current Practices

"To cause a woman to stop [terminate] pregnancy in the first, second or third period [trimester]: Unripe fruit of acacia; Colocynth; Dates; Triturate with 6/7th pint of honey. Moisten a pessary of plant fiber [with the mixture] and place in the vagina." Recipe for abortion on a papyrus scroll in Egypt dated about 1550 BCE, in John M. Riddle, *Eve's Herbs*

Abortion is probably the principal means by which women throughout history have limited their fertility. Even today, with high levels of contraceptive use in most developed countries and rising levels in most developing nations, abortion plays a major role. Among the many traditional methods on which people throughout the world rely for avoiding an unwanted pregnancy, many are harmless, some are dangerous, and almost all are ineffective. Among the modern methods with which we are most familiar, most are safe to use (with certain precautions) but almost all carry some risk, however slight, of accidental pregnancy. In addition, many couples who say they don't want to have a child right away are not using any method to avoid conception, or are using it only sporadically. The sex act itself may be unplanned or unwanted, which often means that the woman is not protected.

For all of these reasons and more, accidental pregnancies are bound to occur. In the United States and Canada *about half* of all pregnancies are unintended, either coming at the wrong time or not wanted at all.

Among typical couples in the United States who rely on contraceptive methods such as periodic abstinence (rhythm), withdrawal (pulling out), or diaphragms, sponges or cervical caps, from 20 to 25 percent will get pregnant within one year. Fourteen percent of regular condom users will have an accidental pregnancy within the year, compared with 5 percent of pill users and fewer than 2 percent of women with an intrauterine device (IUD). Reported in Robert A. Hatcher and colleagues, *Contraceptive Technology*

In this chapter we consider abortion as one among many fertility-regulating practices. By placing it in this context, we hope to demonstrate not only why the option of safe early abortion will always be needed as a backup in cases of contraceptive failure or nonuse, but also why, for some women at some point in their lives, having an abortion may be the most logical choice when compared with other methods of family planning. In subsequent chapters we examine more closely how women make the decision of whether or not to terminate an unwanted pregnancy, how various laws and policies serve to limit their options, and what the consequences are of these limitations to women, families, and society at large.

Setting the stage

Most human beings have a remarkable natural capacity to reproduce. If a woman has her first menstrual period before age fifteen and enters menopause after age forty-five, she has a potential reproductive span of at least thirty years. If she is sexually active throughout this period, if she and her mate have no fertility impairments, if they are not practicing any method of birth control, and if she does not breastfeed, she could get pregnant every eighteen months or so and bear twenty children. Even if she has her first baby at age twenty and breastfeeds each one for a year, she could give birth twelve times. Is it any wonder, then, that women have always had an interest in regulating their fertility? That down through the ages they have whispered recipes to one another for "women's medicines" intended to prevent conception or "bring down" the menstrual period?

Induced abortion was a familiar practice in classical Greek and Roman times. The oldest known medical texts describing techniques of abortion appeared in China about 2727 BCE, more than four thousand seven hundred years ago. From Norman L. Himes, *The Medical History of Contraception*

In most societies, of course, women do not have sexual relations throughout all of their reproductive years. Social norms relating to the age at which people marry or start living together, the likelihood of the relationship's ending in divorce or the death or departure of one partner; whether women marry or remarry at all; and negative attitudes toward sex and reproduction outside of socially approved arrangements can limit a woman's potential childbearing years considerably. Even within socially accepted sexual unions, most women clearly do not produce children every eighteen months. Indeed, the array of traditional methods identified throughout the world for avoiding this outcome—plus those created by modern science—reveals a remarkable degree of human ingenuity.

Most of us think of family planning as consisting of contraception and abortion. But the range of possibilities is broader than that.

At one extreme, one may abstain from sexual intercourse entirely and live a celibate life. At the other extreme, one may take certain steps following the birth of an unwanted child such as giving the baby away, committing infanticide, or letting God or Fate "take" those who are sickly, or of the wrong sex, or born at the wrong time or in the wrong circumstances. In pre-industrial Europe and North America, for example, it was not unusual for one in every five or six newborns to die within the first year. Although most deaths were of natural causes, some were undoubtedly due to deliberate exposure and neglect. Practices of concealed infanticide and child abandonment are still found in many countries today.

In Paris in the second half of the eighteenth century, even given the common practice of aborting unwanted pregnancies, there were twenty to forty "foundlings" for every hundred births. In the decade before the Revolution, about forty thousand infants were abandoned every year on the doorsteps of orphanages, convents, and hospitals. Reported in Rosalind Pollack Petchesky, *Abortion and Woman's Choice: The State, Sexuality, and Reproductive Freedom*

"In Bombay at least one hospital has a small cot at the entrance where a mother may come secretly at night and abandon her child. Sometimes mothers flee the maternity ward leaving their newborn infants behind as they have no prospects of supporting yet another child." Malcom Potts, Peter Diggory, and John Peel, *Abortion*

In between these extremes of abstinence and infanticide or abandonment, the distinction between preventing and terminating a pregnancy—that is, between contraception and abortion—is not always as clear or culturally meaningful as we might expect. A woman in pre-industrial Europe or America who took herbal potions to ensure that her menstrual period was regular was unlikely to think of this practice as abortion. Rather, it was *animation* or *quickening*—the first recognizable stirrings of the fetus in the womb—that defined the beginning of life. The marker of quickening is also used in some abortion laws and religious interpretations today. Indeed, the time that passes between the onset of a menstrual delay and the clear establishment of a pregnancy (or non-pregnancy) is an extremely interesting one from the scientific and cultural points of view.

Of all women worldwide who get pregnant each year, only 63 percent give birth to a live baby. Among the remainder about 15 percent miscarry or have a stillbirth while another 22 percent—more than one in five—end their pregnancy by induced abortion. From the Alan Guttmacher Institute, *Sharing Responsibility: Women, Society and Abortion Worldwide*

For most people, the choice of a birth control method (if one is desired) has never been easy. In considering the role that abortion plays in this age-old human drama, let's begin at the beginning. If one does not live a celibate life, then we must begin with sex.

" . . . this whole business of sexual intercourse"

Every society recognizes certain types of relationships in which intercourse is permitted and others where sexual contact is frowned upon or strictly forbidden. The punishment for violating the rules in conservative cultures may be ostracism or even death, usually for the woman. In addition, the nature and frequency of sexual acts within recognized unions are typically regulated by a variety of social norms and taboos. What amount of sexual activity is considered excessive, what "normal"? When should intercourse be avoided? What particular sexual practices are shunned? How do these expectations differ across cultures, among couples, and from one individual to another?

The frequency of sex

"I am told by my girlfriends, I guess he is like all men, they only care for their own satisfaction, and they want it all the time, every night, and you . . . you get fed up, I am fed up because I'm fed up." Gabriela, a young woman in Sonora, Mexico, quoted in Rosalind P. Petchesky and Karen Judd, *Negotiating Reproductive Rights: Women's Perspectives Across Countries and Cultures*

The frequency of intercourse offers an interesting example of variation in human behavior. A survey of three thousand women in the United States by Robert Michael and colleagues found that 39 percent of wives said they have sex twice a week or more, compared with 56 percent of unmarried women living with their partners. As we might expect, sexual activity declines somewhat with age and duration of the union. In Alfred Kinsey's study of *Sexual Behavior in the Human Female* in the 1950s, for example, women reported overall averages of two to three times a week, ranging from 3.7 acts of intercourse among those ages fifteen through nineteen to 1.7 at ages forty-one through forty-six.

Perhaps it goes without saying that the more often a woman has unprotected sex the more likely she is to get pregnant, but the statistics are interesting. Among American couples with no fertility impairments, about *one-half* of all women having intercourse two or three times a week will get pregnant within six months. This compares with one-third of those having sex once a week and one-sixth of those having sex just a few times a month.

"The average woman in an industrialized country is actually pregnant or attempting to become pregnant for only 10 percent of her reproductive life; for the other 90 percent, she is trying to postpone giving birth or avoid having more births." Jacqueline Darroch Forrest, *in Contemporary Obstetrics and Gynecology*

American women in the nineteenth century who had few options for limiting their fertility were only too aware that any act of intercourse could result in yet another pregnancy. At a time when many wives suffered ill health or died young from the consequences of repeated childbearing, early feminists promoted the revolutionary concept of *voluntary motherhood.* "Man in his lust has regulated long enough this whole question of sexual intercourse" wrote crusader Elizabeth Cady Stanton in 1853. Men were urged to practice "cooperative self-denial" while women were told, perhaps unrealistically, that they had the right to refuse their husband's sexual demands.

This notion of voluntary self-restraint regarding the frequency of intercourse is sometimes extended to longer periods of sexual abstinence within marriage as a means of spacing or stopping childbearing. In some sub-Saharan African cultures, for example, sexual taboos require that couples abstain following the birth of a child. Although the practice is declining under the impact of modernization and the spread of other methods of contraception, a husband may avoid having sexual relations with his wife (although not necessarily with other women) for anywhere from a few months up to two years. In other societies—in parts of South Asia, for example—a woman is expected to stop having intercourse once she becomes a grandmother. This may happen when she is still in her early thirties if she and her sons or daughters marry young.

Whereas some sexual practices and taboos reduce the possibility of pregnancy, others raise it. An example of the latter is the menstrual taboo. Many people share the belief that it is wrong to have sex during the days of a woman's menstrual period or even past that time if she is still considered "impure" or "unclean." Indeed, intercourse on these days is condemned in the Old Testament. Other cultural taboos forbid intercourse on certain holy days, or during periods of mourning, or preceding or following other important events. To the extent that such restrictions serve to concentrate sexual intercourse in the time of the month when conception is most likely to occur (assuming no contraception), more pregnancies will inevitably result.

The risk of pregnancy from a single act of unprotected intercourse of a fertile couple runs as high as 26 to 30 percent at or near the midcycle. Eight or nine of every ten fertile couples having frequent unprotected sexual intercourse will conceive within a year. From Robert A. Hatcher and colleagues, *Contraceptive Technology*

The timing of sex

This brings us to the practice of periodic monthly abstinence, otherwise known as rhythm, fertility awareness, or natural family planning. Is it really possible to prevent pregnancy by avoiding intercourse on the woman's most fertile days?

During a woman's monthly cycle, the average likelihood of conceiving following a single act of unprotected intercourse rises from zero on the fifth day before ovulation to as high as 30 percent on the day *immediately preceding* ovulation. If the couple has sex on this day, perhaps one or two hundred of the millions of sperm deposited in the woman's body will have arrived at their destination high in the fallopian tubes. Here they will be ready to fertilize the egg (although only one will succeed, if any do) within hours if not minutes of its release by the ovary. The probability of conception drops to 15 percent on the *actual* day of ovulation, however, because the ovum has only a few hours to be fertilized as it moves down the fallopian tube. Sperm deposited on that day may not reach the ovum in time. The probabilities decline to zero for intercourse on the third day following ovulation and continue at zero through the next menstruation.

It was not until the early 1930s that researchers identified the precise time during the woman's monthly cycle in which sexual intercourse is most likely to result in conception. Even now, many couples who think they are practicing "rhythm" have got it all wrong. Norman E. Himes, *The Medical History of Contraception*

The big question for those attempting to avoid conception is, of course, what day will ovulation occur? Typically, this will be fourteen days before the *next* menstrual period. The problem with this guideline is that it's something like telling a friend to turn left to your house half a mile *before* the bridge. If a woman's period always arrives on the predicted day regardless of the length of her cycle, then it is possible to calculate backwards from the expected day of the next period. A woman with a twenty-eight-day cycle should be able to avoid pregnancy by not having intercourse (or by using contraception) for seven full days, that is, from day ten since the beginning of her last menstrual period to day seventeen. With a thirty-day cycle, from day twelve to day nineteen, and so on. If she is lucky.

For the majority of women who do not have regular periods, however, circling the safe and unsafe days on a calendar is a tricky business. The greater the irregularity, the larger the number of unsafe days. Two weeks of total abstinence or alternative forms of sexual expression or contraception are not unusual. This is why couples are urged to use more scientifically accurate methods of assessing the time of ovulation, such as measuring very slight changes in the woman's basal body temperature (the Billings method) or in the consistency of her cervical mucus.

Among hypothetical perfect users, failure rates will range from about 1 to 9 percent per consistent year of use, depending on the method. (The calendar is the least reliable.) Among typical users the failure rate is about 25 percent per year. True, avoiding intercourse on possibly fertile days is better than nothing. We noted earlier that among couples with no fertility impairments who have frequent unprotected intercourse, eight or nine of every ten will have a pregnancy within the year. In fact, failure to achieve pregnancy under these conditions is taken as a sign that there may be fertility impairments. Nevertheless, those who really don't want to have a baby right away and will not consider abortion as an option should be using a more effective method.

From crocodile dung to RU 486:

recipes for all seasons

It hasn't always been understood exactly how conception occurs, but most cultures have seized on the idea that the male ejaculate "plants the seed" in the woman even if her own contribution may be unacknowledged. Some embellish the description with the belief that a man should have repeated intercourse with his pregnant wife in order to nourish the growing fetus with his "milk." Thus it is not surprising that accounts of contraceptive practices through the ages include many methods of preventing the semen from entering the woman's body, such as withdrawal and ejaculation outside the vagina (coitus interruptus), the use of penis sheaths (condoms), and some quite ingenious vaginal plugs and douches.

Diverting the sperm from their course

Like periodic abstinence, relying on "pulling out" just before the man ejaculates can be a challenge. Mentioned in the Old Testament as the sin of Onan who spills his seed on the ground to avoid impregnating his brother's widow (which he was required to do under the rules of levirate marriage, or "widow inheritance"), withdrawal is still widely practiced among married couples in some Eastern and Southern European countries and in parts of the Middle East. Although it is unreliable as a method for particular couples, when widely used in a population it can have an observable impact on the birth rate.

Pulling out in time requires practice and self-control, however. Moreover, the concentration of sperm in the first emissions that precede the male orgasm ensures that some transmission will occur even if the sex act is interrupted. Among perfect practitioners of the art, scientists estimate that perhaps 4 percent of couples will get pregnant in the first year of consistent use. Compare this with a failure rate of almost 20 percent—one in five—among the rest of us.

As early as 1564 AD, the Italian anatomist Fallopius (whose name now graces certain parts of the female anatomy) described the use of linen penis sheaths for protection from pregnancy. The invention of vulcanized rubber in the 1840s allowed the mass production of condoms (or "rubbers") which were widely advertised in Europe and North America for protection from disease and "bastardy." Norman E. Himes, *The Medical History of Contraception*

Penis sheaths made from linen cloth, animal intestines or other substances for the purposes of contraception (not just for masculine adornment, which is quite another matter) are described from early times. Now, of course, thin latex and polyurethane condoms treated with lubricants and spermicides, some in rainbow colors, some with molded ribs and other sensual accouterments, are sold almost everywhere.

With the worldwide crisis of sexually transmitted infections and HIV/AIDS, condoms have become the method of choice for disease protection as well as contraception in non-marital relations. Unfortunately, their association with casual sex and prostitution has worked against their adoption by couples in long-term relationships. In very few countries are condoms commonly used by married couples, Japan being the major exception. Current estimates of failure rates during the first year are about 3 percent among perfect users, but 14 percent among typical users who may not wear the condom correctly or use it every time.

The federal Comstock Law in the United States, which was passed in 1873 and not repealed until 1971, forbade the importation or distribution of birth control information or supplies such as condoms or diaphragms on the grounds that they were obscene. In the early 1960s it was still a felony in some states for physicians to give out contraceptive information. Not until 1965 did the US Supreme Court, in the case of *Griswold v. Connecticut,* establish a married couple's right to privacy in the use of contraception. See Ellen Chesler, *Woman of Valor: Margaret Sanger and the Birth Control Movement in America*

Sperm can also be stopped in their course by cutting and tying or clamping the *vas deferens* through which they pass to mix with seminal fluid at the time of ejaculation. The technique of performing a vasectomy is now quite simple and quick; it can generally be done in twenty minutes or so in a clinic or doctor's office. A test is done a few weeks later to make sure that the ejaculate contains no sperm, which are still produced in the testicles but are harmlessly absorbed. Vasectomy is virtually 100 percent effective if the surgery was performed correctly and the *vas* does not spontaneously reconnect.

Vaginal barricades and douches

Just as men try to prevent their semen from entering the woman's body, women have traditionally relied on their own devices. These include barricading the cervical opening with pessaries or suppositories (wax and opium balls have been cited in the historical literature) or with primitive diaphragms (hollowed out halves of lemon, for example), wads of elephant or crocodile dung (if you can find it), leaves, sponges, and whatever else is at hand. After having sex some women douche themselves with oils, lemon juice, bicarbonate of soda, tannic acid, or Coca-Cola. Like the practice of withdrawal, however, postcoital douches typically come too late. Coughing, sneezing, jumping up and down, wiping out the vagina, urinating, and other efforts to expel the semen are as common as they are ineffective, especially among teenage girls who lack the information they need.

Most of these vaginal methods of diverting sperm from their course have more reliable scientific equivalents, such as the newly developed female condom. Rubber diaphragms (more popular in the 1950s before the advent of the contraceptive pill), cervical caps, and vaginal sponges treated with chemical spermicides such as nonoxonal-9 derive from ancient cervical blocking methods. Most vaginal barriers require correct fit, faithful use, careful insertion, and continued placement for up to eight hours following intercourse if they are to do their job. Because failure rates—averaging about

20 percent per year for typical users—vary significantly by method and in different populations, experts recommend that women who have frequent intercourse should *not* rely on these methods if they really want to avoid pregnancy. Spermicidal creams, jellies, foams, and suppositories available from pharmacies are even less reliable when used alone than are most barrier methods, with a first-year failure rate among typical users of up to 25 percent.

Suppressing ovulation

Frequent and intense breastfeeding has the natural physiological effect of suppressing ovulation (and thus menstruation) for an unpredictable length of time. Women in many cultures have relied on prolonged breastfeeding to lengthen the time between pregnancies, but it is never certain just when ovulation will resume. Unfortunately, it can occur two weeks *before* the first menstrual period which would normally serve as a warning sign. The longer a woman breastfeeds, the more likely it is that she will ovulate before her periods resume.

Most breastfeeding women do not ovulate for four to twelve months after delivery, and up to twenty-four months if they are not supplementing breast milk with other foods. In contrast, many women who are not breastfeeding resume ovulation *one or two months after childbirth*, which exposes them to the risk of immediate pregnancy. Robert A. Hatcher and colleagues, *Contraceptive Technology*

On a society-wide basis where prolonged and frequent nursing is common and couples are not using other methods to prevent pregnancy, as in parts of South Asia or sub-Saharan Africa, the overall contraceptive effects of breastfeeding are quite remarkable. For individual women, however, relying on breastfeeding to prevent pregnancy—and on the return of bleeding to signal when fertility has resumed—is not a good idea. This is especially the case in North America and Europe where new mothers who do breastfeed (and many don't) use supplementary feedings almost from the beginning.

Ovulation can also be suppressed artificially with the use of hormones that mimic a state of pregnancy. The introduction of combined oral contraceptive pills in the mid-1950s reflected a major breakthrough in our scientific understanding of the role of progesterone and estrogen in the natural cycle. Although oral contraceptives work primarily by inhibiting ovulation, synthetic hormones also interfere with the movement of sperm by thickening the cervical mucus as well as altering the uterine lining, which hampers implantation. The side effects reported for earlier pills have been almost eliminated with the development of low-dose pills and some that are estrogen-free.

"**Progestin-only pills (POPs) are variants** of the more commonly used combined (estrogen and progestin) oral contraceptives. Because POPs have no estrogen and only very small amounts of progestin, they are sometimes called 'minipills.' . . . A POP is taken every day of the month, even during menstrual periods. It can be started as early as a week after childbirth or immediately after a miscarriage or abortion." Beverly Winikoff and Suzanne Wymelenberg, *The Whole Truth About Contraception*

When used perfectly, the pill is a highly effective method with a first-year failure rate of only one woman in one thousand. Yet many factors can interfere with its effectiveness, such as taking other medications at the same time. The low-dose (mini) pills are particularly demanding of correct use, which means not only taking them every day but also at the *same time* every day. No forgetting, no skipping, no waiting until later. After missing one or more pills—especially at the beginning of a cycle—a woman may be fertile for the rest of the month even if she resumes taking the pill. This is why among typical users about 5 percent, or one woman in twenty, will get pregnant within the year.

Even more effective are the injections, subdermal (skin) implants, and treated vaginal rings that transmit a very low but steady supply of synthetic progestin into the body. Depo-Provera and other injectables such as NET can provide three to six months of protection depending on the brand. Norplant, consisting of six flexible match-like tubes that are inserted under the skin of the inner arm, provides seven years of protection, while other treated subdermal implants are designed for equivalent or shorter periods. Once the implanted capsules are removed, the contraceptive effects wear off quickly and a new pregnancy can be started. Implants are as effective as male or female sterilization (virtually no accidental pregnancies) and can be reversed (removed) or extended (replaced when the protection ends) as one may wish. Injectables are also reliable but only if the woman returns to the clinic at the specified time for her next shot.

The ultimate method for blocking the ovum, of course, is to cut and tie the fallopian tubes that lead from the ovaries to the uterus. Ovulation takes place but the released egg, having nowhere to go, is absorbed and dissipated, just like the sperm in the man's blocked *vas deferens*. Although tubal ligation is more complicated than vasectomy, it is very safe when performed by trained clinicians. A woman can be sterilized with the use of a local anesthetic immediately after giving birth or having an abortion or, at other times, on an outpatient basis with local anesthesia and light sedation. When the procedure is performed correctly, accidental pregnancy rates are close to zero.

Despite legal restrictions that limit access in many countries, contraceptive sterilization among women and men has become the most widely used method of family planning in the world. Almost everywhere, more women than men choose this method. In the US alone, over one million procedures are performed every year. See Robert A. Hatcher and colleagues, *Contraceptive Technology*; United Nations, *Levels and Trends in Contraceptive Use*

Inhibiting implantation

Not only must the sperm pass through the uterus to reach the fallopian tubes, but if fertilization does occur, the fertilized egg, or *blastocyst*, must attach itself successfully to the uterine lining and stay there. For this reason, anything that alters the uterine environment may inhibit the establishment of a pregnancy.

It is said that camel herders in the Saharan desert insert smooth pebbles into the wombs of their she-camels so that they will not get pregnant on long treks, and that in Japan, high-class geishas had apparatuses inserted to prevent pregnancy. If these and other such stories are true, then the intra-uterine device (IUD) has a colorful history. Nowadays, IUDs are rather neat little gadgets of different shapes made from polyethylene (the Lippes loop, for example), copper (the Copper T), silver, or stainless steel (the single-coil ring). Some models release synthetic hormones or other contraceptive substances. Only two types are approved for marketing in the United States. One is treated with progesterone, which lasts for one year; another with copper that lasts up to ten years. Because of its high level of use in China, the IUD is the second most common contraceptive in the world, after sterilization.

Scientists still do not fully understand precisely how these small devices work. The consensus so far is that they interfere with the migration of sperm, disrupt the passage of the ovum, and stimulate the natural production of inhospitable prostaglandins in the fallopian tubes and uterus. Their effectiveness depends on a number of factors relating to the design, material used, and technique of insertion. Failure rates range from close to zero up to 2 percent. Although the most frequent cause of failure is undetected partial or full expulsion of the device, pregnancies can also occur with the IUD in place. About half of such pregnancies will abort spontaneously.

Aside from such mechanical interventions, synthetic hormones can be taken to inhibit the movement of sperm, block fertilization of the ovum, or (possibly) interfere with implantation. The most common technique is the so-called morning-after pill, a form of emergency contraception in which two sets of pills are taken twelve hours apart within 72 hours (three days) of an act unprotected intercourse. Available in pharmacies and from family planning clinics in many countries, including Canada and the United States, emergency contraceptives consist of extra strong doses of hormones typically present in oral contraceptives. The pills do not induce immediate bleeding, however; rather, the next menstruation should arrive at the regular time. Emergency contraception is not recommended for frequent use because it doesn't always work. The insertion of a copper-bearing IUD within five days of having unprotected intercourse is another early option, but only if a woman intends to keep the device in place.

The fertilized egg, which consists of a microscopic cluster of cells, takes about five to seven days to travel down the fallopian tube and several days more to implant in the uterine wall. The American College of Obstetrics and Gynecology, among other medical bodies, defines pregnancy as beginning not at fertilization but at completed *implantation*. According to this definition, interventions that inhibit implantation are not abortions. From Rebecca J. Cook, in *Women's Health in the Third World: The Impact of Unwanted Pregnancy*

When her period is late

Menstruation symbolizes many things for women. The monthly appearance of blood can be a reassuring sign that all is well, a shameful mark of pollution that must be concealed, or a sad message that a desired conception has once more failed to happen. Its delay can elicit joy at the promise of a wanted pregnancy, panic at the possibility of an unwanted one, fear of illness, confusion, and dismay.

A woman's period may be overdue for many reasons besides pregnancy, of course. Normal irregularities in the length of the cycle, the use of contraceptive methods such as Depo-Provera or Norplant, the onset of menopause, and other factors can cause menstrual delays or missed periods. In one study of women requesting menstrual regulation services by vacuum aspiration within a week of a missed period, half were not pregnant; in another, one-fifth of those presenting within ten days of their missed period had not conceived even though all thought that they might have done so.

As many as half of all conceptions may be lost naturally *before* implantation, that is, before the menstrual period is overdue and before a woman suspects a pregnancy. On the other hand, a woman may have a light period even though she *is* pregnant. F. Gary Cunningham and colleagues, *Williams Obstetrics*; see also Canadian Abortion Rights Action League, "About the fetus," *www.caral.ca*

Today, pregnancy can be reliably determined by some laboratory tests as early as six to eight days following fertilization—that is, even before a missed period—once implantation has occurred. For most women, however, the first week or two without bleeding is a time of uncertainty. A woman's response will depend very much on whether she wants to be pregnant or not.

The notion of "removing female irregularity" or "bringing down the menses" as distinct from abortion is widespread in many cultures. A study conducted by the World Health Organization found that women typically view menstruation as a natural, vital bodily occurrence indicative of good general health. The monthly period is widely believed to rid the body of bad blood and poisonous wastes; thus, its absence or stoppage could lead to—or be a sign of—serious illness.

The possible causes of a delayed period and the ways they may be interpreted are revealed in a study by anthropologist Carole Browner of indigenous fertility regulation methods in Cali, Colombia. For these and other Latin women, delayed menstruation is an ambiguous sign. It may indicate pregnancy, or a natural change in the body, or a potentially harmful *atrazo* (menstrual delay). The *atrazo*, in turn, may be caused by accumulated impurities in the menstrual blood or the womb. Because women believe that delayed menses should be remedied to maintain good health, and since it is difficult to distinguish a late period from an early pregnancy, unwanted pregnancies may be terminated surreptitiously by taking herbal remedies and calling it something else.

"We've got to use the medicine at the beginning, not to let the baby grow" explains a woman in Brazil about the use of herbal teas to bring on menstruation. "Take it when one is in doubt, after one month of pregnancy. Then the menstruation comes and it's not abortion." Quoted in Rosalind P. Petchesky and Karen Judd, *Negotiating Reproductive Rights: Women's Perspectives Across Countries and Cultures*

An astonishing array of menstrual-inducing recipes has been identified throughout the world. In indigenous cultures, botanical agents include preparations of pineapple, crocus, mung bean, banana, cinnamon, oregano, chamomile, thyme, celery juice, parsley, and lemon, among hundreds of others. Where patent medicines are available women take quinine pills, chloroquine, ergonovine, metrigen, anti-worm medicines, "boiled beer mixed with aspirin three consecutive days upon rising", epsom salts, laxatives, extra oral contraceptives, injections of estrogen or progesterone, and other medications obtained from pharmacists, herbalists, market vendors, neighbors, and friends.

More drastic measures such as inserting leaves, roots, sticks, knitting needles, wire, or rubber catheters into the uterus; assaulting the abdomen with heavy massage or traumatic blows; tying it tightly with cloth or rope; pouring hot coals or scalding water on the abdomen; introducing caustic substances into the vagina; or taking pharmaceuticals to bring on uterine contractions may be resorted to if milder methods fail. These latter extremes are more clearly intended to cause miscarriage, however, whereas the former recipes are "menstrual inducers" of ambiguous interpretation.

In the mid-nineteenth century Queen Victoria's obstetrician described the use of a uterine syringe to bring on menstruation. The use of a hand-operated syringe to prevent pregnancy by inducing menstruation was reported in Russia in 1927, and for inducing abortion was used in the United States as early as 1935. Reported in Forrest G. Greenslade and colleagues, *Manual Vacuum Aspiration: A Summary of Clinical and Programmatic Experience Worldwide*

The old concept of menstrual regulation has found its modern equivalent in the development of two important technologies. These are the simple and inexpensive hand-operated vacuum aspirator consisting of a flexible plastic cannula and syringe, and drugs that can induce very early miscarriage and cause uterine bleeding.

Described in Chapter Three as methods of abortion, both of these techniques can also be used when menstruation is overdue but before a pregnancy has definitely been established. For many women this is a distinct advantage.

Hard choices

Choosing a contraceptive method clearly isn't easy. Some methods require doing something every day (taking the pill); others require something whenever you have sex (using a condom or diaphragm, say) or not having sex how or when you want to (withdrawal, periodic abstinence). Some involve the collaboration of the sexual partner; others can be used alone. Some methods are free and always available, yet unreliable (withdrawal) while others are costly, sometimes unavailable, but effective (pills, injections, implants). Some actions require frequent decision-making and can be reversed or stopped if you change your mind, others are taken once and for all (sterilization). Some methods require medical examinations, screening, prescriptions, refills, checkups. Some have side effects, such as altering the frequency or flow of the menstrual period. Any one of these characteristics—and more—can encourage or discourage people from practicing contraception in a diligent manner.

Women who seek abortions often insist that they were using contraception but it failed. In the United States, for example, six of every ten women having abortions in 1995 said they (or their partners) were using a contraceptive method during the month they became pregnant. But what does this really mean? Some were undoubtedly using a method correctly (the statistician's "perfect users") but had bad luck. Others were using it sporadically. Perhaps they were "resting" from the pill for a few weeks (a common but mistaken practice), or they had temporarily run out of supplies, or a condom slipped off, or their partner didn't quite pull out in time. Still others who say they were practicing contraception were using one of the many folk methods that someone had told them about. They thought they were "taking precautions" but they weren't.

Still others were not using anything at all. There are many reasons for this. Some women say they have had bad experiences with contraception in the past. Many fear the possibility of side effects, dislike certain aspects such as inserting an object in their vagina or having an injection, do not know what method is best for them, or are ashamed or cannot afford to go to a clinic. Some cannot get their partners to cooperate or, in some cultures, fear the social disapproval of relatives or neighbors if their contraceptive use is discovered. Some women were not expecting to have sex when they became pregnant—whether the act was consensual or coerced—and so were unable to protect themselves. This is especially the case among adolescents. Often women believe that they will not get pregnant because this was their first time, or because they didn't really go "all the way," or because they were breastfeeding and had not yet resumed menstruation, or because they were too young or too old or had been told by a doctor that they would have difficulty conceiving. Some have had a history of successful risk-taking in the past and think they can afford to take chances.

"**Did you think you might get pregnant?**" an interviewer asks a young woman in an abortion referral service in California. "No," she replies, "because I went for six months without taking pills and I didn't get pregnant." Quoted in Kristin Luker, *Taking Chances: Abortion and the Decision Not to Contracept*

The result of this complex mix of technical failure, human vulnerability, and common miscalculation is startling. According to demographic and health surveys in which such questions are commonly asked, women worldwide report almost as many unintended pregnancies each year as planned ones. Surprisingly, both the rate of unplanned pregnancies and of abortion are higher on average in the more developed countries, including Canada and the United States, than they are in the developing regions of the world. This is because the fewer the children one plans to have and the more concerned one is about their timing, the more likely it is that a given pregnancy will be defined as unplanned, and the less tolerance there will be for mistakes.

Half of all pregnancies (49 percent) occurring every year in the developed countries (Europe, North America, Japan, Australia, New Zealand) are unplanned and an estimated 36 percent end in abortion. In the developing regions (most of Africa, Asia and Latin America) about 36 percent of pregnancies are unplanned and 20 percent end in abortion.

From the Alan Guttmacher Institute, *Sharing Responsibility: Women, Society and Abortion Worldwide*

There are striking differences among the regions of the world in the proportions of all pregnancies that end in abortion. Women living in Eastern Europe and Russia are most likely to terminate a pregnancy. The combination of very low family size desires (one or two children at most) and scarce, costly, and unreliable contraceptive supplies means that a woman may have four or five abortions in her lifetime. On average, 57 percent of pregnancies in Eastern Europe end in abortion rather than miscarriage or a live birth, compared with only 21 percent in Western Europe. The lowest ratios, about 12 percent, are found in sub-Saharan Africa, where large families are still highly valued (or at least tolerated), especially in rural areas. In Canada and the United States 23 percent of known pregnancies end in abortion, about the same as for the world as a whole.

Comparing the costs of contraception and abortion

Some pregnancies will always be unplanned in any population. The high rates of contraceptive failure typical of methods such as vaginal foams or barriers, periodic abstinence, and condoms—combined with higher than usual failure rates, risk-taking, or lack of access among groups such as adolescents, ethnic minorities and the poor—mean that safe abortion services will always be needed as a backup. This is true even of couples using some highly effective methods, because the odds can go against them. According to the probabilities, seven out of every ten women using a 95 percent effective method of fertility regulation will require at least one abortion in their lifetime to achieve a two-child family.

Abortion is not only a last resort if all else fails, however. Some women at some point in their lives may well prefer it over other methods of fertility regulation. The relative costs and benefits depend on a woman's personal circumstances and on the social environment in which she lives. Why might a woman prefer abortion to contraception? Let's consider some possibilities.

> " . . . [C]ontraception may *not* be . . . the least costly and most rational method of fertility control for all women at all times . . . The reality of the situation is that the costs associated with contraception are often so high that abortion becomes de facto the only acceptable method of fertility control for many women." Kristen Luker, *Taking Chances: Abortion and the Decision Not to Contracept*

First, contraceptive use requires a sustained commitment to behavior that may or may not be effective in preventing pregnancy and may not even be necessary. Would a pregnancy have occurred in the absence of contraception or not? Who knows? Probabilities are exactly that: *probabilities*, not certainties. In contrast, there is something very concrete about the decision to continue or terminate a particular pregnancy at a particular time. For couples who are ambivalent about having a baby or who are living in uncertain circumstances, making a decision at the point at which a pregnancy is confirmed offers the opportunity to decide whether they are prepared and genuinely committed to raising a child *at this time.*

Second, contraception can be costly on a day-to-day basis, not only economically (purchasing cycles of pills, for example, or getting an implant, if such methods are not covered by a health plan or otherwise subsidized) but also physically, psychologically, and socially. And whereas the costs of having an abortion are hypothetical, the costs of obtaining and using a contraceptive method consistently—or of being contraceptively prepared "just in case" one has sex—are ongoing, current, and real.

Third, for a woman who is trying to avoid pregnancy but cannot persuade her partner to use a contraceptive method or to agree to her own use, abortion offers the possibility of taking action without his knowledge or consent. Even when abortion is unsafe and illegal, many women will interrupt the pregnancy secretly rather than confronting the man and risking resistance, violence, or abandonment as a result.

"I had an abortion once" says Soheir, an Egyptian woman, to an interviewer. "I was using the loop [IUD] but I got pregnant. My neighbor advised me to drink boiled Coca-Cola and take an enema. I had bleeding for fifteen days, then I was transferred to the hospital and they did a small operation on me. I never told anybody that I did it to myself, not even my husband. He is a religious man." Quoted in Rosalind P. Petchesky and Karen Judd, *Negotiating Reproductive Rights: Women's Perspectives Across Countries and Cultures*

Fourth, for women in developing countries in particular, the traditional (and now updated) "curative" ways of bringing on menstruation or inducing miscarriage may be more acceptable than the unfamiliar "preventive" approach to long-term protection such as taking a pill every day, getting periodic injections, having a device inserted into the uterus or under the skin, or being surgically sterilized. This is especially true where women have heard rumors about the side effects of modern contraceptive methods and greatly fear them. Some of these fears are realistic given the poor health and living conditions of many women; others are exaggerated and even bizarre. Whether true or false, however, they affect women's perceptions of their choices in fundamental ways.

"**A recurring theme in the discussions** [with Nigerian adolescents] was the view that 'women who use contraceptives will find it difficult to conceive when they eventually get married.' . . . In contrast, side effects from abortion were thought to be few, with the possibility of damage to the womb and infertility being most frequently mentioned. Participants often perceived these risks as remote, however, especially when doctors perform the abortions."
Valentine O. Otoide and colleagues, in *International Family Planning Perspectives*

Fifth is the safety factor. In the United States, an abortion performed with manual or electric vacuum aspiration up to twelve weeks from the last menstrual period is far less risky as measured by the number of deaths than taking the pill, having a tubal ligation, using an IUD, or even having sexual intercourse (deaths per year resulting from sexually transmitted infections and pelvic inflammatory disease). Potential health complications from hormonal contraceptives (pills, injections, implants) include increased risk of cardiovascular disease (especially among older women and heavy smokers) and, depending on the formulation, duration of use and the woman's age, of breast and cervical cancer. For IUDs they include uterine perforation and infection resulting in pelvic inflammatory disease, ectopic (tubal) pregnancy, and infertility. Many women complain of headaches, weight gain, or depression when they are on the pill, while some IUD users complain of heavier monthly bleeding and menstrual cramps. Ironically, the lowest health risks of all derive from the combined use of a less effective contraceptive method such as the condom (which also protects against sexually transmitted infections), vaginal diaphragm, periodic abstinence, or withdrawal, backed up by a safe early abortion in case of method failure.

In most developing countries, excluding China and a few others, the balance sheet is quite different. Sex, contraception, and abortion all carry high risks for women and their choices (if any) are hard ones indeed. Heightened risks of sexual activity include acquiring a sexually transmitted disease that will not be diagnosed or treated and, in many countries, of HIV/AIDS, to which the female is more biologically vulnerable to sexual transmission than is the male. The use of contraceptive methods such as hormonal pills, IUDs, and surgical sterilization is also riskier where the socioeconomic and health status of the population is poor and clinical services are costly or scarce. As for abortion, in countries where it is highly restricted and thus clandestine, as in most of Africa and Latin America and in parts of Asia, women attempt to induce miscarriage themselves, turn to midwives or quacks, or seek out private doctors if they can afford them.

The death and hospitalization rates following botched abortions are staggering. Up to half of the scarce funds available for hospital obstetrical care in some countries are spent on the emergency treatment of complications from unsafe abortion, which can cost up to three times more than a normal delivery. An estimated 15 to 25 percent of all women who try to induce a miscarriage are hospitalized for complications in some Latin American countries. In Brazil almost 300,000 women were hospitalized in 1991 alone for complications resulting from clandestine procedures. Sub-

Saharan Africa represents the worst-case scenario, however. In Nigeria, for example, unsafe abortion currently accounts for about 20,000 of the estimated 50,000 maternal deaths that occur each year. In the developing regions as a whole (again excluding China, where abortion is legal), one woman of every 300 who attempts an abortion will die. This compares with a death rate of one woman for every 165,000 abortion procedures performed in the United States.

"So many women die, they have a hemorrhage, arrive at the hospital and [the staff] don't care, they don't give a damn" explains a woman to an interviewer in São Paulo, Brazil. "Then, what happens? That bleeding woman will die for the lack of medical attention in the hospital, and this happens every day." Quoted in Rosalind P. Petchesky and Karen Judd, *Negotiating Reproductive Rights: Women's Perspectives Across Countries and Cultures*

Comparing the risks of abortion and childbirth

As shocking as the story is of unnecessary death and suffering of girls and women from unsafe abortion in so many developing countries, the story of childbirth is even worse. In the developing regions as a whole, *the risks of childbirth are higher than for abortion.* Whereas one woman will die for every 300 abortions, one will die for every 200 live births and, in sub-Saharan Africa, one in 100 live births. Because an African woman incurs this terrible risk each time she has a baby, and because she has babies so frequently, her lifetime risk of dying in childbirth can run as high as one in sixteen. Prolonged and obstructed labor (especially among young girls), hemorrhage, infection, eclampsia, anemia, and other complications are major killers. Women living in urban poverty or in isolated rural areas, those under age eighteen having their first child, and those over thirty-five having their sixth baby or more are especially vulnerable.

"All of [the woman's] body systems, including her mind, are affected by the pregnancy . . . . The load on her heart alone is increased by 40%. Pregnancy always involves some costs to women's health, ranging from shortness of breath, backache, nausea, insomnia, hypertension, and edema, to risk of eclampsia [convulsions and coma], obstructed labour, injury, and death in childbirth." Canadian Abortion Rights Action League, "About the fetus," *www.caral.ca*

Even in the United States, where death during childbirth is rare, a woman who carries a pregnancy to term runs ten times the risk of dying than a woman who has an abortion. Whereas the death rate for all abortions is one per 165,000 procedures and for those done within the first nine weeks is one in every 260,000 procedures, in childbirth the risk of the mother's death is one for every 15,000 live births. The discrepancies in these risk factors have led some doctors to suggest that *all* abortions should be considered medically warranted (that is, therapeutic) because they protect women from the health risks of carrying an unwanted pregnancy to term and delivering a baby.

Whether we consider our ancient customs ("triturate with honey . . .") or current practices, it is clear that abortion has always been important in the regulation of human fertility. Even with the increased use of contraception, the situation is unlikely to change significantly. Better sex education and access to contraceptive information and services, especially among underserved groups such as adolescents and the poor, can help to prevent unwanted pregnancies. But from a social and medical viewpoint it makes sense to ensure that good abortion services are also there for all who want and need them.

Deaths from unsafe abortion account for one-eighth of all pregnancy-related deaths (maternal mortality) worldwide and even more in some countries. *Virtually all of these deaths are avoidable with safe and simple medical practices* as are the uncounted injuries that often result in emergency hospitalization or in no medical care at all. The provision of abortion care as a routine aspect of health care and family planning could prevent not only all deaths from unsafe abortion, but also untold numbers of deaths of women resulting from the delivery of unwanted children. As we shall see, however, the laws and regulations of most countries—even those that offer abortion "on request"—delay or prevent many women from obtaining the safe services they need.

But first let's look at what happens to a girl or woman whose life has taken an unexpected and perhaps terrifying turn because she finds herself accidentally pregnant. Under what conditions is she likely to define the pregnancy as unwanted? What options does she have? What will she go through in her search for a safe method or practitioner if she decides to terminate the pregnancy? How will the people she consults react? We turn to these questions in the next chapter.

CHAPTER TWO

Making the Abortion Decision

"I am a fifteen-year-old Latina woman. When I got pregnant I couldn't tell my mother. In my family my pregnancy would be considered a disgrace and an insult to the family. I would have to leave the house. My boyfriend thought I should have an abortion and so did I. I didn't really feel that I had a choice. We did not have the time or money to bring a child into this world. I know what I did was right. I also know that after the abortion I wept tears of sadness and tears of satisfaction."
Quoted in Boston Women's Health Book Collective, *The New Our Bodies, Ourselves*

Almost every one of the eighty million women in the world who has an accidental pregnancy every year could tell her own story. She could tell us whether she had been trying to prevent the pregnancy or not. She could explain what she and her partner were doing or using to avoid conception or why they weren't using anything. She could tell us how she felt when she realized that she was pregnant, what thoughts flashed through her mind, what she hoped for or feared most. She could tell us about the reaction of her partner (if he knew), her parents (if they knew), of others in whom she confided. And she could tell us whether she thought about terminating the pregnancy or not, if she tried to do so but failed, or if she succeeded. But if she is one of the almost eighty thousand women who die unnecessarily every year from the complications of unsafe procedures, she cannot tell us anything at all.

Eighty million misconceived pregnancies. Forty-six million legal and illegal abortions. How can one even begin to appreciate the complexities involved as women confront these decisions? What makes a woman decide to terminate a pregnancy even under the most difficult and dangerous conditions? Does she believe she has any choice, one way or another? How does she feel afterwards about having the abortion? About having the baby? About herself, her partner, her family, her future?

What makes a pregnancy unwanted?

The question of whether a pregnancy is wanted or unwanted is not always easy to answer. At one end of the spectrum are those situations in which a woman clearly does not want to have a child, or another child, at all. At the other end of the spectrum are those pregnancies that are not only planned ("We've been trying for months!") but are eagerly anticipated. In between there may be doubts and dilemmas. Joy and sadness. Anticipation and dread. Indecision.

The problem with using the word "unwanted" is that it does not describe reality very well. For one thing, not all pregnancies that end in abortion are unwanted. A woman may desperately want a child but she simply cannot have it, for economic, health, or personal reasons. An unwed teenager may be longing to have her baby but her parents refuse to allow it.

"I debated keeping the baby because I wanted it. Yet, in my situation . . . I didn't feel like there was really any way that I could have [had it]."

"It's not that I didn't want it. It was my husband's child, you know. [But] I just couldn't see it. It was just too much for me to handle with no help." Quoted in Mary Kay Zimmerman, *Passage Through Abortion: The Personal and Social Reality of Women's Experiences*

A pregnancy may be wanted in general, or in the future, but this particular pregnancy is problematic. Perhaps it happened too early in the marriage or too soon after the previous birth and is thus mistimed. Perhaps the circumstances are all wrong at the moment—an unstable relationship, joblessness, illness—but once they improve, a baby will be welcome. The pregnancy may have resulted from unwanted intercourse (rape, incest, psychological coercion) and the thought of having the baby conceived in this way is intolerable. Or it resulted from unprotected or casual sex—just taking a chance—or from contraceptive failure, and was never intended to happen when (or with whom) it did.

A pregnancy may be very much wanted by one partner but not the other, or wanted at the time of conception but not a month or two later when the implications of having a child are clearer or the situation has changed. If a teenager sees pregnancy as a way to leave home, to test the seriousness of a relationship, or to demonstrate her independence, she may very quickly realize that she has made a terrible mistake.

"I thought I would probably get married, that he would want to. I never, ever thought I'd go through an abortion. That never entered my mind at all." Quoted in Kristen Luker, *Taking Chances: Abortion and the Decision Not to Contracept*

It is one thing to fantasize about being pregnant and to anticipate its benefits, quite another to face the reality of it. Pregnancy confirms a woman's femininity. It confirms her fertility, a sort of "mother earthness." It represents the *possibility* of bringing a child—or another child—into the world. But how will others react? Husband? Boyfriend? Parents and other family members? Friends? Employers? Will the imagined benefits become real, or will they "vanish with the verdict of a positive pregnancy test" as sociologist Kristen Luker remarks of the women in her study who ended up seeking abortions in California?

A woman may be ambivalent about whether she wants to become a mother. The non-use or failure of a contraceptive method ("forgetting" to take the pill every day, for example) may reflect her unconscious desire to have a baby—or at least to see if she can get pregnant—despite what she claims to herself or others. In a sense she is testing the waters, perhaps of her own commitment, perhaps of her partner's. She may insist that the pregnancy was accidental, but it is not entirely unexpected. Is it, then, a wanted pregnancy or not?

When is pregnancy a problem? Two scenarios

Both at the personal level and in the society as a whole there are two very common situations in which a pregnancy is particularly likely to be defined as unwanted, or at least as a *problem pregnancy*. This is not to say that the pregnancy will necessarily end in abortion, however, for that path can be jammed with legal and administrative as well as social and personal obstacles.

The first situation is a pregnancy that occurs *outside of a socially approved reproductive union* such as marriage or, in some cultures, a recognized common-law union or cohabiting relationship in which childbearing is accepted. At risk are single women who are not living with a partner, married women whose husbands were absent (as migratory workers, for example) at the time they got pregnant, and those who are separated, divorced, or widowed.

In some countries very few women who are not currently married will admit to having sexual relations. Indeed, in the conservative cultures of North Africa and the Middle East, questions about sexual and contraceptive activity are rarely asked of unmarried women in demographic and health surveys. In most developed countries, however, and in sub-Saharan Africa and some other developing regions, premarital, extramarital and postmarital sexual relationships (especially among divorced women of reproductive age) are common. In the United States, a national survey conducted in 1995 found that 59 percent of single women between the ages of 15 and 44 said they had been sexually active at some time in the past (even if they did not currently have a partner). Sixty-seven percent of separated and divorced women under fifty years of age said they were sexually active within the past three months.

Almost three-quarters of Canadian women and over four-fifths of American women who obtain abortions are unmarried. In contrast, in developing countries such as Bangladesh, Malaysia, Turkey, Vietnam, Peru, and the Dominican Republic, more than nine of every ten women having abortions are married, and most are already mothers.

From The Alan Guttmacher Institute, *Sharing Responsibility: Women, Society and Abortion Worldwide*

Higher levels of sexual activity outside marriage raise the odds that an unwanted pregnancy will occur even if couples are contracepting. Yet many are not. In the American survey mentioned above, 28 percent of unmarried sexually active women ages 15 to 24 said that they or their partners were using *no* contraceptive method the last time they had sex. In some Latin American and Caribbean countries the figures run as high as 50 to 75 percent (the Dominican Republic, Bolivia, Paraguay, for example) and in sub-Saharan Africa up to 80 to 90 percent (Liberia, Zambia, and Tanzania).

What happens if an accidental pregnancy occurs in these situations? Under what conditions is a woman most likely to try to terminate? Although the scenarios are numerous, some common themes can be identified.

One theme relates to the nature of the sexual relationship. If it is highly illicit or taboo, then the evidence of its existence (a pregnancy) must be concealed at all costs. The story may involve the loss of a girl's virginity in a conservative Islamic society, for example, which (if known) will destroy her marriageability and bring dishonor to the entire family, or it may involve an adulterous affair. Another theme is male responsibility. Is the man willing to acknowledge paternity, contribute some support, and live with or marry the mother? Or is he someone else's husband and father, or a restless teenager, or a person in authority such as a teacher or employer who refuses to admit his part in the pregnancy?

Still another theme is the acceptability of single motherhood. If the pregnancy cannot be legitimized through marriage, how easy is it for a woman to raise a child in the society in which she lives? Will she be treated harshly, even stigmatized? Will her child be labeled illegitimate? Or is unmarried motherhood a more-or-less normal course of events, as it is in parts of the Caribbean, for example, where a woman may have babies by several fathers (who also have children with other women) and rely on her own mother to help raise them? In some areas of Europe, especially in Scandinavia, social norms are quite liberal and governments may offer housing, child-care subsidies or other special allowances to single women with babies. All of these factors contribute to the woman's perception of whether it is feasible or not for her to have a baby outside of marriage.

The second situation in which a pregnancy is likely to be unwanted arises *within marriage* or in a less formal reproductive union. A pregnancy comes too quickly, or too soon after the previous baby.

Both the husband and wife are working and there is no-one else to care for a baby. They have economic, health, or personal problems. There are too many demands from the children already born. Other family members—aging parents, perhaps—require care. Or they already have the number of children they want (or more)—or at least, *she* does—and definitely intend to stop.

"**Isabel always viewed abortion as a sin.** She tried using the pill early, after her first child, but was advised to discontinue using it when she started to lose weight. She then had seven more children in quick succession. When she got pregnant for the ninth time her youngest was less than a year old. So she decided to have an abortion. 'I cannot continue with this pregnancy. I am already forty-two, too old to [have] another child.'" Interviewed in the Philippines, in Rosalind P. Petchesky and Karen Judd, *Negotiating Reproductive Rights: Women's Perspectives Across Countries and Cultures*

Throughout the world, many women will deliver what they hope is their last child by the time they are twenty-five years old. This leaves another twenty or more potentially reproductive years in which, if they or their partner are not sterilized, they will have to contracept very carefully indeed. Yet surveys show that in some countries in sub-Saharan Africa, Asia, and Latin America, from 50 to 90 percent of married women who say they want to postpone having a child or stop altogether are not using any method at all. Many are fearful that contraceptives will make them ill or (ironically) infertile.

The "typical" abortion client
is not always who you think

Different combinations of the two scenarios described above help to explain the characteristics of women in different countries who obtain abortions and their reasons for having them.

Although there are many exceptions to this general pattern, the majority of women in Canada, the United States, and Western Europe who have an abortion are *unmarried and have never had a child*. In most developing countries the majority are more likely to be *married with children*. This latter situation is changing in some places, however, as girls' marriages are increasingly delayed under the impact of social and economic changes and unmarried young people become more sexually active. In Nigeria, for example, where abortion is highly restricted by law, half or more of patients treated in hospitals for the complications of illegal botched attempts are young and single, typically still in high school. This would have been extremely rare two or three decades ago when girls were married as soon as they reached puberty. In China, where late marriage is the rule, physical contact between unmarried couples was prohibited in the Maoist regime. Nowadays, although sexual norms are changing, a single person still cannot easily obtain contraception. As a result, 25 percent of all women having abortions in the Shanghai region are unmarried, most of them in their early twenties.

The typical abortion client in the United States is often portrayed as a teenager—a high-school dropout, perhaps—who "got herself in trouble." True, the teenage pregnancy rate is higher in the United States than in most other developed countries, despite the decline in the past decade. This is not because American teenagers are more sexually active than their counterparts in, say, Sweden, but because they tend to have less accurate contraceptive information and more limited access. Ignorance and misinformation about contraceptive safety and effectiveness, especially concerning the alleged dangers of the pill, are partly responsible. Although the use of contraceptives among adolescents at the time of first intercourse reached almost 80 percent in the late 1990s (due mostly to an increase in condom use), teenagers are still less likely than older couples to use contraceptives every time they have sex. As a result, four of every five teen pregnancies in the United States are unplanned and two out of five (half of all unplanned pregnancies in this group) end in abortion.

Although teenagers are especially prone to unplanned pregnancies and abortion, their representation among abortion clients has been shrinking. Only 20 percent or so of all abortion clients in the US are now under age twenty. Almost half are twenty-five or older. The same is true of Canada where clients are increasingly older, single women who have had a previous abortion or birth.

On the other hand, the proportion of abortion clients who are currently unmarried has grown to 80 percent. This is a group in which the pregnancies that do occur are particularly likely to be unintended. In the US in 1987, 88 percent of pregnancies among never-married women were unintended (of which three-quarters ended in abortion) and 68 percent of pregnancies among women who were separated, divorced or widowed (of which over half ended in abortion). Thus the typical client—if there is one—is a currently unmarried adult who may or may not be living with her partner and is probably in college or employed. Whereas teenage clients are more likely to be single, white, middle-class and childless, clients over thirty are more likely to be nonwhite, poor, and already mothers, whether they are currently married or not.

These North American age and marital patterns are repeated in many Western European countries. Fewer than one abortion client in every five is under age twenty in England and Wales, Norway, Denmark, Finland, Sweden, Germany, the Netherlands, France, and Spain as well as in Australia and New Zealand. From 50 to 80 percent are currently unmarried, however, and about half have not had a baby before.

In the Netherlands, a country noted for its tolerance of responsible adolescent sexuality, the teenage pregnancy rate is only one-tenth that of the United States and the teenage abortion rate one-eighth of the US level. Because sex education in the schools starts at an early age and contraceptives are widely available to young people, almost all Dutch teenagers (unlike American teenagers) use contraception when they first have sex. From Henry P. David and Jany Rademakers, in *Studies in Family Planning*

What women say about why they had to terminate

What reasons do women give for having an abortion? This is a more difficult question to answer than it might seem. First, some surveys are set up so that a woman simply checks off a reason on a list of pre-coded responses that rarely reflect the complexity of most personal situations. Second, some answers such as "contraception failed" or "didn't want the baby" simply beg the question of why? Third, some respondents may give what they think is a socially acceptable reason rather than one that makes them appear to be thinking only of themselves. Fourth, even reasons such as "can't afford another baby" or "am not married to the father" don't really get at the question of why one woman will accept an accidental pregnancy under these circumstances and another will not.

In any case, for most women the decision to terminate a pregnancy is the result of a cluster of problems and not a single issue. In a study by Aida Torres and Jacqueline Forrest of almost two thousand women who filled out a questionnaire in selected US abortion clinics in 1988, virtually none gave just one reason for her decision. Respondents cited almost four reasons on average; some gave six or more. For a young unmarried woman these would typically include explanations such as she is not ready to have a child, does not want to or cannot marry the man, is in school or working, cannot afford to raise the baby alone, believes that a baby should have a father, parents disapprove. Other clusters of explanations reflect other situations. Too old. Too many children already. Children are grown. Husband doesn't want any more. And so on.

What many women are saying is that they simply cannot, in their present or foreseen circumstances, give a new baby the quality of care that it needs and deserves. Those who are already mothers are concerned about maintaining a level of care for the children they already have, not to mention their husband and other family members for whom they may be responsible. The reasons for terminating are almost never "frivolous" or "trifling," as some critics claim.

"The majority of women who have abortions do so for mature reasons based on careful self-assessment of their economic ability to support themselves and their children and of their psychological readiness to take on the responsibility of rearing a healthy, cared-for child." Alice S. Rossi and Bhavani Sitaram, in *Studies in Family Planning*

How quickly are women likely to come to a decision? An in-depth study conducted by Paul Sachdev of unmarried Canadian women between the ages of 18 and 25 who had abortions in the early 1990s found that half chose to terminate the pregnancy as soon as they discovered it while the other half decided only after vacillating between abortion, having and raising the child as an unwed mother, or marrying the man responsible for the pregnancy. *Not one* considered having the baby and giving it up for adoption. When asked why not, most said they believed that giving birth and then relinquishing the baby would be far more traumatic than having an abortion. A study by Mary Kay Zimmerman of forty abortion clients in the American midwest in the mid-1970s came to similar conclusions. Adoption was not considered seriously by any of the women studied. Both unwed motherhood and marriage to the baby's father were quickly rejected as well.

Turning to the rest of the world, a review by Akrinola Bankole and colleagues summarizes the results of surveys on reasons for abortions conducted in twenty-six countries in Asia, Latin America, sub-Saharan Africa, and Europe plus the United States.

In countries where the majority of women having abortions are married, the dominant reasons will naturally differ from those where the majority are not. In Malaysia, Nepal, Singapore, and Taiwan, for example, where most women having abortions are married, 80 percent or more simply said that they wanted to delay having the next child or wanted no more children. In India and Bangladesh the standard reasons were economic (cannot afford to have another baby) or worries about the mother's health.

In Kenya and Nigeria, however, where most women who get abortions are *unmarried*, three-quarters of those interviewed said they were too young, that having a child would disrupt their education or job, that their parents disapproved, or that their partner did not want the pregnancy. In Chile, Mexico and Honduras about two-thirds gave these same responses. Because the surveys ask somewhat different questions and provide different possible responses, the results across countries are difficult to compare.

Giving a reason in a survey for choosing abortion tells only a small part of the story. As we know, many women will carry an unplanned or even unwanted pregnancy to term. The option of abortion may be considered but rejected, attempted without success, or blocked by someone else. Perhaps it is simply out of the question. Nor do the reasons given in surveys tell us much about what a woman goes through in making her decision. Even in countries where abortion is legal on all grounds, someone who decides to terminate an unwanted pregnancy may face social disapproval and personal isolation. No matter how compelling are her motives, she may be criticized and even rejected by her family and friends or condemned by her religion. She may feel that the pregnancy is her fault and that she is being punished whatever she decides to do.

"The lack of formal social acceptance of abortion [in Latin America] makes the woman who aborts an outcast. Even the male partner or the mother may not be supportive, and most of the time the pregnant woman feels that the entire burden is on her shoulders. Forced marriage, single motherhood, giving the baby up for adoption or adding an unwanted child to the family are all stressful and traumatic solutions." J. A. Pinotti and A. Faúndes, in *Women's Health in the Third World: The Impact of Unwanted Pregnancy*

Moral dilemmas and subversive acts

"Abortion is the most highly subversive thing that we women can do . . ." María Ladi Londoño E., in *Women's Health in the Third World: The Impact of Unwanted Pregnancy*

In every society, sexual and reproductive events are highly charged with social and personal meaning. Pleasure and pain, anticipation and dread, honor and shame: the human emotions surrounding our sexual and reproductive lives are deep and complex. The sexual act itself can elicit joy or fear—the fear of discovery, for example, or of rejection, of physical harm, of disease, of an unwanted conception. We like to think of the creation of a new life as a natural human condition, an event to be celebrated. But for many women it is a time of discomfort, danger, and vulnerability.

An unintended pregnancy is an exceptionally stressful event. Whereas even a planned and much-wanted pregnancy can cause a great deal of anxiety ("Can I endure the pain of childbirth? Will the baby be all right?"), the unintended or unwanted pregnancy comes at a very bad time or should never have happened at all. This volatile situation can create a high level of psychosocial stress. Expressed in feelings of depression, anxiety, or hostility, stressful states are often accompanied by physical symptoms as well.

Depression is usually characterized by feelings of despair, helplessness, worthlessness, shame, having "the blues", and by physical symptoms such as lethargy, difficulty sleeping (or sleeping too much), and loss of appetite (or eating too much). Anxiety is typically expressed in feelings of generalized or specific worry, fear, panic, and dread or foreboding as well as in physical symptoms such as raised blood pressure or increased heart rate. Hostility is represented by feelings of anger, conflict or hatred, which may pour out in violent, erratic or abusive behavior toward oneself or others (partner, parents, medical personnel) or in social withdrawal (refusal to talk to anyone).

"**It seemed like a punishment.** I used birth control and got pregnant anyway. I no longer trusted my diaphragm, my lover, my body. My guilt about being pregnant turned into anger when I learned that no method of birth control is 100 percent effective! I took all the precautions and still needed an abortion. At the clinic, so many women had similar experiences." Quoted in Boston Women's Health Book Collective, *The New Our Bodies, Ourselves*

None of these feelings is surprising when we consider what a woman may be facing at this point in her life. Deciding whether to carry the pregnancy to term or to have an abortion presents a painful dilemma. She may not be mentally or physically prepared to bear a child. If she is young and unmarried she may have to leave home or school, give the baby up for adoption, or be forced to marry. A mother living in poverty has to weigh the needs of the children she already has against the economic consequences of another pregnancy. If a woman chooses to terminate she faces continuing conflict. Is abortion legally restricted, unavailable, expensive? Will she have to look for a clandestine provider or attempt it on her own? Even if she finds someone who will perform a safe abortion, how will she be treated? Who can she turn to for moral support and sympathy?

Personal moralities and the decision to abort

Compounding the emotional stress of having to make a decision under difficult circumstances are the ethical dilemmas that many women face.

Not all women have moral qualms about terminating a pregnancy even though they may feel sad about having to do so. In a secular society where abortion is widely practiced as a method of family planning, as in Russia and much of Eastern Europe, China, and Vietnam, abortion may become more or less routine for some women. A study of four thousand married women undergoing early pregnancy terminations in six rural counties of Sichuan province in China, for example, found that 85 percent had had at least one abortion before.

But even in the United States, a society with very high levels of church attendance when compared with most European countries, almost half of the women interviewed in a national survey reported by Stanley Henshaw and Greg Martire said that, for them, abortion was either not a moral issue or else that they had no opinion. Among respondents who acknowledged having had at least one abortion, three-quarters said that it was not a moral issue from their personal point of view.

Moreover, the dominant religion, if there is one, may not define the termination of a pregnancy as morally wrong. In some religions an abortion performed early in the pregnancy is not considered a sin. Different schools of thought in Islam define the period during which abortion is permitted as, variously, up to forty days, up to 120 days, or (more vaguely) before the "ensoulment" or quickening of the fetus. Until the mid-nineteenth century most Christian societies also shared the view that abortion was wrong only if it occurred following the first discernible movements of the fetus, which could be as late as the fourth or fifth month of pregnancy.

For those women whose ethical values do define the interruption of a pregnancy of whatever duration as morally wrong or who share a religious belief in the sanctity of human life from the point of conception, the decision to abort becomes an especially difficult one.

Although many Christian churches tolerate abortion and, indeed, were an important part of the movement to liberalize abortion laws throughout much of Western Europe and North America in the mid-twentieth century, others still strictly condemn it under all conditions. The Roman Catholic Church has remained particularly strict on this question and, at the Papal level, at least, on the continued prohibition of all artificial methods of birth control as well. Yet it is interesting to observe that in the United States, Canada, and Europe generally, Catholics are just as likely as non-Catholics to use modern methods of contraception and to have an abortion. In addition, some of the highest abortion rates in the world are found in Catholic countries in Latin America such as Brazil, Colombia and Chile, even though abortion is illegal there under almost all conditions.

Catholic women in the United States are just as likely as anyone else to terminate a pregnancy. They are *more likely* to do so than Protestant women, especially those who are Evangelicals. These religious differences persist even after Hispanics and nonwhites are excluded from the comparisons. See Catholics for a Free Choice, *Catholics and Reproduction: A World View*; Stanley Henshaw and Jennifer Van Vort, in *Studies and Family Planning*

For some women, then, their personal conviction that abortion is unacceptable whatever the circumstances, or the convictions of others who have control over their fate, will outweigh all other considerations. Other women struggle with their conscience and decide—sometimes with the support of their partners, friends, and family members and sometimes alone—that abortion is justified under the circumstances. In *Negotiating Reproductive Rights: Women's Perspectives Across Countries and Cultures*, Rosalind Petchesky and Karen Judd describe a kind of situational ethics or "practical morality" that many women express, in which matters of personal desperation override religious teachings. The process of rationalization may be helped by the belief that the religious teachings are themselves outmoded with regard to abortion (as well as other practices such as nonmarital sex, contraception and divorce), or else that a compassionate and loving God will understand and forgive. "Which is the greater sin?" one woman asks. "To have an abortion or to have a child I cannot take care of?"

"I was afraid of God's punishment," admits a Muslim woman to an interviewer in Egypt, "but at the same time I wonder, does God accept the suffering of the whole family if I have to stop work [to have another baby]?"

"When I was bleeding profusely [from an attempted abortion], I begged God for everything to be okay," a Catholic mother says in Brazil. "I asked for much forgiveness because I knew it was a sin. But I knew only God could understand my need." Quoted in Rosalind P. Petchesky and Karen Judd, *Negotiating Reproductive Rights: Women's Perspectives Across Countries and Cultures*

If at first you don't succeed . . .

A woman may know exactly what she is going to do if she gets pregnant accidentally, especially if she has had the experience before. Thus, at the first signs that her period is delayed she may, under the best of circumstances in a country where abortion is legal and she has the personal resources, buy a pregnancy test kit at the drugstore or consult a gynecologist for confirmation. If the results are positive and she plans to terminate, she can make an appointment right away at a nearby clinic, pay for the procedure or have it covered by insurance or a government subsidy, and go on with her life. Yet for every woman who has this experience, hundreds do not.

First, denying the obvious

A woman who does not want to be pregnant may go into a state of denial in which she attributes even the most obvious signs of conception to something else. A missed period can be ignored or, if vaguely acknowledged, blamed on stress or some other cause. It may take a second missed period to make the point. Signs of breast tenderness or even of fatigue and vomiting, which can appear as early as two weeks after fertilization, may be blamed on the flu, perhaps, or exhaustion from overwork or the pressure of school examinations. A temporary upset. Anything but pregnancy.

The tendency to ignore or explain away signs of a possible pregnancy is especially high among adolescents, among breastfeeding women who have not resumed menstruation, and among women who believe for other reasons that they are unlikely to be pregnant (infrequent sex, perceived fertility impairments, consistent contraceptive use, and other reasons). This failure to perceive and act on early signs makes it more likely that if a woman does eventually choose to terminate, she will do so at a later gestational stage with all of the physical, emotional, and legal consequences that this entails.

For adolescents the denial may be particularly profound as all sorts of difficult questions arise, even when services are generally available. "Do I tell my parents that I'm having sex? What will they think? How will my boyfriend react when he learns that I'm pregnant? What about my friends? How can I tell my doctor—he's my parents' doctor! How can I pay for this?" When combined with teenagers' relative lack of coping skills and tendency to engage in magical thinking, questions such as these can cause significant delays in seeking help.

During those first ambiguous days of a late period a woman who does not want to be pregnant and who lives in a place where safe services are inaccessible may begin to think about taking something—herbal teas or heavy doses of contraceptive pills or injections—to "bring down" her period. Perhaps the woman will get her period, perhaps not. If she doesn't, she may let the matter rest there and make no further effort to intervene. She may say that it is up to Fate or God to decide.

"**It does not work**" insists an Egyptian woman in a group discussion. "A woman can drink onion juice or garlic juice, or she can get anything from the herbs man. I know a woman who tried everything and nothing ever worked. God did not wish it for her." Quoted in Dale Huntington and colleagues, in *Studies in Family Planning*

Second, trying more drastic measures

For those who do decide to take the next step and cannot afford safe services, interventions become more drastic. In Cali, Colombia, anthropologist Carole Browner interviewed a sample of women—some married or living with their sexual partners, some not—about how they dealt with their unwanted pregnancies. In only twenty-eight of a total of 122 unwanted pregnancies did the woman make no attempt to intervene. In ninety-two cases the woman tried at least one minor method such as strong herbal teas or douches, commercial pills or injections, and other special preparations thought to induce bleeding. In forty-two of the pregnancies the woman also made a major attempt to terminate such as inserting a rubber catheter in her uterus and leaving it there until she miscarried, or going to a clandestine provider for dilation and curettage (D&C).

This sequence of increasingly drastic steps is typical of countries where safe services are not available to most women. A study of adolescent girls in Mexico City by N. Ehrenfeld found that those who succeeded in inducing a miscarriage made between one and four attempts each. Others tried but failed. Aside from various injections and infusions obtained in the marketplace, the girls had tried high dosages of quinine tables, carrying water in heavy containers for long distances, and falling down steps. "The point is," explains one to an interviewer, "you have to fall down several steps, abruptly, so that you land on the little bone, with open legs. It should be a fall of more than four steps, of course."

Where women turn first to folk remedies to bring on their periods or a miscarriage and thus lose precious time, the result can be self-defeating. Clinicians in Bangladesh, for example, will reject a woman who is too advanced in her pregnancy to receive a legal menstrual regulation, which can be performed manually only up to eight or ten weeks after the onset of the last menstrual period. Once rejected, the client will be forced to carry the pregnancy to term or seek an illegal abortion elsewhere.

Who can help?

The stress of trying to decide what to do about a crisis pregnancy may be alleviated if the girl or woman has someone to confide in and help her through the process. The confidant may be her husband or lover, a close friend or family member, a sympathetic advisor (clergy, teacher, social worker), a health worker, or someone else. Yet where abortion is legally restricted or considered highly immoral there is a risk even in seeking counsel. Who can she confide in? Who will give her advice about where to go and what to do?

Who will try to dissuade her from having an abortion or even insist that she bear the child, no matter what?

"I told my husband that I didn't want to have the baby and that a friend had offered me some shots to have a miscarriage" explains Pilar to an interviewer in Mexico City. "He said it was a sin, that God sends children to us. To be honest, I wanted to rebel against that. I said, 'Why do you say God sends children? They come because we had sex, not because God came to me and touched my stomach!' But then he called my in-laws and they said that what I wanted to do was against nature." (Pilar had the baby.) Quoted in Rosalind P. Petchesky and Karen Judd, *Negotiating Reproductive Rights: Women's Perspectives Across Countries and Cultures*

For many women in this situation, the best thing from their point of view is not to confide in anyone. Consider the case of women hospitalized for complications of illegally induced abortions studied by Chizuru Misago and Walter Fonseca in the city of Fortaleza in north-eastern Brazil. Fewer than half of the women were married or living in a stable union; one-quarter were under age twenty. Almost all were admitted to the hospital with vaginal bleeding caused by taking the ulcer medication *Cytotec* (generic name misoprosol) alone or in combination with something else. There they were treated for incomplete abortion by dilation and curettage (D&C). Although 40 percent said they had talked with family or friends about their decision, only 3 percent had consulted a medical professional. Half had not sought anyone's advice before making the attempt.

In Colombia, too, among the women of Cali with unwanted pregnancies, very few talked to close female relatives about their intentions even though most tried at least one method to induce a miscarriage. Rather, it was the reaction of the male partner that influenced the decision most directly. Most went along with their partner's wishes, either continuing the pregnancy if he was not actively opposed or terminating if he refused to accept responsibility or threatened to leave her. Women who were not in stable relationships were most likely to try to terminate.

Consulting a health practitioner

In many developing countries, the front line of the health care system for poor women with reproductive health problems consists primarily of practitioners who do not have formal training in their fields. These include indigenous healers, herbalists, traditional birth attendants or untrained midwives, and others who offer creative if often ineffective and even dangerous products and advice.

Increasingly, however, formal public health systems are reaching into previously underserved urban slums and remote rural regions. In these areas, the front line may also include trained community health and family planning workers who make home visits or serve in health posts or clinics, licensed nurses, trained midwives, and pharmacists and physicians. Women in wealthier circumstances who live in metropolitan centers will typically have access to private gynecological and obstetrical care.

What happens when a woman with a crisis pregnancy asks one of these practitioners for help? Responses will be influenced by the legality of abortion in the country in question, of course. But they are also influenced by the social and cultural environment, by the personal values of the practitioner, and by the situation of the woman herself. Let us begin with the worst case: a woman who approaches an unsympathetic physician in a country in which abortion is a criminal offense on virtually all grounds.

"The scene repeats itself over and over in physicians' offices throughout the world," writes a Colombian obstetrician/gynecologist. "A woman asks a doctor for help with an unwanted pregnancy. She hears, 'Sorry. Abortion is illegal. It goes against my moral and religious principles and professional ethics.' The physician, who once swore to place his patient's interest before his own, may or may not confront a tormented conscience. The woman, devastated and confused, confronts isolation and despair . . ." Jorge Villareal, in *Women's Health in the Third World: The Impact of Unwanted Pregnancy*

Not only is the client refused, she is told that she is a immoral: first, for breaking the law; second, for being sexually active if she is unmarried, and third, for considering abortion as a means of resolving her dilemma, whether married or not. This attitude is not restricted only to doctors, of course, although their professional opinion is likely to carry great weight. Studies in countries as diverse as Mexico, the Philippines, Indonesia, and Sri Lanka have found that across the range of formal and informal health practitioners there can always be found those who, on religious or moral grounds, blame the woman for her condition and refuse to refer her to someone who could help.

There are others, however, whose initial response will be to try to talk her out of an abortion, but who will ultimately relent. When asked what assistance they gave to women asking for help with an unwanted pregnancy, for example, two-thirds of traditional birth attendants and licensed midwives interviewed in a Philippines study said they advised the woman not to have an induced abortion. (Abortion is illegal on all grounds in the Philippines.) Yet, despite what the researchers describe as an "overwhelmingly negative attitude towards induced abortion" among both the traditional and trained practitioners, a significant number admitted that they gave women information on abortion methods or on how to locate an abortion provider. A few offered services themselves, the traditional birth attendants typically administering deep abdominal massage and/or herbal concoctions for drinking, the trained midwives giving pharmaceutical pills or injections. Often the exceptions were based on personal sympathy, such as an unmarried girl likely to be beaten by her father for becoming pregnant, or an older woman with health problems, too many children, a troubled marriage, or too little money.

In Mexico City, the front line of reproductive health care for poor women consists of drugstores and market vendors. In interviews with pharmacy workers (both trained professionals and untrained clerks) and market herb sellers, researchers found that almost all practitioners acknowledged having been asked for a method of inducing menstruation (a common euphemism) and that most held quite negative views of such women. Because abortion in the Federal District is legal only to save a woman's life or in cases of rape, the workers were understandably reluctant to admit that they might comply with their clients' requests. Yet when female interviewers posing as clients went to each person asking for treatment for a menstrual period that was three weeks overdue, 40 percent of pharmacy workers offered them injections or pills of various types (some of which are not advised for this purpose) and 66 percent of the herb vendors had something to sell. The rest refused or maintained they knew of nothing that would work. Those who did offer something included a substantial number who had said in earlier interviews they believed that such women are "bad."

The practitioner's initial reluctance to suggest a method may also be motivated by an honest desire to protect the woman from what may be, in the circumstances, an ineffective or dangerous clandestine procedure. Yet even where services are legal and safe, some providers falsely believe that abortion is riskier than childbirth or that it can result in permanent fertility impairments. They will try to talk the woman out of her decision on these grounds. If she decides to go ahead, then her anxiety is likely to be heightened by her fears of the long-term consequences.

"[T]here is a common belief among Chinese doctors of obstetrics and gynaecology . . . that the experience of induced abortion may adversely affect the outcome of the subsequent pregnancy, with increased risks of spontaneous abortion, premature delivery (or low birth weight) and maternal morbidity . . . . Doctors with this opinion routinely try to persuade pregnant women, especially those who have never had a live birth . . . not to have an induced abortion." Zhou Wei-jin and colleagues, in *Abortion in the Developing World*

The reverse side of this assessment is found among practitioners who are aware of the dangers of clandestine methods and who want to protect their patients, not by trying to talk them *out* of their decision (which is probably futile) but by acknowledging the urgency of their need and referring them to a safe provider or doing it themselves. In a country such as Indonesia, where abortion is against the law but menstrual regulation by vacuum aspiration is widely practiced in public and private clinics and hospitals, the referral process is fairly easy. In contrast, it is more difficult to refer a woman to a known safe provider in countries such as the Philippines where they must keep a low profile for fear of prosecution, and where few but the elite may know of their existence.

"The willingness of many providers [in Indonesia] to assist a woman who requests termination of pregnancy was ultimately practical—that it is better to help a woman than to have her go to an unqualified person. Otherwise, she will come after she has had an unsafe abortion, usually in a critical condition and possibly with fatal consequences." E. Djohan and colleagues, in *Abortion in the Developing World*

A woman searching for a safe provider where abortion is a criminal offense may have to persist in her efforts before she finds one willing to comply with her request. Given that she is likely to be in a state of emotional distress, this is not easy. In the end she may find someone who is willing to help her, perhaps for humanitarian reasons, perhaps to earn some extra money. In the meantime she may confront disapproving or punitive treatment, outright refusals, and many dead ends. Her pregnancy is advancing, day by day, week by week. When she finally does find someone the abortion will be more difficult, dangerous, and expensive. If she is young and unmarried, she may have an especially hard time.

"Although the greatest number of illegal abortions [in Latin America] are undertaken by married women in their late twenties or early thirties . . . the experience of unwanted pregnancy and illegal abortion may be more severe for single adolescent girls. They have less social support, greater doubts, less financial capacity to pay for an interruption and take longer to realize that they are pregnant. Consequently, they have more severe complications, a higher rate of infection, and greater risk of mutilation and death." J. A. Pinotti and A. Faúndes, in *Women's Health in the Third World: The Impact of Unwanted Pregnancy*

These stories are typical not only of developing countries, however. Consider the case of women living in the United States before abortion was decriminalized in 1973 by the Supreme Court. What did they do? Who did they talk to? How did they find someone who would help them?

Searching for an illegal provider:
an American story

In the late 1960s, anthropologist Nancy Howell Lee interviewed 107 women in the United States who admitted to having a recent illegal abortion. Most were unmarried, highly educated, and living in urban areas. As they were trying to make up their minds about what to do and where to go, only two of them did *not* talk with anyone, and half consulted four or more people. Most often their confidants included the man involved in the pregnancy, a few of whom were strongly opposed to termination and tried to convince her not to do it. In descending frequency they also included a close female friend, a personal doctor who was asked for assistance, other friends, and a parent. Many of these contacts involved requests for specific, practical help in finding a provider, however, rather than for general advice or support.

Most had to search far and wide for an abortionist or tried to induce themselves. The search typically entailed a long chain of human contacts—or rather, several chains, some of which led nowhere—before a provider could be identified. In the end, fewer than one-third of the women had the abortion locally. Two-thirds traveled outside the city in which they lived, and half of these went outside the country to illegal providers in Canada, Mexico, or Puerto Rico.

Of the 107 women included in the study, fourteen said they inserted a catheter into their uterus at home to induce bleeding or had it done by the abortionist; fifty-one had dilation and curettage (D&C)

with anesthetic, some in a clinic but more often in a doctor's office or secret location; and forty-two had curettage *without* anesthetic in a doctor's office outside regular hours or in a hidden place such as a rented apartment, hotel or motel room, or the abortionist's home. One-fifth had septic or incomplete abortions. One-tenth ended up in a hospital with complications. Others did not obtain competent post-operative care because they feared prosecution if the doctors or hospital administrators reported them to the authorities, as was required by law in most states. Perhaps the most surprising finding, however, is that despite the harrowing difficulties that some experienced, three-quarters of the women said they were generally satisfied with the treatment they received from the abortionist, whom they believed was performing an important service. Most recovered from the physical effects in a few days and from the emotional effects of the entire clandestine experience, including their search for a provider, within a few months.

"In general, one gets the impression from these women that the abortion was extremely disruptive for a few months but did not have lasting social consequences for their lives, especially in comparison with the changes which would necessarily have occurred if they had continued the pregnancies." Nancy Howell Lee, *The Search for an Abortionist*

In sum, whether abortion is more or less restricted by law in the country in which she lives, the decision to terminate a pregnancy is for most women not an easy one. Many strong feelings come into play. Moralities must be disentangled from practicalities, sense from sensibilities. A woman may be longing to have a child—even this particular child—but it is simply not possible under the circumstances. She has other children demanding her care. She hasn't any money. Her boyfriend has taken off. She is still in school.

There are as many stories as there are women, young or old, married or not, who find themselves with an unintended pregnancy that they must cope with as best they can.

Where abortion is illegal on most or all grounds, inaccessible, and largely unsafe, the path is a rocky one indeed. A woman may try to induce bleeding but fail. She may succeed, but only by doing herself great bodily harm. She may find a safe provider who is willing to help her, or she may not. She may be refused, condemned, shamed. She may turn to an unskilled practitioner and endure unspeakable pain. This is the price she pays for making her own moral decision to avoid bringing a child into the world that was conceived unintentionally and that she knows she cannot care for.

Under the best of circumstances, a woman may still wrestle with her conscience or with the wishes or her boyfriend, husband, or other family members in deciding what to do. The decision may still be a difficult one. But whatever her personal situation, she will know that she has the right to obtain a safe, legal, and affordable abortion and to be treated with compassion. In the next chapter we look more closely at how abortions are performed in medical settings under these "best" circumstances. What techniques are used for early and later procedures? What methods do women say they prefer, and why? How long will it take? How much will it hurt? What are the risks? What should a woman expect?

CHAPTER THREE

The Procedure

"**When I was an intern we'd see these women coming in with illegal abortions,**" explains an American physician. "And what bothers me now is that at that stage of my career we were all so indoctrinated how terrible abortion is. If someone came in with an illegal, we would grill her, 'Who did it? Who did it?' We were treating her like a criminal, instead of treating her like a patient. And I participated in that too, and then I thought, 'Am I crazy?! What's going on here?!'" Quoted in Carol Joffe, *Doctors of Conscience: The Struggle to Provide Abortion Before and After Roe v. Wade*

While women in many developing countries are terribly damaged from the consequences of clandestine abortions or die in the attempt, the majority of women in most developed countries now have access to high quality services. Every year, approximately 100,000 Canadian women and 1.3 million American women make the decision to have a legal abortion. During their reproductive lifetimes, an estimated four of every ten American women will terminate at least one pregnancy. For them, abortion is a fact of life and a low-risk decision. Having an early abortion is safer than having a tonsillectomy or appendectomy and far safer than having a baby.

It hasn't always been that way. The National Center of Health Statistics reported that 193 women died in 1967 from illegal abortions in the United States, accounting for almost 17 percent of all maternal deaths that year. Because the official cause of death is usually attributed to something else, this figure is probably low. Some estimates of deaths when abortion was illegal in the United States go as high as 1,000 per year. Of course even this figure pales in comparison to the estimated 20,000 women of Nigeria who die annually from the complications of unsafe illegal abortions. But that is another story.

In this chapter we explain how safe abortions are performed by physicians or other trained personnel in settings such as women's health centers, family planning and specialized abortion clinics, doctors' offices, medical centers, and hospitals. We focus primarily on the United States and Canada, although the procedures are similar in other developed countries. What methods are used most frequently? How can a woman decide what is best for her?

The preliminaries

The first question a client is likely to face when she consults a gynecologist, nurse practitioner, family planning worker, or other health professional is "What makes you think you are pregnant?" followed by "How many weeks?"

Establishing the pregnancy

The old joke that you can't be "just a little bit pregnant" fortunately does not apply here. For someone considering an abortion, "a little bit" is much better than "a whole lot" when it comes to choosing a method and provider, avoiding complications, reducing the cost, and ensuring that the procedure can be done. Past the first thirteen weeks (first trimester), restrictions on abortion can tighten up considerably, the number of willing providers shrinks, and costs and complications multiply. Abortions late in the second trimester or beyond, which are extremely rare, are almost always reserved for cases of severe fetal abnormalities or other medical emergencies. Despite the propaganda of antichoice demonstrators who display lurid photographs of aborted fetuses in advanced stages of development, almost all abortions in developed countries are performed during the embryonic or very early fetal stages.

Over half of all abortions in the United States are performed within the first eight weeks of pregnancy and almost 90 percent within the first twelve weeks. In both the US and Canada, the trend is toward earlier procedures. Almost all are done on an out-patient basis in clinics or doctors' offices; fewer than one percent require an overnight hospital stay. See Robert A. Hatcher and colleagues, *Contraceptive Technology*; Rachel Benson Gold, *Abortion and Women's Health*; and Paul Sachdev, *Sex, Abortion and Unmarried Women*

The duration of pregnancy is expressed in standard obstetrical terms as the time elapsed since the first day of the woman's last regular (that is, not unusually light or spotty) menstrual period. Although this is called the *gestational age*, the term is misleading because fertilization does not occur until about two weeks later and implantation for another week or more after that. This means that a woman is never as far along in her pregnancy as the gestational age implies.

At the time of implantation the fertilized egg is a tiny cluster of cells called a *blastocyst* that is no larger than the dot at the end of this sentence. It does not become an *embryo* until the fifth week after the last menstrual period nor a *fetus* until the tenth week. By the sixth week it is still less than one-quarter of an inch (5 mm.) in length. With its tail and primitive gill structures, the human embryo is not easily distinguishable from that of other vertebrates at this stage, including fish and other mammals.

Counting the weeks from the first day of the last period assumes that a woman can remember the date. If not, she will have to guess. It also assumes she has a regular cycle; if not, the estimate may be off by a week or two. In any case, the health provider will conduct a manual pelvic examination to assess the size and position of the uterus and the softness of the cervix. If the estimates of gestation from the two sources differ by a substantial margin, if an ectopic (tubal) pregnancy is suspected, or if the physical exam suggests some structural abnormalities, an ultrasound may be used to see what is inside. This is a painless procedure in which the technician moves a monitoring device slowly across the lubricated surface of the stomach and scrutinizes the image that appears on a screen. The choice of abortion technique depends on the results of these estimates as well as on the methods available to the provider and the client's preferences.

Next steps

Once the pregnancy and its duration are confirmed and a woman has decided that she will terminate, what does she do? This depends on whether the person she consulted about the pregnancy is also an abortion provider or works in a hospital, group practice, or family planning clinic that provides them. If not, she will have to request a referral or find a provider on her own. Abortion services are typically advertised in the yellow pages of the telephone directory. Agencies listed under the heading "abortion alternatives" are not providers, however; rather, they are usually prolife activists who try to persuade every woman to carry her pregnancy to term.

Although the sequence varies, a typical licensed abortion facility—

whether it is a women's health center, family planning clinic, specialized abortion clinic, or a medical center with gynecological services—is likely to include the following steps. These will be taken either at the initial consultation or at the time of the procedure itself.

- Review of legal requirements relating to issues such as parental consent or notification for minors, waiting ("reflection") periods, required counseling (if any), and other regulations imposed by state, provincial, or federal law;

- Review of all costs, including required or optional tests and medication; discussion as to method of payment such as private insurance, state assistance (in some states), provincial health plans (in some Canadian provinces), cash or credit card; eligibility for subsidies if available, and so on;

- Standard personal and medical history, including recent menstrual history; previous births, miscarriages and abortions; serious health conditions such as severe asthma, diabetes, heart problems or bleeding disorders; allergic reactions to medication; current drug use including over-the-counter and prescription drugs of any kind, anti-coagulants, and the use of recreational (street) drugs;

- Brief general physical exam, including pulse, blood pressure, heart and lungs;

- Blood test to determine whether patient is Rh negative (if so, Rh immune globuline is given following the abortion) or anemic (if so, iron supplement may be given beforehand);

- Blood test for HIV/AIDS, possible screening for gonorrhea, syphilis, chlamidia, other sexually transmitted infections;

- Pelvic examination to confirm gestational age and position of the uterus; PAP test for cervical cancer if not done within past year; inspection of vagina and cervix for evidence of infection (if an active infection is identified the abortion may be deferred until the condition is controlled, in order to prevent pelvic inflammatory disease and possible resulting infertility);

- Standard dose of antibiotics as a routine precaution for surgical procedures, or stronger therapeutic measures if infection is present;

- Counseling to ensure that the decision to terminate is freely taken and that other options have been considered; discussion of who may accompany the client during the procedure and who is responsible for her afterwards;

- Advice about possible delay in the return of menstruation (five to six weeks is common) and the possibility of another immediate pregnancy; post-abortion contraceptive advice and services (some clinics offer contraceptive implants, IUD insertions or even tubal ligation at the time of abortion, if requested);

- Complete explanation of the abortion procedure, including the choice of method, with the possible risks involved, what to watch for afterwards, and how and where to deal with any complications; arrangement for followup visit;

- Signing of document in which client gives the provider legal permission to perform the abortion and states that she has been told of the risks and benefits and gives her fully informed consent to the procedure agreed upon; for medical abortions (see below), a signed statement that the client agrees to have a vacuum aspiration in case of method failure;

- Review of options for pain medication, including risks and benefits of each.

"**Informed consent and counseling are two different processes.** The goal of informed consent is to assure that the woman's decision is voluntary and informed, and to obtain legal permission for an abortion. Counseling is a discussion of the feelings and concerns expressed by the woman who finds herself in a crisis situation. . . . [It also prepares her for the] procedure by reducing her level of anxiety. Counseling must not create a barrier to service and must be voluntary."

National Abortion Federation, *Clinical Policy Guidelines*

How to diminish the pain

During an abortion, the uterus will be emptied of its contents: the endometrius (clotted blood and mucous) and the embryo or fetus in its protective sac. This will be done either by *surgical* means, in which an implement is inserted through the cervical opening into the uterus to suction or scrape out the uterine lining, or by *medical* means, in which drugs are taken orally or vaginally to detach the products of conception from the uterine lining and to stimulate contractions of the uterus and expulsion of its contents.

The amount of pain or discomfort the woman experiences will depend on the length of gestation, the method used for termination, the skills of the practitioner and support staff, the woman's physical and emotional condition, her tolerance of pain, and the use of medication, among other things. If she comes to the clinic already frightened by exaggerated or lurid stories as in the Chinese case in the box below, she is likely to have an especially hard time.

"When someone said that her menstruation was late,"
explains a woman in Shanghai, "the whole group of workers
in the textile shop would be alarmed. Induced abortions,
like a delivery, may be one of the most agonizing experiences
in a woman's life." Zhou Wei-Jin and others, in *Abortion in the
Developing World*

What choices of medication are there? For surgical procedures such as
vacuum aspiration there are three: *anesthetics, analgesics,* and
tranquilizers. Experts strongly advise the least possible use of general
anesthesia for safety reasons. Without it, the patient is more alert and
responsive to what is happening to her, recovers more rapidly, and
runs less risk of allergic reaction. On the other hand, some abortion
providers prefer to use heavy sedation—what they call "twilight sleep"—
either because the patient demands it or because sedated patients are
easier to manage during the procedure even if they do feel faint or
nauseous afterwards and take a bit longer to recover.

The use of general anesthesia such as pentothal which is given
intravenously increases the risks of complications from the surgery
(such as perforation of the uterus or heavy bleeding) as well as
from the anesthesia itself (heart or respiratory failure, serious allergic
reaction). It also requires careful monitoring of the patient's vital
signs throughout the procedure and during recovery by a certified
technician who is *not* the person performing the abortion. The
need for an anesthetist substantially raises the costs.

In the United States, even under good conditions, the use of general
anesthesia in first-trimester abortion raises the risk of death from
two to four times that of local anesthesia. The danger of death
from general anesthesia is far greater in settings, such as those in
many developing countries, that may lack trained specialists,
emergency equipment, and backup hospital care. For this reason,

experts recommend either no anesthesia in the case of early vacuum aspiration or a locally injected anesthetic (paracervical block) such as lidocaine to minimize the pain that is stimulated by the probing and opening of the cervix. The local anesthetic will not block the sensation of abdominal pain and cramping from the uterus, though, which can be alleviated with analgesics such as aspirin or ibuprofen taken an hour or so before the procedure. Some providers give small doses of narcotics intravenously.

The more apprehensive a woman is before she undergoes an abortion, the more pain she is likely to feel. Indeed, the management of pain has a lot to do with the control of anxiety. A tranquilizer such as diazepam (Valium), which works best if injected, can help to lower anxiety, relax muscles, encourage a feeling of calm, and cloud the memory of the procedure afterwards. These responses may aid both the patient and the clinician. An even better approach to reducing anxiety is for an empathetic nurse or counselor to explain to the woman exactly what is happening to her at each stage of the procedure, provide reassurance and comfort throughout, and make sure that she is recovering well. For many women receiving this kind of support the pain is much less than they expected and the recovery period brief.

"**I felt real good about my decision** not to be put to sleep for my abortion. I found out that I have the strength to face my fear of pain. My cramps were bad for a few minutes, but I concentrated on deep breathing and held my counselor's hand. Ten minutes later I felt fine and ready to go home." Quoted in Boston Women's Health Book Collective, *The New Our Bodies, Ourselves*

"**I thought there would be more pain**. I just had slight cramps afterward. It went really fast. It wasn't horrible as I had thought." Quoted in Paul Sachdev, *Sex, Abortion, and Unmarried Women*

Choosing a method of early abortion

For an early procedure the main choice a woman will face is between a medical (if available) and surgical abortion.

Recently approved for release in the United States (but not yet in Canada), mifepristone, formerly known as RU 486, has been widely used in France, the United Kingdom, and Sweden since the late 1980s and early 1990s. Up to the year 2000, when about a dozen European countries had approved its use, well over six hundred thousand European women had terminated their pregnancies with mifepristone. It has now been approved in about two dozen countries worldwide, including China. Some providers in the US and Canada have been using other abortion-inducing drugs, which are described below. These are by no means the magic pills that some people thought they might be, however. Typically limited by regulatory agencies to pregnancies of no more than seven weeks (but nine weeks in Britain and Sweden), the window of opportunity slams shut very quickly. The standard regimen of pills and followup is strictly controlled and requires several clinic visits, at least one involving several hours of supervision.

Studies by Beverly Winikoff and colleagues at the Population Council in New York of women's experiences with medical and surgical abortion in several countries show that although some women think that medical induction is more natural and allows them to avoid an intrusive mechanical procedure, the abortion takes longer to complete and for many is more painful and produces heavier or longer bleeding than they expected. Often it is the *expectations* that are unrealistic, however. French women, for example, say that the new method "was not so easy and quick" as they had been led to believe.

"**The most profound significance** of the availability of safe and effective medical abortion is choice for women in a domain where previously there was none . . . . Not only is medical abortion acceptable, for some it is markedly preferable. The task now is to improve the technology and make the service delivery even more convenient and responsive to women's needs." Beverly Winikoff, *Acceptability of First Trimester Medical Abortion*

In contrast, many women prefer vacuum aspiration because, although the pain of dilation and cramping can be breathtakingly intense, it is over and done with in just a few minutes and the recovery period is brief. In addition, vacuum aspiration can be performed past the seven week deadline for mifepristone; indeed, it is often deferred to seven or eight weeks but can easily be managed up to ten or twelve weeks.

Early procedures I: the "abortion pill"

Medical options for early abortion involve the use of drugs taken orally or by injection that interfere either with the cellular development of the pre-embryo or with the ability of the endometrium (uterine lining) to sustain it. The initial medication is followed by a drug that causes the muscles of the uterus to contract and expel the contents. The most common of the medical agents used for these purposes are the "three Ms:" *mifepristone, methotrexate,* and *misoprostol.*

Mifepristone (formerly called RU 486) was synthesized in 1980 by researchers at the French pharmaceutical firm Roussel-Uclaf (thus the RU). Although it was first tested in the US in clinical trials in 1984, the request for approval from the Food and Drug Administration was not made until 1996 and was not granted until 2000. The major obstacle to its approval was not medical or scientific, however; it was political. See Planned Parenthood Association of America, "Mifepristone," www.planned parenthood.org

---

The first M: mifepristone (RU 486)

An antiprogestin, mifepristone (US trade name *Mifeprex*) blocks the transmission of the hormone progesterone that is necessary to nurture the implanted pre-embryo or embryo. Experimental trials also suggest that it may be effective in the treatment of certain brain tumors, breast and ovarian cancers, uterine fibroids, and endometriosis. Although low-dose mifepristone can be used by itself as an emergency contraceptive or menstrual regulator, its effectiveness in terminating a pregnancy is greatly improved when combined with a prostaglandin such as *misoprostol* that causes uterine contractions and expulsion of the products of conception.

Up to seven weeks the combined mifepristone-misoprostal regimen is at least 95 percent effective. At seven weeks the embryo is still very tiny, less than one half inch in length (8-10 mm.). At nine weeks the drug has a slightly lower success rate, although complete abortions have occurred in 80 to 95 percent of women, depending on the study. Because of the possibility of fetal damage from the prostaglandin, the client must agree to terminate with vacuum aspiration if the method fails. Facilities must be available for this, and she cannot change her mind.

According to clinical standards in Europe and the United States, a patient typically takes three 200-milligram pills of mifepristone in the clinic or doctor's office, after which she is free to leave. Studies in many countries have demonstrated that a single 200-milligram dose is equally effective, however. She returns thirty-six to forty-eight hours later for treatment with misoprostol (usually two tablets of 200 micrograms) or another prostaglandin taken orally or as a vaginal suppository. She may have started bleeding before she takes the misoprostol and there is a very slight possibility that the abortion has already occurred. If not, she waits four hours under supervision in the clinic for the drug to produce the cramping (which can be quite intense) and bleeding (heavier than normal menstrual flow) that signify that the process is working.

Discomfort may be alleviated with an analgesic such as Tylenol (acetominofen), but products such as aspirin or ibuprofin are not recommended because they may counteract the spasmodic effects of the misoprostol. Feelings of dizziness and nausea may surge immediately following the intake of misoprostol, although these are common symptoms of early pregnancy as well.

About two-thirds of women pass the products of conception within four hours of taking the misoprostol. Most will recognize that they have done so even though the embryo at this stage is still very tiny. Three-quarters will abort within twenty-four hours, but for the those who do not, the wait can cause considerable anxiety.

If the patient has not started bleeding within twenty-four hours she may be given a second dose of the prostaglandin. In a few cases (about 5 percent) expulsion will not occur at all or will be incomplete. This is why it is essential to return to the clinic about twelve days later to make sure the abortion is complete and, if not, to have a surgical procedure. Bleeding will continue for anywhere from a few days up to two to four weeks. The next menstrual period will arrive in five or six weeks. About one percent of women will

require aspiration or curettage to stop a v
flow.

In adapting the regimen for use in develoj
countries such as Tunisia and Vietnam de
financial costs and number of clinic vi
reduced without affecting safety or effi
women the lower dose of mifepristone (200 mg) and offering them
the option of self-administering the misoprostol at home. Clearly
this is a significant advantage in resource-poor settings where neither
providers nor clients can afford the investment of time required by
the European and American protocols.

"**If women desire and are able to use medical abortion
methods safely** and effectively without supervision, they
should be given the opportunity to do so. If safe and simple
abortion technologies could be available without medical
barriers, the cost of abortion to women would decline, and
women's sense of control over their fertility would increase."
Charlotte Ellertson, Batya Elul and Beverly Winikoff in *Reproductive
Health Matters*, based on the results of clinical trials of mifepristone-
misoprostol in China, Cuba and India.

The second M: methotrexate

A second method of inducing abortion medically is with an
injection of methotrexate followed five to seven days later with
misoprostol tablets inserted vaginally. Prescribed for the treatment
of certain malignancies, severe psoriasis and rheumatoid arthritis,
methotrexate hinders cell division which is essential for embryonic
development. It has not been properly researched or approved for
abortion, however, and so its use for this purpose raises questions
of medical liability. Nevertheless, prior to the approval of

...e by the Food and Drug Administration in the United ... the year 2000, as many as 20 to 30 percent of all abortion ...ders may have been using methotrexate with clients who ...eferred a medical option. In Canada, hospitals and clinics in several provinces use the methotrexate-misoprostol regimen for medical termination. Methotrexate is also an effective non-surgical method of terminating a dangerous ectopic pregnancy when injected directly into the conceptus in the fallopian tube.

Although its success rate approximates that of mifepristone, methotrexate takes significantly longer to destroy the products of conception and the follow-up dose of misoprostol is not taken for up to one week. The misoprostol suppositories can be inserted at home, during which the patient is advised to prepare herself carefully and to anticipate twelve hours of hard cramping and brisk bleeding (with the use of pads, not tampons) during which she should rest. Even then, some women must wait several days or even a week or more for the abortion to result. A second dose of misoprostol may be required for those who do not miscarry. If induction fails, the fetus carries a high risk of severe malformations. For this and other reasons, the World Health Organization has recommended against the use of methotrexate for pregnancy termination despite its advantages of relatively low cost and wide availability.

The third M: misoprostol

Misoprostol used by itself rather than as a followup to mifepristone or methotrexate can also cause abortion by stimulating strong uterine contractions. Now marketed by the pharmaceutical firm Pharmacia (formerly Searle) under the brand name Cytotec, misoprostol is a synthetic prostaglandin approved for the treatment of gastric and duodenal ulcers in more than seventy countries worldwide. The fact that it is contra-indicated for women who are pregnant or trying to conceive has tipped off pharmacists and consumers—most notably in Brazil but also elsewhere in Latin America and the Caribbean and in some Asian countries as well— that Cytotec can initiate bleeding and possible expulsion in the absence of safe legal services. Doses reported from Brazil range from four to sixteen pills, often with two taken orally and two inserted vaginally. Unlike mifepristone or methotrexate, misoprostol is *least* effective in the first trimester (although that is when it is typically taken, often repeatedly until it works) and improves with the duration of gestation. In small doses it is used therapeutically for the induction of labor at full term and to help prevent post-partum hemorrhage, among other uses.

In Brazil, two-thirds of women hospitalized for incomplete illegal abortions in the city of Fortaleza said they took misoprostol (Cytotec) alone or in combination with something else. The sale of Cytotec in Brazil, which was once brisk, is now restricted because it is so widely used to terminate pregnancies in the absence of legal services. Reported by Chizuru Misago and Walter Foncesca, in *Abortion in the Developing World*

Where abortion is highly restricted by law, as it is throughout most of Latin America, misoprostol has offered an accessible, inexpensive, and relatively safe alternative to harmful traditional methods. By stimulating bleeding and uterine contractions, it produces what appears to be a spontaneous miscarriage which buys women a "ticket" to hospital admission. Perhaps 10 to 20 percent of women who take Cytotec must report to a hospital for a follow-up D&C. Physicians may suspect that the abortion is induced but bleeding and incomplete expulsion are far easier to treat than the uterine perforations, cervical trauma, sepsis, hemorrhaging and shock that they otherwise confront. Because of unknown effects on women's health and fetal development if the pregnancy continues, however, the method is not recommended under uncontrolled conditions.

Early procedures II: vacuum aspiration

Introduced in the US in 1967, the practice of vacuum aspiration of the uterus, also known as *suction curettage*, now accounts for about 97 percent of all first-trimester abortions. Throughout the world, vacuum aspiration by manual syringe or electric pump has proved to be an extremely safe and simple way to empty the uterus with minimal discomfort when performed early.

Vacuum aspiration is used for at least nine of every ten abortions in countries such as Canada and the United States, England and Wales, France, the Netherlands, Italy, Norway, Sweden, Denmark, Finland, Hungary, and China. Yet, despite its simplicity and safety, physicians in many developing countries are trained only in the use of dilation and curettage (D&C), which carries far higher risks. Forrest D. Greenslade and colleagues, *Manual Vacuum Aspiration: A Summary of Clinical and Programmatic Experience Worldwide*

Following a bimanual exam to assess the size and position of the uterus, the clinician washes the external genital area and swabs the vagina and cervix with antiseptic solution. She then introduces a speculum into the vagina, which remains there throughout the procedure, to provide a clear view of the cervix at the upper end. An implement called a tenaculum is used to hold the cervix steady for the administration of a paracervical block (if used), a local anesthetic that is injected in two or three spots on the cervix. Once the anesthetic has taken effect in a few minutes, the cervical opening is dilated (slowly opened) so that a tube can be inserted through it.

The lower the gestational age, the less dilation is required. For menstrual regulation procedures done from four to six weeks gestation or for early evacuations from six to eight weeks neither dilation nor anesthetic is necessary, although the procedure will hurt. Women who have never given birth will experience more pain because the tight muscles of the cervix are more resistant to stretching.

The clinician gently pushes a flexible, narrow transparent tube called a cannula through the cervical opening, plumbs the depths of the uterus, withdraws the tube slightly, attaches the outer end to a hand-held plastic syringe about the size of a turkey baster or to a clear plastic container or glass jar connected to a mechanical or electric pump, releases a valve to create a vacuum, and moves the cannula slowly back and forth in a sweeping motion within the uterine cavity. The suctioning of the uterine contents into the jar or syringe takes only five minutes or so. The patient will experience cramping as her emptying uterus contracts around the cannula. The procedure is finished when the clinician feels this contraction and sees that only a little red or pink foam is being extracted. For most women the strong cramps ease within a few minutes, although some will feel milder cramps for several hours or even, sporadically, for several days.

"The abortion was amazingly quick and painless (considering the propaganda to the contrary). I spent an hour lying down to recover. I remember being elated—it was over and it had been so simple!" Quoted in Boston Women's Health Book Collective, *The New Our Bodies, Ourselves*

After the procedure the woman rests for anywhere from a few

minutes to an hour or so until she feels ready to leave. Some clinics serve fruit juice or sugared tea. She is checked to make sure everything is well; advised of danger signs such as prolonged bleeding (beyond two weeks) or severe pain, fever or chills; given a contact number; and told to return in a week or two to make sure the abortion is complete. Although vacuum aspiration is 98 to 99 percent effective on average, it is slightly less reliable in the very early stages up to six weeks when the products of conception may be missed.

For gestations of up to twelve weeks or longer, more cervical dilation is required because the fetus is larger. By twelve weeks it has grown to about two and one half inches (60 mm.) in length and weighs about half an ounce (14 grams). Whereas a cannula of only 4-6 mm. diameter is used for early evacuations, more advanced procedures will require diameters twice that size (that is, up to half an inch). Dilation will also take longer and the aspiration itself may last for ten to fifteen minutes. Afterwards, the clinician will inspect the evacuated contents, including the fetal tissue, to make sure that the abortion is complete. If there is some doubt she may use a curette—a long narrow metal implement with a loop at the end—to scrape the uterine walls.

"**It hurt so much. It was incredible.** The people at the clinic were really sweet and helpful but they should have told me how much it was going to hurt. What hurt the most was that I could feel when they were scraping around inside. I've talked to a lot of girls who said the same thing happened to them when they were really far along. That's why it pays to have an abortion as early as possible." Quoted in Boston Women's Health Book Collective, *The New Our Bodies, Ourselves*

Early procedures III: dilation and curettage (D&C)

There was a time when early abortions were routinely performed by what is now called *sharp curettage* but was formerly referred to as *dilation and curettage* or D&C. In some social circles the phrase "She had a D&C, you know" was a euphemism for abortion. However, like vacuum aspiration, D&C is also used to obtain diagnostic material for uterine biopsies, to treat excessive bleeding, and to clean out the uterus following a miscarriage. Most medical students routinely learn how to do a D&C for these purposes and some doctors still do them for abortions from twelve to sixteen weeks.

Complications from vacuum aspiration in the first trimester are about half those from sharp curettage. In the United States, deaths from legal abortion dropped fivefold between 1973 and 1985—that is, from 3.3 to 0.4 deaths per 100,000 procedures—and they're still going down. This drop reflects better physician training, improved medical technology, and a trend toward earlier terminations. Forrest D. Greenslade and colleagues, *Manual Vacuum Aspiration: A Summary of Clinical and Programmatic Experience Worldwide*

Sharp curettage involves the use of a rigid metal curette, as noted above, rather than a flexible plastic cannula. The procedure is thus not only more risky than aspiration but is also more painful. The curette is introduced through the cervix and manipulated to loosen and remove the tissue from the uterus. D&C also takes longer to perform and causes more bleeding. Nowadays it is typically done under general anesthesia, which involves the use of costly facilities and personnel. In the days when abortion was illegal in the United States, however, physicians were often reluctant to use anesthesia for fear of complications and discovery. They simply performed the D&C without it.

A word about the use of D&C in developing countries. In many areas of the world, ob/gyns are trained only in this procedure even though vacuum aspiration is simpler, safer, and quicker. The World Health Organization recommends the use of vacuum aspiration over sharp curettage for the treatment of incomplete abortions, whether spontaneous or induced. It requires less use of surgical facilities and anesthesia, needs no electricity (for manual vacuum aspiration), and can be performed in rural health posts by trained non-physicians.

In many developing countries, emergency medical care is beyond the reach of the majority of women who suffer from the complications of induced or spontaneous abortion. Concentrating treatment in a handful of urban hospitals that are inaccessible to most people, which the technique of surgical D&C involves, does not help. Replacing D&C with vacuum aspiration not only reduces the waiting period for emergency treatment in hospitals but also alleviates pressure on hospitals by decentralizing services to other centers. Several US-based and international organizations have launched intensive efforts to retrain and equip physicians in developing countries in the technique of vacuum aspiration as part of an overall campaign to improve the quality of abortion care.

"**Prior to the introduction of manual vacuum aspiration** to treat abortion-related complications at Kenyatta National Hospital in Kenya, bed occupancy in the emergency gynecology ward was 300 percent (i.e., three patients per bed), and 90 percent of these women had been admitted for incomplete abortion."

At the Dr. Aurelio Valdivieso General Hospital in Oaxaca, Mexico, up to four women present with incomplete abortion or related complications every day . . . . Senior ob-gyn staff were taught to use manual vacuum aspiration (MVA) with local anesthesia, instead of sharp curettage . . . . Partly as a result, women spent an average of 11 fewer hours in the hospital . . ." Ellen Brazier and colleagues, *Prevention and Management of Unsafe Abortion*

Beyond the first trimester

Approximately 10 percent of all abortions in the US and Canada are performed beyond twelve weeks gestation. This compares with 13 percent in England and Wales but lower proportions in most of the rest of Europe. In Denmark, fewer than 3 percent of all abortions are performed beyond twelve weeks.

Many obstacles can prevent a woman from obtaining an early procedure. These include her inability to recognize the early signs of pregnancy, difficulty in deciding whether to terminate, experiencing a sudden change of circumstances after she has initially accepted the pregnancy, conflicting advice or lack of social support, the opposition of parents, husband or partner, fear of discovery or of the procedure itself, lack of information about how or where to get an abortion, absence of providers in her area of residence, and lack of money.

"Finally, I had to tell my friend that my periods are six weeks late," a young Canadian woman tells an interviewer. "She decided for me to go to the drug store. I was too scared to go, because I was afraid to face the fact that the druggist will come to me and actually say to me, yes, you are [pregnant]."

> "I waited for eight weeks before I went for the pregnancy
> test," says another. "I knew I was pregnant, but I just had to
> figure out what I was going to do about it. When I pretty
> well knew what I was going to do, I went to my doctor."
> Quoted in Paul Sachdev, *Sex, Abortion and Unmarried Women*

Delays can also result from difficulties in making travel arrangements (where necessary), arranging to take time off work, obtaining parental or judicial consent if required for minors, and other procedural delays. Although the overall trend in the US and Canada has been toward earlier abortions, some women are invariably left behind. These include disproportionate numbers of teenagers, nonwhites, low-income women, girls and women who are pregnant as a result of rape or incest, and those living in rural areas or states or provinces with few abortion providers.

Except in cases of genuine medical need, most private physicians and hospital-based clinics will not perform second-trimester abortions. More and more, advanced elective procedures are done in free-standing abortion clinics. Some of these also set quite early limits; others do not. Clinic advertisements in the yellow pages of a telephone book serving one major US city with a large low-income nonwhite population offer "abortion up to 18 weeks" and "standard abortions (from 3 to 24 weeks)". The most likely surgical procedure for late cases such as these is *dilation and evacuation*, or D&E.

Dilation and evacuation (D&E)

Considered the safest and briefest method for a second trimester abortion, D&E employs a combination of methods for evacuating the uterus. These include vacuum aspiration, sharp curettage, the use of forceps to extract the fetus and placenta, and sometimes an injection of sodium chloride into the fetal sac prior to its removal. The technique requires special equipment and training. It can be done in an office or clinic as long as backup hospital care is close by. Later in the second trimester D&E is more often performed in a hospital although on an outpatient basis (no overnight stay).

Given that the pregnancy is more advanced and the instruments used are larger, the cervix will need to be opened much farther. This may be started the day before with the insertion of several absorbent matchstick-size *osmotic dilators* that slowly expand, which can cause cramping. (Some providers also administer Cytotec to soften the cervix.) The dilators are removed following the administration of a paracervical block or heavier sedation just before the procedure. Additional dilation may be needed using instruments of graduated size at this time. The aspirator is then introduced into the uterus to loosen the tissue and remove what it can, followed by scraping with a curette, perhaps more aspiration, and the use of forceps to remove any remaining parts of the fetus or placenta. D&E takes significantly longer than vacuum aspiration, ordinarily twenty to thirty minutes or more, and produces heavier bleeding. A drug may be given to help the uterus contract and to slow the loss of blood.

At sixteen weeks gestation, which is within the mid-range of a D&E procedure, the fetus is about five inches long (120 mm.) and weighs less than four ounces (110 grams). A sonogram would reveal its delicate features: large head with tiny eyes, ears, nose and mouth; distended abdomen; thin arms and legs with long fingers and toes; a beating heart. It has no awareness of pain at this stage because the neocortex of the brain is not sufficiently developed to transmit signals. But it does look distinctly human. For this reason among many others, terminating a pregnancy this late can be profoundly disturbing for everyone involved.

Nevertheless, there can be compelling reasons for performing late abortions. A woman in extreme emotional distress who is determined to terminate the pregnancy or who has tried and been unable to do so earlier will need help. In addition are those difficult cases when severe fetal deficiencies or deformities are revealed in the second trimester by amniocentesis (extraction of fluid for analysis from the amniotic sac surrounding the fetus), ultrasound (sonogram), or some other test.

D&E is widely recommended over other methods for second-trimester abortions because it has fewer complications and side effects when performed by trained medical personnel in a properly equipped facility. National Abortion Federation, *Clinical Policy Guidelines*

Medically induced late abortions

Although surgical D&E can be performed throughout the second trimester, a physician may prefer an *induction abortion* for pregnancies of sixteen weeks or more. This is a medical method that usually requires a one- or two-day hospital stay. Formerly more common, it now accounts for fewer than one percent of all abortions in the United States. A solution is injected with a long narrow needle through the abdominal wall directly into the amniotic sac. Fluid may also be extracted from the sac. Hours later the patient has severe contractions similar to labor pains that dilate the cervix and expel the intact fetus and placenta. Often she is alone in the hospital room when this occurs. The doctor is not typically in attendance, although he or she may return to do a followup D&C if there is any suspicion that the abortion is not complete.

"**With respect to second trimester abortion**, providers seek to distance themselves from an unpleasant procedure: physicians prefer medical abortions (where they need not be present at the expulsion of the fetus), and nurses prefer D&E procedures (where the physician does the 'distasteful' surgery)." Beverly Winikoff, *Acceptability of First Trimester Medical Abortion*

It used to be that saline (salt) solution was always used for late inductions. The injection causes the death of the fetus, which is then naturally expelled. The patient must wait a long time before contractions begin, however—sometimes from eight to twenty-four hours or more—and if she has a medical condition such as high blood pressure or liver or kidney problems she cannot use saline at all. There is a slight risk of medical emergency if salt is injected into a blood vessel. Yet on the whole, saline has a relatively low rate of complications including incomplete abortion requiring followup D&C.

The direct injection of a prostaglandin solution into the uterus or the repeated insertion of vaginal suppositories of misoprostol (Cytotec) causes labor contractions to occur sooner than does saline. The contractions, which can be sharp and fast, are often accompanied by nausea, vomiting and diarrhea. Not advised for women with conditions such as severe asthma or epilepsy, the prostaglandin has a higher failure rate than saline and a higher rate of excessive bleeding and retained placenta requiring D&C. Moreover, unless the prostaglandin is combined with a solution of saline, urea, or some other ingredient, the expelled fetus may briefly show signs of life even if it is not viable.

Somewhere between twenty-four and twenty-eight weeks gestation—that is, around the beginning of the third trimester—the fetus is considered *viable*. This means that although it is by no means fully developed the fetus may have the capacity to survive outside the womb for a brief period of time. If it has attained a minimum weight of slightly over one pound (500 grams) the fetus has a slim possibility of being saved with emergency life support but with a very high risk of incurring serious permanent disability. The lung capacity is inadequate at this stage and the brain synapses are not all in place. If the fetus is expelled spontaneously without signs of life it is considered a miscarriage up to thirty weeks and a stillbirth from that point on.

It is not surprising that abortion opponents target late termination procedures for elimination, which they misleadingly refer to as "partial-birth abortions." A number of states now forbid the use of certain techniques for terminating late pregnancies or require a test of fetal viability before an abortion can be performed. Yet removing the legal option not only intrudes on the physician's medical judgment but also on the emotionally difficult decision that the woman and those close to her must make if something has gone seriously wrong. Almost all very late terminations are due not to choice but to heartbreaking necessity, either because the pregnant woman has developed a life-threatening medical condition or because the fetus is afflicted in some terrible way.

In one to two percent of all pregnancies, fetal anomalies are sufficiently serious to require termination. Amniocentesis, the most common test for certain fetal defects, is typically performed between the sixteenth and eighteenth week of pregnancy and the results may not available for two to five weeks after that. Some developmental abnormalities may not be revealed until much later with the use of ultrasound. Canadian Abortion Rights Action League, "Pre-natal development," *www.caral.ca*

Followup

The chance of having serious complications following a legal abortion performed by skilled personnel in a clean environment is very small. Standards of care stress that a patient should leave the clinic only when she is in stable condition, both emotionally and physically, with good vital signs and with cramping and bleeding under control. She should know what to watch for (including what is normal and abnormal) and how to care for herself, especially with regard to preventing vaginal infection and another unwanted conception. Clinicians should be available for telephone or in-person consultations to answer any questions. A pelvic examination should be routinely performed in a couple of weeks, either by the abortion provider or another clinician, to make sure that everything is fine.

Short-term care

Some complications may arise in the days immediately following the procedure. What are the warning signals? Fever (100.5 degrees F or more) or chills. Intense abdominal pain, cramping, backache or abdominal tenderness. Prolonged or excessive bleeding (soaking through a thick pad in an hour or less) or passing large clots of blood. A foul-smelling vaginal discharge. Breast tenderness, nausea, or fatigue, which may suggest an ongoing pregnancy. This is more likely if a vacuum aspiration has been performed within the first five or six weeks.

All require further consultation. They could be signs of infection (sepsis) that may require a dose of antibiotics; perforation of the uterus or cervical tears that might require stitching; retained tissue (incomplete abortion) or continuing pregnancy (missed abortion) that will require re-aspiration; or the stopping of the cervical opening with blood clots that, when accumulated in the uterus, cause cramping and bloating. This last condition may be handled with deep massage, drugs, or re-aspiration. Finally, the possibility of an ectopic pregnancy that will have to be terminated by drugs or surgery, if not definitively ruled out previously, must be assessed.

Long-term effects

One of the main worries that many women express following abortion is about their future fertility. Will they be able to get pregnant again, if and when they wish to, and carry the pregnancy to term? This concern is not surprising considering that only 30 percent of women who have an abortion in the United States say they do not intend to have any more children. About half are under age twenty-five, and half have never had a baby. But even mothers of several children can be strongly motivated to protect their reproductive options for the future. Yet, just as misconceptions persist about the effects of contraceptive use on future fertility (the fear that a woman will have difficulty getting pregnant when she stops taking the pill or contraceptive injections, for example), so too do misconceptions about the effects of abortion.

Of course an unsafe abortion that is self-induced or performed by an unskilled practitioner in unsanitary conditions can have negative consequences. Damage to the reproductive tract (cervical trauma, perforation of the uterus) or infection (sepsis) that is transmitted to the uterus and the fallopian tubes can cause chronic pain, pelvic inflammatory disease (PID) and infertility from tubal scarring. It is possible, although by no means well documented, that repeated abortions using dilation and curettage could impair future childbearing capacity in some way. However, scientific reviews of evidence from a number of countries conclude that first-trimester abortion by vacuum aspiration does *not* increase the risk of subsequent miscarriage, of premature delivery or stillbirth, of producing an underweight or congenitally malformed infant, of having a subsequent ectopic pregnancy, or of not being able to conceive at all.

One of the best studies of post-abortion pregnancy attempts was conducted on a large sample of women in Great Britain by Peter Frank and colleagues over a period of eleven years. They found no differences between women who had induced abortions and those who delivered a baby in how long it took to get pregnant again once they started trying. Exactly 61 percent of the women in both groups conceived within three months and 97 percent within twenty-four months. Moreover, women who had abortions showed no difference in time to pregnancy due to the abortion technique employed, the gestational age at termination, or even whether they had experienced any complications.

The physical effects of a properly performed abortion, especially if it is done early in the first trimester of pregnancy, are minor both in and of themselves and when compared with the effects of term delivery. The contrasts between abortion and childbirth are especially striking when we consider that about one-quarter of all deliveries in the US and Canada and even more in some countries are performed by Cesarean section, which adds to the risks. For this reason among others, it is unfortunate that abortion opponents have adopted a strategy of trying to block women's access to methods of early pregnancy termination such as mifepristone as well as to the use of emergency contraception, which is not considered abortion at all.

But what of the emotional consequences? Critics often argue that the psychological costs of abortion are high and that a girl or woman who interrupts a pregnancy will inevitably experience deep feelings of guilt and regret. Is this true, or is it yet another example of wrong information? We turn to this important question in the next chapter.

CHAPTER FOUR

Psychological Consequences of Abortion and the Myth of Regret

---

"**Research studies indicate** that emotional responses to legally induced abortion are largely positive. They also indicate that emotional problems resulting from abortion are rare and less frequent than those following childbirth." Fact Sheet: "The emotional effects of induced abortion," *www.plannedparenthood.org*

"**What is striking is the unspoken assumption** that such careful consideration [to pre-abortion counseling] need only be given to the decision *not* to become a mother; that the only 'wrong' decision would be to have an abortion; that it is only over the decision to abort that women are likely to experience regret or worse." Mary Boyle, in *Re-Thinking Abortion: Psychology, Power, Gender and the Law*

One of the most common misconceptions about abortion is that every woman will undergo shockwaves of remorse, feel guilty and ashamed at what she has done, and forever regret her decision. Perhaps all her life she will wonder about the child she never had, even if she was already a mother or had children later when she was better able to cope. Yet carefully designed studies that have looked at this question end on a very different note. On the whole, they conclude, most women report quite positive emotions following the procedure, such as *an overwhelming sense of relief.*

Yet the antichoice movement is highly vocal on this topic. "Abortion destroys women psychologically and physically," declares a member of the British parliament during the 1990 debates on legal reform. "Many women . . . have been emotionally and psychologically scarred by abortion," insists another. The antiabortion literature is filled with assertions that women who have interrupted a pregnancy are afflicted with "abortion trauma syndrome" or "post-abortion syndrome" with its associated symptoms of intense guilt, regret, and suicidal tendencies. This imaginary syndrome is not recognized by the American Psychiatric Association, however, nor by other scientific bodies. Quite the contrary: they have rejected it outright because there is no supporting evidence.

The popular impression of regret may be due in part to the conviction held by many people that a woman's most important role in life is to bear and nurture children and that interrupting a pregnancy is invariably wrong. On both of these counts a "normal" woman *ought* to feel remorse about what she has done because she is rejecting the very essence of her femininity: *motherhood*. In a social context such as this, a woman who has terminated a pregnancy may feel obliged to express doubts or sorrow to her friends or family whether she feels them or not. She is *supposed* to feel them. After all, who wants to appear inhuman, unfeeling, unfeminine? As a woman who walks away from an abortion *free from guilt*?

"**The first thing that must be said about guilt** is that it does not exist in a vacuum but in a context shaped by history, politics, and religious and moral codes. A century of legal and religious condemnation, along with the lived reality of abortion as sinister, secret, dirty, and dangerous, inevitably stamps women's 'moral sense' of abortion as wrong or deviant." Rosalind Pollack Petchesky, *Abortion and Woman's Choice: The State, Sexuality, and Reproductive Freedom*

Reflections on the abortion experience

Many of the early investigations of the psychological consequences of abortion published in the 1950s and 1960s contributed to a perception of the inevitability of regret. Yet on closer scrutiny they often reveal major flaws in their design and interpretation. Reviewers point out that the results tend to reflect the prejudices and preconceptions of their authors more than the actual experiences of the women involved.

For one thing, many of the early studies consisted of impressionistic reports in psychiatric or medical journals of cases that were selected *because* they revealed interesting psychological disturbances. Other limitations included short periods of follow-up (asking women how they felt immediately after the operation, for example), vague and poorly defined questions that could not elicit identifiable psychological symptoms, a disease-oriented bias toward describing negative physical or psychological symptoms without acknowledging the positive (and therefore not even asking), and a failure to inquire about why the woman had had an abortion or to explore her feelings leading up to her decision, which would influence her later reactions.

Moreover, much of the early research in the United States was done at a time when abortion was restricted in most states—if it was permitted at all—to women who could demonstrate in a psychiatric or medical consultation that their physical or mental health would be significantly threatened by a continuation of the pregnancy. The same is true of the Canadian and European studies. Women with convincing symptoms such as a history of psychiatric treatment (or whose doctors were sympathetic or well-paid) were granted permission to terminate on therapeutic grounds, while mentally healthy women were denied. It would be hard to imagine a more biased sample of cases.

Yet, despite this selectivity, the few reliable studies that measure symptoms accurately on a standard psychological scale (including physical complaints and signs of depression, anxiety or hostility), and that make comparisons over time, demonstrate that the highest levels of distress are found just *before* the abortion and tend to disappear entirely within six months to a year if not right way. Indeed, most studies of therapeutic abortion even immediately following the procedure show that women's positive feelings far outweigh their negative ones, and that the abortion itself was a significant factor in resolving their distress. Very few express feelings of guilt or self-reproach.

The therapeutic abortion

Canadian researchers Harry Brody, Stewart Meikle and Richard Gerritse collected interviews and psychological test results from a group of women who applied to a hospital therapeutic abortion committee for permission to terminate and from a sample of women who accepted their pregnancies and were seeking prenatal care. Both groups were interviewed within the first three months of pregnancy, six months after the abortion or delivery, and one year later. Among the women requesting a termination, 60 percent were currently married while 30 percent were single and 10 percent were separated or divorced. In the second group, all were married.

"Individuals applying for a therapeutic abortion at this hospital followed a standard routine. An application form completed by a physician and requesting an abortion was forwarded to the Chairman of the Therapeutic Abortion Committee, who then arranged a meeting to consider the case. The patient, husband (if any), and the referring physician were all expected to attend. Having deliberated on the merits of the case, the committee members then individually and independently completed voting forms. The decision was based on a straight majority rule, and all members of the committee, consisting of at least 3 physicians plus a social worker and a psychologist, carried equal voting rights." Harry Brody and colleagues, in the *American Journal of Obstetrics and Gynecology*

Not surprisingly, abortion applicants interviewed just before their committee hearings revealed a marked degree of psychological distress. (Indeed, the prospect of the hearing itself, which is described in the box, could easily have caused anxiety.) The tests showed especially elevated levels of "hypochondria," "depression," and "schizophrenia" among abortion applicants compared with women who planned to deliver. Among applicants who were granted permission to terminate (80 percent of those requesting it), symptoms of distress dropped markedly within the first six weeks following the procedure. After one year their psychological profiles were identical to those of the women who had accepted their pregnancies and had the babies; all were within the range of normal variation. The very different situation of women denied permission for abortion is discussed later.

When abortion is available on request

More recent studies of women who had access to abortion on request (although certain restrictions always apply) reveal a similar pattern of findings. Immediately before the procedure a woman is more likely to show signs of emotional distress due to the circumstances that caused the accidental pregnancy or that led her to interrupt it. Some anxiety may also relate to the impending procedure itself, although this is not clear. After the abortion, however, symptoms of distress decrease quite rapidly.

"As I regained consciousness I felt relieved that I was no longer pregnant. It was a nice feeling to have it all over, because it was a problem and now this was out of my way. I was totally transformed from my former state of depression."

Abortion client quoted in Paul Sachdev, *Sex, Abortion, and Unmarried Women*

Although most studies analyze women's psychological scores on a battery of standard tests, one study of almost six hundred women by Joy and Howard Osofsky and Renga Rajan describes patients' emotional reactions directly following the procedure. The setting is a hospital in Syracuse, New York, soon after abortion was legalized there in 1970. Whereas 10 percent of the post-abortion patients apparently reacted with "moderate crying" or "much crying," one-quarter reacted with "moderate smiling" and one-half reacted with "much smiling." And although 40 percent of the abortion patients were Catholic, only 15 percent reported post-operative guilt feelings while 73 percent expressed relief.

In virtually all such studies, the most common words used to describe women's immediate post-abortion responses are "positive," "happy," "relieved," and even "euphoric." Only a small minority express mild guilt, sadness, or doubt. Moreover, researchers note that for most women who have had abortions and for their partners as well, the procedure represents a maturing experience because they have successfully resolved a personal crisis. Even when the abortion decision elicits ambivalence in the couple or a clash of values, it can lead to a deepening sense of self-awareness and responsibility for oneself and for others. Rather than being a source of stress, the decision to terminate an unplanned pregnancy appears to have a genuine therapeutic effect. It can also lead to positive behavioral changes such as the decision to finish high school or college and to practice more effective contraception in the future.

Who is most vulnerable to negative reactions?

This is not to deny that some women do go through a period of distress, and particularly of depression, following the abortion. There are several reasons for this.

"One of the main conclusions of the study [in the Netherlands] is that the psychological consequences of abortion are less alarming than imagined by some. There is no reason, nevertheless, to belittle the problems or dismiss them entirely. About 10% to 20% of women go through a period of distress after abortion, 10% explicitly need help during this period. In general, short-term counseling will prove adequate." Marie Schopman, in Stimezo Nederland, *Abortion Matters*

First, although the abortion may have helped to resolve an immediate crisis, the problems leading up to the abortion (social, economic, personal) often persist. A woman may have to cope with a broken relationship, for example, or with the grim persistence of poverty or ill health. This is not to say that she necessarily regrets having had the abortion, but rather that she must still must face the harsh realities of her life.

Second, the evidence suggests that post-abortion symptoms of depression or hostility are associated with the circumstances of the decision and whether the woman feels in control. Adolescents pressured by parents to have an abortion or women whose husbands or lovers did not want the baby are more likely to be depressed or hostile afterwards than those who make the decision on their own. In a related vein, women who have negative feelings toward their partner, who face opposition from their parents in the decision to abort, or who make the decision without consulting anyone, are also likely to show higher levels of emotional distress both before and immediately after having an abortion.

Women forced to terminate for medical or genetic reasons are particularly prone to depression, hostility, or anxiety following their abortions. Often this happens very late in the pregnancy when the results of amniocentesis become known. For a woman in this position the abortion is not a choice but a cruel stroke of fate, especially if the pregnancy was a particularly wanted one or was difficult to achieve. Following the stress of a late-term procedure she must then worry about whether she can get pregnant again and have a normal baby. She may wonder if she made the right decision to terminate after all.

Women who are more ambivalent about their pregnancies and have more difficulty making the abortion decision are also more likely to have negative reactions afterwards. Because their ambivalence often leads to delays, such women are more likely to undergo a second-trimester procedure which is far more physically and emotionally stressful. The combination of ambivalence, a longer period of pregnancy in which to identify with the fetus, and the delivery-like abortion procedure if labor is medically induced compounds the usual stress factors to produce an especially disturbing outcome.

An early study of low-income abortion patients in a Philadelphia hospital by Joy and Howard Osofsky and Renga Rajan found that women having second-trimester procedures took a significantly longer time to recognize that they were pregnant and had more difficulty in finding a medical facility that would perform the procedure. Abortion was still restricted in Pennsylvania at this time, although the hospital's therapeutic committee refused no one. They were also more likely than first-trimester patients to say they were "very scared" when they realized that they were pregnant (half admitted to this) and that the decision to terminate was a difficult one. Although post-abortion feelings of guilt and depression were uncommon, about 10 to 12 percent of second-trimester patients reported such feelings compared with only 2 percent of the first-trimester group.

Women with a history of pre-existing psychological problems including psychiatric treatment are also more likely to show signs of emotional distress following abortion than are those with no such history. One study found that women exhibiting significant post-abortion distress use a great deal of denial and repression, as well as projection onto their partner or the medical staff, in dealing with the stress of their pregnancy and subsequent abortion. These women also tend to "blur the boundaries" between themselves and the aborted fetus and maintain an ongoing, high level of attachment to the fetus, despite its loss. Another study found that women with lower self-esteem and a sense of alienation before the abortion experience greater post-abortion distress. In contrast, those with higher levels of self-esteem and a clearer sense of control over their own lives show more favorable responses.

What about regret?

Perhaps the question of greatest interest to many is that of long-term regret. Is this a common reaction? As time passes, do many women wish they had not decided as they did? We are speaking here of those who decided on their own, of course, and not of those who had to terminate for other reasons.

A review of women's feelings after abortion in studies that specifically address the question of regret shows that in most cases, 5 percent or fewer say they were sorry they had the abortion and almost all say they would make the same decision again.

"**Often, it is not the abortion itself they regret** but rather the fact that they have had to come to this decision: the patient feels faced with a situation that she could not or cannot change. Only an insignificant percentage [1 to 2 percent] mention afterwards that they feel they made the wrong decision after all." Maria Schopman, in Stimezo Nederland, *Abortion Matters*

Interestingly, it may be among those women whose lives did not turn out as badly as they expected who are more likely to have later regrets. Although most studies show that women react most positively when they have strong social support, one found that women whose partners accompanied them to the clinic for the procedure were more likely to feel depressed afterward. Another found that single women who maintain a strong relationship with their partner after the abortion are more likely to feel regret a year later. These findings suggest that the woman may be asking herself "Is it possible, given how things turned out, that I could have had the baby after all?"

What happens to women
denied permission to terminate?

A major limitation in playing this guessing game about the might-have-beens is that most studies of the psychological consequences of abortion do not cast the same analytical eye on the consequences of being forced to carry an unintended pregnancy to term. What happens to a woman whose request for a therapeutic abortion is denied?

Where legal grounds for abortion are restricted to certain mental, physical, or socioeconomic indications, a woman with a problem pregnancy typically must solicit permission from one or more physicians or a hospital committee and wait for its response. Even where abortion is legally available on request, as in the United States, an underage girl who lives in a state where parental or judicial consent is required may not get permission to terminate. It should not be difficult for us to imagine how this dependence on the decisions of others in authority must feel to the woman involved. What will she do if she is told that she must have the baby, regardless of her own wishes?

Many women who are denied a legal termination go on to have an illegal abortion elsewhere even though they have lost time by the delay. As many as 15 percent to *half or more* do so, according to evidence from therapeutic abortion systems in the United States, Great Britain, Sweden, Czechoslovakia, and New Zealand. And the rest? Some will place the infant for adoption—as many as 8 to 20 percent of those denied permission to terminate, according to some early surveys. Others will try to adjust.

"I don't think she should get an abortion just because she doesn't want [the baby] . . . I think that women should suffer the consequences and go ahead and have the baby. And, if she doesn't want that baby, she should just put it up for adoption. But I don't feel she should have an abortion if she really doesn't have a good reason for doing it." Young woman quoted in Mary Kay Zimmerman, *Passage Through Abortion*

It is interesting to see how casually some people will say that a woman who doesn't want to have a baby should have it anyway and give it up for adoption. Sometimes this proposal is phrased as though she has an *obligation* to infertile couples. In the 1990 British debates about abortion law reform described by Mary Boyle in her book *Re-thinking Abortion*, for example, some members of parliament argued that all abortions except those performed for therapeutic reasons should be prohibited in order to benefit couples who were unable to conceive. Other members claimed that "women could easily give up their babies for adoption rather than have an abortion, and so bring happiness to a childless couple."

Yet adoption can be a bitter pill to swallow. It is hard on the birth mother and often hard on the adopted child who wonders *who* she or he really is and *why* she was "abandoned" or "given away." In Scotland, social researcher Gordon Horobin found that women who gave up their babies were doubly resentful at their predicament. Sadness at having to give up a child they knew all along they couldn't have was mixed with anger at having been forced by hospital authorities to carry the pregnancy to term in the first place. The emotional consequences for them were far more severe than for women granted an abortion on therapeutic grounds.

In Canada, too, Paul Sachdev found that 95 percent of birth mothers who gave up their babies for adoption reported feelings of grief and loss after signing the consent forms; two-thirds still had these feelings five to fifteen years later. Many, in retrospect, wished they had raised their babies themselves. Yet as we have seen, feelings of distress (if any) following an early abortion tend to dissipate quickly for almost all women, who can then get on with their lives without wondering every day how and where their child is.

"It's hard to . . . [terminate] when you are two or three months pregnant. But I can't imagine to go through the birth and sign papers and say, 'Look, someone else can have my baby; he is yours, he is no longer mine.' I would think the rest of my life that . . . someone [else] is bringing up my child . . . . I think it is better for a girl to have an abortion than to have to give her baby up for adoption." Quoted in Paul Sachdev, *Sex, Abortion, and Unmarried Women*

The intent of a therapeutic abortion is ideally to make things better for the person in distress. A therapeutic abortion *denied* can make things worse. In the Canadian study by Harry Brody and colleagues that compared women who applied for a therapeutic abortion with women who had their babies, 20 percent of the abortion applicants were refused permission to terminate. Of the twenty-three women who were turned down, twelve left the city and could not be located. Others obtained illegal abortions locally and were afraid to be reinterviewed. "Some wanted nothing more to do with the hospital," say the researchers, "feeling that since they had been refused help in their time of need they were under no obligation to continue in the project." In the end, only four women could be reinterviewed. All four had the baby and showed symptoms of psychological distress six months later that were as high as those measured preceding their request to terminate.

Similar findings are reported from other studies in the United States, England, Scotland, and Sweden. In a strange twist of logic, mentally and physically healthy women whose request for termination was rejected suffered more than did those who were judged on mental health grounds to be "sufficiently disturbed" and whose abortions were approved.

"**Patients who were denied an abortion** [in the United States] because of insufficient psychiatric problems fared considerably worse postdelivery than did the apparently more emotionally disturbed individuals following abortion."
Joy D. Osofsky and colleagues, in *The Abortion Experience: Psychological and Medical Impact*

The Scottish study in the City of Aberdeen in 1968-69 compared women denied therapeutic abortion with those whose cases were accepted. Interviews sixteen months later revealed that single women who had been granted an abortion were the *least likely* to exhibit lasting symptoms of mild or severe depression. The worst off were married or divorced women who were made to continue their pregnancies, among whom 30 percent showed signs of mild or severe depression long after giving birth. Typical of most such studies, we learn little if anything about the effect on the fathers.

An even longer time perspective was used in an early study by Hans Forssman and Inger Thuwe of 249 Swedish women who were refused a therapeutic abortion. Interviews seven years later showed that one-quarter of the women had been able to cope fully with the pregnancy and the child. Half experienced symptoms of great emotional strain for a period of time following the birth but seemed to have overcome these problems. One-quarter still showed signs of mental distress and poor adjustment after seven years. In Great Britain in 1970, seventy-three women were interviewed one to three years following the denial of their request for termination who had the baby. Although sixty percent reported that they accepted the child and were ultimately glad that they had not ended the pregnancy, one-third said that the child was a burden they frequently resented.

Admittedly quite subjective, these findings nonetheless show that, although an unwanted pregnancy does not always result in an unwanted child, there is reason to be concerned that a woman who is denied her request for termination may harbor quite negative feelings toward her children. Having tried her best to avoid having a baby in the difficult circumstances in which she found herself, she is told by her doctor or by a committee of anonymous "experts" that she is not eligible to terminate and *must* have the child. The child is punishment. Her feelings of resentment and frustration at not being in control of her life are easily elicited by skilled interviewers long after the event.

Born unwanted: effects on children and families

"Large proportions of married women all around the world report that in the past five years, they had a birth sooner than they had wished to (a mistimed birth) or at a time when they had wanted no more children (an unwanted birth). The proportion of women who describe a recent birth as mistimed or unwanted is striking everywhere, but it is particularly high in Kenya and Zimbabwe, in the Philippines, in [Brazil, Colombia, Mexico, and Peru], and in Japan." The Alan Guttmacher Institute, *Sharing Responsibility: Women, Society and Abortion Worldwide*

Couples throughout the world increasingly want to have small families—often no more than two or three children, if that—and are practicing contraception more diligently. Yet although in the developing world the average number of births per woman has dropped from 6.0 in the early 1960s to 3.4 in the mid-1990s (excluding China, where the birth rate is much lower) and is still going down, the proportion of all births that are unwanted is going up. This is because couples' desired family size is dropping even faster than their actual fertility, resulting in the birth of babies that are unwanted because they exceed the couples' family planning goals.

A review of surveys from twenty developing countries by demographer John Bongaarts reveals that even after aborted pregnancies are excluded, *one in every four babies born was not wanted at all* (that is, was not just mistimed). But this happens not only in the developing world. In the US, the proportion of *births* (not just pregnancies) that were unwanted at the time of conception ranges from under 10 percent among currently married women to almost 30 percent among those who are still single. It is even higher among women in low-income households who can least afford the psychological and financial burdens of an unwanted baby.

What does it mean to a child to be born of an unwanted pregnancy? How might it affect the child's sense of self in his or her surroundings? Is it possible that a child's awareness, conscious or subconscious, that something is "missing" or "wrong" could have a profound impact not only during childhood but also for years afterwards?

Infants and young children are acute observers of the world around them, and particularly of their parents or other primary caregivers. According to psychiatrist Daniel N. Stern, babies recognize the eyes as the center of a face as early as eight weeks. By three and a half months they can control their gaze almost as well as an adult

can, and they actively seek out the faces and eyes of those
them for intense scrutiny. The response of a parent to th
actions from moment to moment can be very revealing during
these periods of mutual gaze. Because the infant at this point has
essentially no other method of close communication or social
connection, these interactions take on a powerful meaning as the
baby begins to build a concept of itself in relation to others.

By four years of age, children begin to create a sense of narrative
about themselves as separate beings in relation to others and to the
larger world. They do this in part by incorporating experiences
from their environment, and especially from those closest to them,
into their developing personalities. Although we know that not
every unwanted pregnancy results in an unwanted child, we can
imagine how hard it could be for a parent to conceal feelings of
ambivalence, annoyance, or despair from the intense scrutiny of
the infant's gaze, and, later, from the struggle of the growing child
who is seeking to understand his or her place in the world. If the
primary caregiver, usually the mother, is depressed or resentful
about the child's intrusion in her life she may simply close down,
withdrawing from all unnecessary interaction with the baby even
immediately following its birth. As we shall see below, avoiding
the infant's gaze is one of several common but damaging behaviors
among depressed mothers, especially if the baby was not wanted.

Born unwanted?
Or born into other disadvantaged circumstances?

One of the many challenges in trying to understand the effects of
birth intention on a child's psychosocial development is to sort
out the effects of being born due to an unwanted pregnancy from
being born into an already disadvantaged situation in which
unwanted conceptions are more likely to occur. Poverty, risk-taking
behaviors, teenage parenthood, single motherhood (at any age),
too many children already, a conflicted or dysfunctional family

situation: all are grist for the mill when it comes to unintended pregnancies, unwanted births, and difficulties in coping with a(nother) child. How can one sort out their effects?

We can't just look at problems among unwanted children and attribute them to their "unwantedness" any more than we can just look at, say, problems among children whose parents have divorced and blame the divorce for the problems. One needs to make careful comparisons with children who are *not* unwanted, or did *not* go through a divorce, but who are otherwise similar in age, sex, religion, racial or ethnic identity, social class, living situations, and so on. Moreover, one must follow the children and parents of both groups for many years and conduct repeated interviews and psychological tests. This is as complicated as it is expensive. Nevertheless, some intrepid researchers have made the attempt, with some success.

"Carefully designed and executed prospective studies . . . reveal long-lasting, broadly based, negative effects of the denial of abortion on the children subsequently raised in the situation that the parents had tried so desperately to avoid." Paul K. B. Dagg, in the *American Journal of Psychiatry*

Children born following a denied request for termination

There are many ways of trying to assess whether a given pregnancy or birth is a wanted one or not. One indicator stands apart because it is so clear: the birth of a baby following a refused request for therapeutic termination. At some point early in the pregnancy we know that the woman was determined not to carry it to term. Now she has had the baby after all. What happens to children born in these circumstances?

Perhaps the most ambitious study to date, and one that is much quoted, was done in Prague by Matijcek, Dytrych, and Schuller who followed 220 children born between 1961 and 1963. That the pregnancies were unwanted is without doubt, for the mothers of these children were *twice* denied permission to terminate (at the initial petition and again on appeal) even under the generous health and social grounds allowed by the 1957 Czechoslovakian law. The main reasons the women gave for not wanting the baby were being unmarried, living in a disintegrating family situation, not having adequate housing, or being in poor health. Why did the committee refuse them? Two-thirds of the refusals were based on "insufficient reason." The rest were due to pregnancies of more than twelve weeks or occurring within six months of a previous abortion. Committee deliberations typically took two weeks; nearly all applicants who were already ten weeks pregnant were denied. (On appeal, the pregnancies were of course even farther along.)

Of 555 pregnant women who were twice denied for the same pregnancy during the time period, only 220 babies were born. The rest of the women admitted to having an abortion elsewhere, claimed a "miscarriage," or could not otherwise be linked with a birth record. Researchers matched the 220 babies born from the unwanted pregnancies with babies of accepted pregnancies born at the same time and of the same sex, socioeconomic class, birth order, and mother's marital status. This is a classic matched-pairs design that allows comparisons to be made between unwanted and accepted babies while controlling for the potentially confounding effects of these other characteristics.

In their many followup interviews, the investigators found that the unwanted babies were breastfed for shorter periods or not nursed at all. They were more likely than the accepted children to have serious physical illnesses, to be maladjusted as preschoolers, to be described as difficult by their mothers, and, by ages seven to nine, to be rejected by friends and teachers and to perform poorly in school. All differences were more marked for boys than for girls. At ages fourteen to sixteen the school performance of teenagers in the unwanted group continued to deteriorate and their relationships with their mothers as measured on psychological scales were worse than those of their counterparts. By their early twenties they had fewer friends, were more dissatisfied with their jobs and with life in general, and had more personal and social problems. Remember that this is in comparison with children who grew up in very similar circumstances, apart from the fact of their mothers' twice-denied request to terminate the pregnancy.

It is difficult to tell from such observations what interpersonal family dynamics might have created problems for the children born of unwanted pregnancies. (In most cases both father and mother had rejected the pregnancy, although many of the women were not married.) What the researchers found is quite interesting: parental rejection was not typically translated into *hostility*, which might have resulted in a pattern of physical abuse, but rather into a generalized *lack of interest and concern* that resulted in the psychological deprivation of the child.

"Acceptance [by the mother] is incomplete, ineffective, and ambivalent, leading to more or less deviant interactions, less maternal empathy with the child's needs, less understanding of his/her behavioral signals, [and] less warm emotional interchange of stimuli . . ." Reactions of mothers to children born unwanted described in the Prague study, in Henry P. David and colleagues, *Born Unwanted*

In Sweden, Forssman and Thuwe found that babies born to women who were denied a therapeutic abortion between 1939 and 1942 were far more likely than those born of accepted pregnancies to have single mothers or, if not, to experience the breakup of their parents while they were young. Comparisons of children born following a refused termination with children of the same age and sex born of accepted pregnancies found that the former were more likely to have an insecure childhood (including family instability, placement in a foster or children's home, trouble reported to child welfare authorities, etc.), to require psychological counseling, to perform poorly in school, and to drop out sooner. As adults they were more likely to marry early and to receive public assistance. Studies in other Scandinavian countries, where there was much early interest in the social policy implications of denying women therapeutic abortions, elicit similar results.

Born unwanted when abortion is an option

Once the legal restrictions on grounds for abortion are removed, it is no longer possible to look at the consequences of a committee's refusal to grant permission to terminate. Yet even where abortion is available on request, many children are born who were unwanted (not just unintended) at the time of conception. How do we know this? Typically, by asking the mother.

An interviewer might ask a series of questions such as this: "Thinking back to your most recent pregnancy, was it planned or not? If it was unplanned, did you not want to have a baby at all, or did you want to have a baby later but not at that time? Did the pregnancy result in a live birth? If not, was it terminated by a miscarriage, or by an abortion?" The woman may not be able to give a clear answer, however. It may be hard for her to say so neatly that a particular pregnancy was *planned* or *not planned*, especially if she was using contraception sporadically or was ambivalent about having a baby.

"I didn't plan [the pregnancy], and then again I kind of knew what was going to happen because I wasn't like really taking the pills like I was supposed to. I couldn't remember every day to take the pill. And I still don't." Quoted in Sarah S. Brown and Leon Eisenberg, *The Best Intentions: Unintended Pregnancy and the Well-being of Children and Families*

An additional problem arises if we ask a mother about whether a child who is now part of the family was planned at the time of conception. In a rush of *ex post* rationalization she is quite naturally likely to say that little Maria or Michael was wanted all along. Some studies try to neutralize the question by avoiding reference to a particular pregnancy. The US National Survey of Families and Households, for example, asked each mother this question: "Sometimes people have (a child/another child) after they intend not to have any (more) children. Has this ever happened to you?" Seventeen percent of women in the 1987-1988 survey admitted that it had happened to them at least once. This figure is really quite high considering that many mothers were still in their childbearing years and thus at risk of having another pregnancy, and that some unwanted pregnancies had undoubtedly been terminated by abortion (that question was not asked).

Seven percent of all babies born to married women in the US between 1985 and 1990 were not wanted at all and another 30 percent arrived at a bad time. Among unmarried women, however, 28 percent of all babies were born unwanted and another 45 percent were mistimed. *Only one in every four babies of unmarried mothers was neither mistimed nor unwanted at conception.* Sarah S. Brown and Leon Eisenberg, *The Best Intentions: Unintended Pregnancy and the Well-being of Children and Families*

Sociologist Jennifer Barber and her colleagues analyzed responses to the National Survey of Families and Households to assess the effects of unwantedness on the relationship between mothers and young children. Women who reported having had at least one child when they hadn't intended to have any (more) were more likely than those with no unwanted births to score high on a series of questions about specific symptoms of depression and low on an overall assessment of their own happiness. Whether such feelings are causes or consequences (or, more likely, both) of having an unwanted pregnancy and of not terminating it cannot be easily sorted out. What is important in this study is their effect on the quality of the mother's interactions with her children and with her husband, if she is not single or divorced. A strained marital relationship associated with unwanted childbearing (among other factors) will clearly affect the children as well.

We know that even an ordinary pregnancy and childbirth, if there is such a thing, is not always an unqualified joyful event. It can cause stress, anxiety, or depression in the mother and perhaps in the father as well, although we know less about this. When the birth is also an unwanted one, a mother's depression can be severe. This is due not only to the arrival of the baby itself, which is disruptive under the best of circumstances, but also to the situation that caused the conception to be unwanted in the first place. What makes the mother's depression especially serious in such cases, quite apart from her own mental health, is her impaired capacity to seek prenatal care and to interact and bond with the baby once it is born.

Women in the US who have unwanted conceptions tend to initiate prenatal care later and to receive less adequate care than women who planned their pregnancy. This is due in part to an inability or refusal to acknowledge the pregnancy early, and in part because unwanted pregnancies occur more frequently among adolescents, the poor, minority women, and other groups with limited access to good health care.

From Sarah S. Brown and Leon Eisenberg, *The Best Intentions: Unintended Pregnancy and the Well-being of Children and Families*

Evidence from a number of studies suggests that depressed mothers often tend either to withdraw from their infants (for example, to touch, look at, and play with them less than nondepressed mothers do), or, alternatively, to respond to the infant's demands intrusively, with irritation and anger. These patterns are especially apparent among adolescent girls coping with their first baby and older mothers who already have a lot of children. "Both withdrawn and intrusive interactions are likely to have negative consequences for infant development," write the authors of the US study, "particularly in terms of emotional and behavioral problems, delayed verbal development, and weaker mother-child attachment." The negative effects can begin within days of the baby's birth and continue indefinitely.

Interviews with mothers in the National Survey of Families and Households reveal both patterns. Women with at least one unwanted child, especially if they showed signs of depression, spent less time interacting with their young children and reported more episodes of physical punishment, such as spanking or slapping. Those who were currently married and had at least one unwanted birth also reported higher levels of marital strain and general unhappiness. Not just the particular child but the entire family was affected.

"**Overall, these findings add to growing evidence** regarding the negative consequences of unwanted childbearing. Having unwanted births leads to outcomes that are problematic for both mothers and their children, including mental health problems for mothers, lower quality relationships between mothers and children in terms of affection and social support, and increased violence and less leisure time interaction during childhood." Jennifer S. Barber and colleagues, in *Journal of Health and Social Behavior*

In sum, the conclusions drawn from this and other studies of unwanted children whose mothers accepted their pregnancies (in the sense that the pregnancies were carried to term and the babies were not given away) appear to differ in degree, but not in kind, from those reported for children born to mothers whose request for an abortion was denied. Although there is no one-on-one relationship between pregnancy intention and the well-being of the child, children born of pregnancies that were unwanted by one or both parents tend to have lower self-esteem and more difficulties in social adjustment, in school, and as adults than do children born of wanted (or at least not *unwanted*) pregnancies in similar social and economic circumstances.

The insistence of abortion opponents that the voluntary termination of a pregnancy is bound to be a physically and emotionally traumatic event for the girl or woman, and one that she will inevitably regret, is clearly mistaken. On the contrary, research shows that by far the most common reaction to a safe early procedure is one of happiness and relief at having resolved a stressful personal situation. It is the women who have been *refused* permission to terminate an unwanted pregnancy who are more likely to experience depression and regret. Either they risk having an illegal, perhaps dangerous, and unnecessarily late abortion somewhere else, or else they must continue the pregnancy and raise the unwanted baby themselves or give it away. These outcomes are far more likely to have negative psychological, social, economic, and health consequences than is a safe abortion. In fact, compared with its alternatives, a carefully considered and early decision to terminate may well be the most sensible and least costly solution in every respect.

This conclusion is of course profoundly upsetting to antiabortion crusaders. Yet their claim that abortion inevitably harms women not only misrepresents the facts; it also ignores the potentially harmful consequences to women, men, families, and communities of the birth of an unwanted child. Indeed, their insistence that every embryo has a "right to life" quite apart from the pregnant girl's or woman's best interests shows a remarkable disregard for the mother's emotional and physical wellbeing as well as that of the child. In the antiabortionist's view, the decision *not* to become a mother at a particular point in her life (or at all) takes on greater significance than the decision to *become* a mother, with all of the economic, social, and personal responsibilities that parenthood entails. This illogical reversal of priorities is reflected in our legal systems as well, for in most cases, the law is constructed to persuade every woman to embrace motherhood no matter how accidental the conception rather than to provide her the means to make an intelligent choice.

In the next chapter we look at the many ways in which a woman's access to safe and affordable abortion care is circumscribed by restrictive laws and policies. Under what conditions is a woman permitted to have a legal procedure, and where? In countries where abortion is a criminal offense, what can a desperate woman do? When *is* abortion against the law, and what difference does it make?

PART II:

PUBLIC SETTINGS

CHAPTER FIVE

When Is Abortion Against the Law and What Difference Does It Make?

"**Any woman who, with intent to procure her own miscarriage,** whether she is or is not with child, unlawfully administers to herself any poison or other noxious thing, or uses any force of any kind, or uses any other means whatever, or permits any such thing or means to be administered or used to her, is guilty of a felony, and is liable to imprisonment for seven years." Section 229 of the Criminal Code of Nigeria; see Adetoun Ilumoka in *Women's Health Issues in Nigeria*

"**Some of the women were placed under arrest** while they were still on the maternity ward and were interrogated there." Lidia Casas-Becerra, in *Reproductive Health Matters*, reporting on her study of 80 women prosecuted in Santiago, Chile, for having an abortion, 40 women prosecuted for performing abortions, and 12 friends and relatives prosecuted as accomplices.

If every one of the estimated twenty million women worldwide who have illegal abortions every year were incarcerated, the prisons would be full of mothers, wives, sisters, daughters, and girlfriends who had broken the law. Not to mention the abortion providers destined to receive more severe sentences—the family physician or pharmacist equally with the market vendor, unskilled midwife, and back-alley quack.

But the prisons are not full of women who have had (or attempted) an abortion, nor are they full of abortion providers. In fact it would be difficult to find such prisoners anywhere, although they do exist. One study of women imprisoned in Nepal found that one-fifth were convicted of illegally induced abortion, which was considered a homicide there up until 2002. In Chile during the Pinochet regime in the 1980s, about one thousand court cases per year were brought against women and abortion providers, although the numbers have dropped dramatically since then. Only a handful of women (mostly very poor) and abortion providers (mostly older and untrained) are actually incarcerated, in part because of the shortage of prison space and lack of facilities to care for their children. In addition, most doctors refuse to report abortion cases to the authorities even if they themselves are unwilling to perform them, and many judges are reluctant to send the women to jail.

Who, then, is likely to be arrested and charged in countries where restrictive laws prevail? Almost no one. Governments and local law enforcement agencies usually close their eyes to known violations unless they are forced to prosecute because of a formal complaint or a woman's death. If a case does come to trial, the defendant may receive a suspended sentence or not be convicted at all. A conviction may also be reversed on appeal. Moreover, juries are often sympathetic to the woman's plight and even to the provider's if she or he meant well and caused no harm.

Occasionally a highly publicized case *is* tried, however, and if necessary appealed to a higher court. It may be a political gesture or a deliberate effort on the part of abortion supporters or opponents to challenge the interpretation or constitutionality of the law. In Canada, for example, Dr. Henry Morgentaler crusaded for safe, legal and humane abortion long before the federal criminal laws were allowed to lapse. In 1968 he started performing abortions in his Montreal office that were illegal because they were not done in a hospital on strict medical grounds authorized by three physicians. His actions set in motion more than two decades of police raids, arrests, trials, jury acquittals, government appeals, convictions, and a ten-month prison term. Incarcerated in 1975, he was released before serving the full eighteen months to which he had been sentenced when the Canadian Minister of Justice set aside his conviction on the grounds that the Quebec Court of Appeals should not have converted a jury acquittal into a conviction.

In the United States, Dr. Jane Hodgson was convicted in 1971 in St. Paul, Minnesota of performing an illegal abortion in a hospital. At a time when Minnesota law permitted abortion only under life-threatening conditions as approved by the hospital's therapeutic abortion committee, she terminated the pregnancy of a married woman with two children who had been exposed to rubella (German measles) and risked having a severely deformed infant. The police were notified and Dr. Hodgson was arrested, tried and convicted. While her appeal to the Minnesota Supreme Court was being processed the US Supreme Court decriminalized abortion and her conviction was overturned.

Does the fact that criminalization rarely sends abortion providers and their clients to jail mean that the laws make no difference? Not at all. The laws can and do make a profound difference, but not necessarily in the ways that were intended.

First and foremost, criminalizing abortion does not substantially reduce the numbers of abortions, it only drives them underground. Estimates for Canada and the United States, for example, suggest that there were almost as many abortions before they were decriminalized as afterwards. If true, this means as many as one hundred thousand illegal procedures in Canada in the 1960s and well over a million in the US. The difference is that more women were injured or died when abortion was concealed.

Second, the physical dangers of abortion rise with its illegality. Most qualified physicians do not want to risk their careers by performing an illegal operation. As a consequence, the majority of women needing services in countries or states where abortion is highly restricted either try to do it themselves or else turn to untrained providers such as midwives or healers who employ the crudest of methods in the most unsanitary of conditions. Emergency hospital wards are filled with the consequences. Not only women and their families but the entire health system bears the costs.

"The risks of abortion result not from medical factors but from its illegality. Therefore, the logical step to prevent deaths among women who have an unwanted pregnancy is to decriminalize abortion." José Aristodemo Pinotti and Anibal Faúndes, in *Women's Health in the Third World: The Impact of Unwanted Pregnancy*

Third, in addition to driving abortion underground where women have no protection from medical malpractice, the criminalization of abortion creates a climate of fear, threat, subterfuge, profiteering, and hypocrisy. The identity of illegal providers is often an open secret, but because there is a need, they are not prosecuted.

Fourth, criminalization creates a two-tiered system in which privileged women have access to private physicians through their social connections or can travel to other states or countries but poor women do not. The same two-tiered system exists at the international level as well. Whereas abortion is now legal and safe in virtually all of the wealthy countries of the world, it is legally restricted and often dangerous in almost all of the poorest ones whose legal systems have been inherited from their former colonial masters.

"The laws against abortion are mainly old laws, and it is worth recalling that part of the rationale for most 19th century abortion laws was to save women from quacks and unsafe and experimental surgery. That these same laws or their derivatives should now lead to the very opposite situation, given the safety and efficacy of currently available technologies, is a cruel irony." Fred T. Sai, in *Planned Parenthood Challenges*

This chapter tells the story of the evolution of these abortion laws and policies. How did this two-tiered international system develop? What do the legal statutes actually say? On what grounds are women able to obtain abortions where it is restricted? And finally, does abortion "on request" always mean what it says?

"With intent to procure"

Let's begin by trying to describe what it is, exactly, that the laws of different countries are attempting to regulate. We refer here not to the grounds on which abortion is legally permitted or prohibited, such as life endangerment or fetal deformity, but to the act itself. What *is* this act? In other words, *what is an abortion*, according to the law?

"The point at which contraception becomes abortion is not clearly delineated in most laws, and it varies according to jurisdiction. While some might consider a procedure to be abortion in fact, it may not necessarily be so in law."[And, we might add, vice versa.] Rebecca J. Cook, in *Women's Health in the Third World: The Impact of Unwanted Pregnancy*

In criminal law, the definition of abortion depends, first, on whether a particular statute declares implicitly or explicitly that a woman must be pregnant in order for an abortion to take place. Second, it depends on whether a particular statute penalizes only the outcome (a completed abortion) or also the attempt (whether or not it was successful). Third, it depends on the definition of when a pregnancy begins.

Does a criminal abortion
require proof of pregnancy?

In order for a person to be criminally liable for having or performing an unlawful abortion, most countries require proof that the woman was in fact pregnant. In the Dominican Republic, for example, the law (which is drawn from the Spanish Penal Code of 1870) imposes punishment on "any person who, through use of any food, beverage, medicine, sounding, treatment, or by any other means, causes or cooperates in causing an abortion *upon a pregnant woman*, even if she consents thereto."

Why would a woman seek an abortion if she were not, in fact, pregnant? Couldn't this simply be assumed? Not really. The appeal courts of Argentina, Brazil, and Mexico have ruled that unless the prosecution could *prove* a pre-existing pregnancy through the testimony of witnesses or the evidence of fetal remains, a criminal abortion could not be demonstrated to have occurred.

From the perspective of recent technological advances in the early identification of pregnancy as well as its early interruption, the issue of proof of pregnancy becomes especially interesting. On the one hand, the best laboratory tests can now accurately confirm conception within a week or so of fertilization, even before a missed period. Yet we know that some women with delayed periods of one or two weeks are *not* pregnant. If a client comes to a clinic during these early days for a menstrual regulation procedure and no test is done, then no evidence of pregnancy exists. It is difficult to obtain physical evidence from inspection of the menstrual extraction at this stage.

Is criminal intent sufficient?

In many countries, however, and particularly those whose legal systems are based on old French or English laws, abortion is a crime regardless of the woman's actual condition. The French penal code, for example, which was suspended in France in 1975 but still applies in the majority of former French colonies in Northern and Western Africa, states that "Any person who causes or attempts to cause an abortion on a pregnant or putatively pregnant woman, regardless of her consent, by means of food, beverages, prescriptions, manipulations, force, or by any other means whatsoever, shall be punished."

Note that a *presumed* pregnancy is sufficient here. Moreover, the intent is as offensive as the result. Similar statutes are in place throughout many former British colonies or protectorates based on the 1861 Offenses Against the Person Act. In its Criminal Code of 1892, for example, Canada reduced the maximum penalty for women procuring their own abortions from life imprisonment to seven years but added a provision that the penalty would also apply to women who were not, in fact, pregnant. This provision lasted until 1954. The Nigerian Criminal Code quoted earlier which condemns the intent to procure a miscarriage "whether she is or is not with child" is another example.

The laws restricting abortion are far more severe in most developing countries than they are in the developed countries. Twenty million *illegal* abortions occur every year in the world. Of these, more than nineteen million occur in Africa, Asia or Latin America and fewer than one million in Europe, in a few countries where restrictions still apply. See The Alan Guttmacher Institute, *Sharing Responsibility: Women, Society and Abortion Worldwide*

Although these English- and French-based statutes penalize abortion or attempted abortion regardless of the condition of the woman, they do require proof of *intent*. That is, the prosecutor must prove that the procedure was intended to interrupt a pregnancy whether or not it did so in fact. For a full-fledged abortion this is not difficult to demonstrate. For very early procedures such as vacuum aspiration, however, a provider or client could insist that the intent of the procedure was not to interrupt a (possible) pregnancy but to diagnose or treat a uterine condition or to extract the menses for some other health-related reason.

How pregnant *is* she?

The definition of abortion also depends on the tricky question of when a pregnancy begins. In Chapter One we referred to the definition by the American College of Obstetrics and Gynecology that a pregnancy starts not with fertilization but with the successful implantation of the fertilized ovum, which could be one or two weeks later. This is also the interpretation of the International Federation of Gynecology and Obstetrics. Trying to avoid confusion, a committee of the International Federation emphasized that there is a basic difference between the definition of the beginning of *pregnancy*, which is a scientific question, and the definition of the beginning of *life*, which is a moral, religious and ethical question that cannot be answered scientifically.

The Roman Catholic church was relatively tolerant of abortion before "quickening" up to 1869, when Pope Pius IX declared that ensoulment occurs at conception. Noting that the Scriptures say nothing about abortion or the origins of the human soul, Saint Augustine speculated that the fetus acquires a soul on the forty-sixth day, which is the time (in years) that it took to build the Temple in Jerusalem. See Gary Wills, *Papal Sin: Structures of Deceit*

According to the medical definition, then, interventions performed between an act of intercourse and the successful implantation of a fertilized embryo (a period during which up to half of all conceptions may be lost in any case) could not be said to induce abortion. These include postcoital emergency contraceptive pills, the insertion of an IUD following unprotected sex, early vacuum aspiration, and early treatments with low-dose mifepristone (RU 486) or its equivalent. The interpretation of "early" in this context is ambiguous. But if implantation can take up to two weeks following fertilization, and if fertilization takes place on day fourteen, then "early" would be (for a twenty-eight-day cycle) about the date that the next period is due. If a woman fears pregnancy, she has to act fast.

Most criminal and civil codes regulate abortion according to the length of gestation. The more advanced the pregnancy, the stricter the conditions. Even liberal laws that permit abortion on request usually do so only in the first trimester, that is, within the first twelve or thirteen weeks. From then on, restrictions such as medical conditions or the approval of two physicians may apply. In Denmark, for example, abortion during the first trimester is available for any reason but later procedures must be approved by a committee of two doctors and a social worker. Without such authorization, a woman terminating her pregnancy is subject to a prison term of up to two years.

Recall that the length of gestation can be counted in at least three ways. The most common usage in medical and legal practice, because it is convenient and known, is to start from the first day of the *last* menstrual period. In a twenty-eight-day cycle, this would be about two weeks *before* fertilization. Gestation could also be counted from the date of *fertilization* (if it were known) or *implantation* (if it were known). The very different outcomes resulting from these three approaches—a span of up to three or four weeks—leave considerable room for maneuver in the interpretation of abortion laws and policies where the counting rule is not specified.

This is not to say that procedures such as manual vacuum aspiration or medical induction of the menses are necessarily excluded from abortion regulations. Regardless of the purpose for which they are used, the *techniques themselves* are sometimes legally restricted to qualified personnel and licensed facilities. In the United States, for example, the approval of the drug mifepristone (RU 486) by the Food and Drug Administration subjects its use to a multitude of regulations that apply to abortion as well. Yet in countries such as Bangladesh (where abortion is restricted to life-threatening conditions) and the Netherlands and Cuba (where it is available on request), menstrual regulation with vacuum aspiration does not technically count as abortion at all.

Permitted or denied? How the law decides

Abortion has been integrated into the repertoire of fertility regulation methods in most if not all of the world's cultures. It was widely practiced in Europe and North America during the nineteenth century, a period when birth rates in some countries fell by half. In the United States the drop in family size from an average of seven children in 1800 to under four in 1900 was due partly to women's widespread reliance on abortion. In the second half of the nineteenth century when the practice surged, ladies' magazines were filled with ads promoting emetics (to purge the body) and remedies for "female irregularity" (which were not advised for pregnant women).

As early as 1860, one American doctor estimated that *one in every five pregnancies* was deliberately aborted despite the dangerous practices current at the time. Another estimated in 1890 that *two million abortions* were performed every year. This compares with a yearly total of 1.3 million abortions today. Reported in Rosalind Pollack Petchesky, *Abortion and Woman's Choice: The State, Sexuality, and Reproductive Freedom*

Making abortion a criminal offense

Alarmed by these trends and determined to put lay practitioners out of business, the American Medical Association (AMA) in 1859 called for the general suppression of abortion. For the next hundred years, the AMA was committed to eliminating the practice except for medical emergencies. Previously, abortion had been tolerated or only lightly punished in most states if it occurred before quickening. This practice reflected women's perceptions that until animation they might not actually be pregnant but only "irregular" and were entitled to do what they wished about the situation. In addition, social historians have discovered that juries often believed that abortion at this early stage was not a serious offense but an "imaginary crime."

Prior to 1821 no American state had a statutory law against abortion. Connecticut was the first. One by one, the states imposed criminal penalties on all abortions except those required to save a woman's life. In the beginning they penalized only the person who administered the abortion agent (a pharmacist, say) or performed the procedure (doctor, midwife, neighbor). By the final decade of the nineteenth century all states had extended penalties to the "consenting woman" as well as to advertisers of abortifacients.

The state laws that made abortion a criminal offense in the United States were by no means the first. In France, a law dating from 1556 made abortion and infanticide (which was also common at the time) a crime punishable by death. A survey of French physicians in 1790 found that many of them blamed the sale of herbs, pills, and other remedies in the country markets and what they called the "unnatural arts of crones and charlatans" for depopulating the country. (The birth rate in France was dropping faster than in neighboring countries, much to their alarm.)

The British parliament criminalized abortion for the first time in 1803 with the passage of Lord Ellenborough's Act. If the abortion occurred after quickening, the person who performed it could be condemned to death. If performed before quickening, the abortionist could be fined, whipped, imprisoned, or transported "beyond the seas" for up to fourteen years. In 1837 the quickening distinction was removed from the law and a maximum penalty of three years imposed on all abortions. Canada, which had picked up the statutory provision of Lord Ellenborough's Act (but had never, it seems, prosecuted anyone) soon copied the 1837 law, but imposed a maximum penalty of life imprisonment for the abortionist. The woman herself was not mentioned. It was not until the Offenses Against the Person Act was adopted in England in 1861 that a woman's attempt to procure her own abortion also became a criminal offense.

In Europe, Spain criminalized all abortions in 1870 and Germany in 1871. The German prohibitions derived from the Prussian Penal Code of 1851 that decreed that a woman found guilty of abortion was liable to up to five years in prison and an abortion provider could be given a life sentence. (Almost a century later, Hitler was to introduce the death penalty for abortion in Germany, except for Jews.) A wave of prohibitions then swept across Europe and North America, through the overseas colonies in Latin America and the Caribbean, across Northern and sub-Saharan Africa, through South and Southeast Asia, and into China and Japan.

The international movement
for abortion law reform

A counterwave of reform began early in the twentieth century but was slow to gather momentum. In the Soviet Union the feminist minister of health, Alexandra Kolontai, introduced a law in 1920 that entitled any woman to procure an abortion in the first trimester for whatever reason, free of charge in a state hospital, from a qualified physician. (Abortion was recriminalized in the Soviet Union in 1936, however, and made available once again in 1955). Supporters agitated for similar laws in Czechoslovakia, Germany, Austria, and Great Britain in the early 1920s, but without success. Several Scandinavian countries and Iceland extended the grounds for legal abortion in the 1930s and 1940s to include broad social and health-related justifications. The English courts recognized what had been common medical practice by legalizing therapeutic abortions in 1938. Japan followed in 1948. Many Eastern and Western European countries liberalized their abortion laws in the 1950s There were holdouts, however. In 1960, Spain, Italy, France, Ireland, Canada, and most of the United States still permitted abortion only to save a woman's life.

After 1960 the grounds needed to justify abortion were expanded or eliminated entirely throughout most of the rest of Europe and in the US and Canada. By the end of the twentieth century, thirty-two developed countries allowed abortion *on request* within the first trimester. Portugal, Spain, Switzerland, Northern Ireland, Australia, and New Zealand allowed abortion on physical and mental health grounds, while Finland, Great Britain and Japan added socioeconomic grounds, which are generously applied.

The two major exceptions to European liberalization are Poland and Ireland. In 1956, Poland adopted the Abortion Admissibility Law which allowed abortion on request during the first trimester. But following the collapse of the Soviet Union and the renewed influence of the Roman Catholic Church, the Polish parliament in 1993 passed the restrictive Law on Family Planning, Human Embryo Protection, and Conditions of Abortion. Declaring that human life begins at the moment of conception, the law prohibits most abortions and rejects all but "natural" methods of avoiding conception. In 1997 the law was tightened still further so that only proven cases of rape or incest (confirmed by the Public Prosecutor) and of gross fetal deformity are allowed.

Ireland has retained its total prohibition based on the English law of 1861. A national referendum in 1983 inserted language into the Constitution guaranteeing that the government will defend the life of the unborn. The circulation of information about abortion (in magazine articles, for example), as well as engaging in abortion counseling or referrals, is prohibited. A woman seeking an abortion can face life in prison.

"The state acknowledges the right to life of the unborn and, with due regard to the equal right to life of the mother, guarantees in its laws to respect, and, as far as practicable, by its laws, to defend and vindicate that right." Eighth Amendment to the Irish Constitution (1983), cited by Brian Girvin in *Abortion Politics: Public Policy in Cross-Cultural Perspective*

Some of these reforms are the result of legislative actions while others have emerged from the courts. Political analysts suggest that the relative stability of the abortion law reforms in Western Europe is due to their having been adopted by legislative bodies that debated the issues for years before settling on what are, in essence, compromise positions. Neither forbidden nor unregulated, abortion in most Western European countries *is* permitted and *is* circumscribed as to length of gestation or justification or facility in which it is performed. Party politics have been relatively unimportant in most cases because European legislators' attitudes about abortion typically cut across political lines except in those countries with religiously-based parties. The situation in the United States is very different. Not only have the major abortion law reforms been decided by the Supreme Court, but legislators at the national and state levels tend to be highly partisan in their approach to abortion access. The Republican and Democratic parties have taken clear and opposite positions on the issue in their official platforms.

Prior to 1973, seventeen states, beginning with Colorado in 1967, had already legalized abortion on therapeutic (health) grounds. New

York, Hawaii and Alaska repealed their criminal laws, thus making abortion generally available for whatever reason. On 22 January of that year, the US Supreme Court held in the case of *Roe v. Wade* that a right to privacy, which had been invoked in a previous case involving the use of contraception by married couples, extended to a woman's decision of whether or not to terminate her pregnancy. State laws that continued to criminalize abortion were suddenly void.

The decriminalization of abortion in Canada also resulted from an action of the Supreme Court, which in 1988 declared the abortion section of the Criminal Code unconstitutional in the case of *Morgentaler v. The Queen*. Although therapeutic exceptions to the general prohibition had been enacted in 1969, their unequal and unfair application in practice were found to violate a woman's right to life, liberty, and security of the person as spelled out in the Canadian Charter of Rights and Freedoms. There is an important difference between this and the American decision, however: unlike the US Supreme Court, the Canadian court did not declare a positive right to abortion. Because the Canadian parliament has been unable to agree on legislation, provincial governments and hospitals have adopted their own policies.

The uneven legal situation in the developing world

"The Philippines provides an example of the irony . . . that many countries retain restrictive abortion laws imposed by earlier colonial powers. The absolute prohibition of abortion in the Philippines, contained in the 1930 penal code, came originally from the Spanish Penal Code of 1870. While Spain has liberalized its own abortion law, her former colony retains the absolute restriction imposed almost 120 years ago." Alfredo Flores Tadiar, in *Women's Health in the Third World: The Impact of Unwanted Pregnancy*

The wave of legal reform that swept across Europe and North America in the second half of the twentieth century scarcely touched most of the former colonies. Long after these nations achieved their independence, their inherited criminal codes penalizing abortion (and, in some countries, the importation, manufacture, sale, and use of contraceptives as well) remain intact. Over fifty developing countries still prohibit abortion entirely or permit it only *in extremis.* The list includes at least twenty-two countries in sub-Saharan Africa (such as Nigeria, Kenya, Uganda); eleven in the Islamic regions of Central Asia, the Middle East and North Africa (Afghanistan, Iran, and Egypt, for instance); eight in South and East Asia and the Pacific (including the Philippines, Sri Lanka, Indonesia); and thirteen in Latin America and the Caribbean (such as Chile, Venezuela and Nicaragua). In many of these countries women still face high risks of death and disability from early and repeated childbearing as well as from illegal abortion.

Yet some of the world's largest developing countries have adopted significant reforms. China, for one. Now containing more than one-fourth of the world's population, China in 1957 legalized abortion in the first six months of gestation. Abortion is available free of charge as an indispensable ingredient of the national policy of population control. Currently, Chinese women account for about eight million of the more than twenty-five million legal abortions performed worldwide every year.

India, with one-sixth of the world's population, is another important example of early reform. The 1971 Medical Termination of Pregnancy Act legalized abortion on mental and physical health and socioeconomic grounds and in cases of rape, fetal deformity, and contraceptive failure. In essence, this means that abortions can be performed on request free of charge in licensed government hospitals in the first twenty weeks of pregnancy. Indian women account for over half a million legal abortions every year. However, they also account for unknown numbers of illegal (and thus undocumented) abortions because they are not performed by specialists in facilities specifically licensed for this purpose.

Other developing countries in which abortion is available on request within the first trimester include Puerto Rico (which is governed by the US law), Cuba, Cambodia, Mongolia, North Korea, Singapore, and Vietnam. In the Islamic regions of what was once Soviet Central Asia, seven countries permit abortion on all grounds (such as Kazakstan and Uzbekistan), as do Armenia, Turkey, and Tunisia.

The Republic of South Africa is the first sub-Saharan African country to legalize abortion on request in the first trimester. The Choice on Termination of Pregnancy Act was passed by the new multiracial South African Parliament in 1996 as part of its program of advancing human rights and social justice following the end of the apartheid regime. See "Choice on Termination of Pregnancy Act" in *Reproductive Health Matters* No. 9 (May 1997); for a comment on accessibility see Sanjani Varkey in *Family Planning Perspectives*

If we consider the restrictiveness of abortion laws not by the number of countries but by the proportion of the world's women who live in such countries, an interesting picture emerges.

At one extreme, 25 percent of the world's women live in countries where abortion is permitted only to save a woman's life or is prohibited altogether. *Virtually every abortion that takes place in one of these countries is illegal.* At the other extreme, 41 percent of the world's women live in countries where no medical or health or social justification is needed to obtain an abortion in the first trimester, that is, where abortion is available (although not necessarily accessible) on request. *Virtually every abortion that takes place in one of these countries is legal.* This leaves another 34 percent—

one-third of the world's women—who live in countries where abortion is allowed on certain grounds such as the protection of her physical health, or perhaps her physical and mental health, or for socioeconomic reasons, or in cases of rape or incest, or if the fetus is deformed. *Every legal abortion that takes place in one of these countries must be approved. Every unauthorized abortion, even if performed by a physician in a hospital, is illegal.*

The key question in this latter group of countries is, who is empowered to decide? In other words, who are the gatekeepers that control the route to safe legal services? We will discuss this and other questions pertaining to the US and Canada later in this book. For now, let us just say that in countries where some restrictions as to indication are in place, a woman must typically seek permission to terminate from a physician, psychiatrist, social worker, therapeutic abortion committee, hospital or clinic administrative committee, or judicial entity. She may also have to obtain the consent of her husband or, if she is an unmarried minor, her parents. In cases where the law allows exceptions for pregnancies resulting from rape or incest she must have proof, which means that she has to file criminal charges against the man who violated her. In the end, if the authorities are not convinced of the merits of her case, permission is denied and she is legally compelled to carry the pregnancy to term. As we saw in the previous chapter, however, whether she does so or not is quite another matter.

Multiple layers, multiple interpretations

Although one may classify countries according to the characteristics of their abortion laws, it is misleading to talk as though each country has one law. In fact, most have multiple laws and regulations surrounding all aspects of abortion. Some are specific to provinces or states or cantons; others to local governments such as counties and municipalities. Cutting across these political/geographical entities are the regulations and policies imposed by ministries of health, by professional associations (physicians and nurses, for example), by medical facilities (private and public hospitals, religious or secular institutions, free-standing clinics), and by insurance companies. Negotiating the maze of regulations can be a challenge for enforcers, providers, and clients alike.

But the multiple layers of laws and regulations don't tell the whole story either. As in most areas of human behavior, the reality can be very different. Those in a position to enforce them do so selectively along the lines of administrative norms, an assessment of the seriousness of the offense, and their own values and priorities. The practices of individuals and institutions can shape the outcomes in quite unexpected ways.

In addition, ordinary citizens obey some laws quite willingly, ignore or defy others. Many people simply do not know whether a particular act is legal or, if it is illegal, what the penalties are. Abortion is a good example of this. A survey of women in five villages in the Philippines in the late 1970s found that more than half believed that abortion was legal when in fact it is strictly prohibited on all grounds. In contrast, in Puerto Rico in 1993, twenty years after abortion was decriminalized under the same ruling as the United States, conversations with low-income women revealed that many still believe that abortion is against the law.

"**Do you think that abortion is legal** or illegal in Puerto Rico?" an interviewer asks a client in an abortion clinic. "It is illegal," the woman replies. "If it were legal, there would be more places like this. There are just a few, you know, as if they are hidden . . . . If it were legal, it would be like hospitals, or lawyers' and doctor's offices, there would be a lot." Yamila Azize-Vargas and Luis A. Avilés, in *Reproductive Health Matters*

There are many ways in which the actual practices "on the ground" will differ from the law—or the multiple layers of the law—as written "on the books." Let's look first at some common ways in which providers and potential enforcers circumvent or simply ignore restrictive laws so that at least some women can obtain the services they need.

Getting around restrictive laws

In virtually every country with restrictive laws there are qualified medical personnel such as physicians, nurses, trained midwives, family planning practitioners, and others, who make the decision on their own, or as a group in the professional organizations or medical facilities in which they work, to offer safe services to women outside the law. Their activities may involve simply stretching the law where some grounds for abortion are permitted, or they may clearly violate the law's intent to punish and eliminate all abortions, whatever their justification.

"In Belgium, where abortion was prohibited until 1990, safe abortion services provided by qualified physicians were so readily available that a large proportion of Belgian women were not even aware of prevailing restrictions." Henry P. David, in *Studies in Family Planning*

Stretching the law—that is, interpreting it in a flexible way—is not difficult in countries that permit abortion in order to protect the physical health (not just the life) of the pregnant woman. As University of Toronto law professor Rebecca Cook points out, doctors, administrative committees, and legal authorities can adopt a broad definition of "health." The World Health Organization, for example, defines health as not simply the absence of disease or infirmity but *as a state of complete physical, mental, and social well-*

being. Of course most restrictive abortion legislation is far more limited in its wording and intent than the WHO definition implies. Typically, a health indication would require strict medical proof that the continuation of the pregnancy would severely compromise a woman's physical condition. But if the law defers to physicians to set these standards, then physicians could in their professional capacity choose to protect the health of their patients, their patients' families, and the community at large.

"Medicine, like law, is filled with probabilities and interpretations. Many conditions pose varying magnitudes of risk of maternal death. The spectrum for legally approved risk is wide. Because the law does not specify 'acceptable risk,' it leaves medical interpretation open at all levels of abortion regulation, from the ministry [of health] to the individual provider." Karen Stein and colleagues, *Abortion: Expanding Access and Improving Quality*

Even in countries where abortion is prohibited entirely or permitted only to save a woman's life, physicians sometimes take matters into their own hands where they see a compelling medical and social need. Ministries of health often cooperate, even to the extent of promoting training. In countries as different as Brazil, Colombia, Egypt, Nigeria, and Indonesia, many health professionals provide safe services and training in doctors' offices, family planning clinics, and private and public hospitals.

In these so-called lapsed-law states, the government essentially closes its eyes to violations of the law. It does this in the interests of lowering unacceptably high rates of maternal mortality associated with unsafe abortion and the high social and public costs of managing complications. Physicians are often motivated to provide services because they see the dreadful consequences of self-induced or botched procedures in their practices. Some have other motives, of course, given that public prohibitions almost always create a lucrative source of private income.

"In Morocco, as in all countries where abortion is illegal, the vast majority of abortions are clandestine; like all prohibitions, it has generated a flourishing secret trade which breeds abuses. Many doctors agree to carry out abortions, in spite of the risks they face, either to help their patients—or to pocket some tax free extra income." Soumaya Naamande-Guessous, in *Planned Parenthood Challenges*

Open violations such as these may or may not be a precursor to a change in the law. In a number of developing countries, political and religious opposition has consistently blocked efforts at reform by legal and medical professionals and women's groups. Because liberalization is unlikely in the near future but the need is urgent, an uneasy but generally acknowledged compromise is often the result. As long as the quality of the services is maintained and there is no negative publicity, the provision of safe services, although far from ideal, is not threatened.

In other countries, however, widespread civil disobedience— that is, a decision to provide forbidden services openly—has helped to trigger a change in the law. In the Netherlands, for example, abortion did not become fully legal until 1985 when the Termination of Pregnancy Act came into effect. Before that time, affluent Dutch women traveled to England for abortions while others had to find an illegal provider at home or bear an unwanted child. Responding to the social inequities of this situation, a group of Dutch doctors began in the late 1960s to perform vacuum aspiration procedures in their own offices, in hospitals, and by the 1970s in a newly formed federation of non-profit clinics. These activities were known to the authorities but they were reluctant to prosecute. Records kept by the early clinics on the numbers and social characteristics of clients and the safety of the procedures helped to inform the public and allay many concerns when the campaign to liberalize the law was finally under way.

> "Virtually all the present clinics [in the Netherlands] were set up in the early 1970s, some in the larger towns, but with a reasonable spread throughout the country . . . . The Medical Committee was mainly important because of the situation in which the clinics carried out their work: they were tolerated but in fact still illegal, and therefore had to be extremely cautious. This was one of the reasons why a high quality service developed." Stimezo Nederland, *Abortion Matters: 25 Years Experience in the Netherlands*

Enforcing the law . . . and then some

Amidst the tangle of laws and policies in many countries one can also find examples in which the practices are more restrictive than the law requires. In conservative legal and social settings, those in a position to do so may take the strictest possible interpretation of the law and close the door to individual exceptions. In countries with liberal statutes or where abortion has been removed from the criminal codes entirely, opponents may adopt policies that prohibit the performance of abortions in the medical facilities where they work, refuse to refer clients to other providers, treat doctors who do perform abortions with contempt, and entangle the laws with so many procedural regulations and qualifications that legal abortion services become all but inaccessible to many women, especially the poor. All of these obstructions and more have been tried in the US and

Canada, as we shall see in the next two chapters. Here, we sketch some general outlines.

The first tactic is the refusal to do abortions even in circumstances where they are legal. Governments are almost invariably reluctant to place health professionals and facilities under a *positive obligation* to provide services. There are exceptions, such as China and Vietnam, in which abortion is part of the national family planning policy. In Sweden, the law penalizes physicians who won't comply with a woman's request for a first-trimester termination or refer her to the National Board of Health to obtain one. But the exceptions basically prove the rule: a woman may be eligible for a legal abortion in the sense that she is *permitted* to have one, but no one is compelled to provide it.

In many European countries and in the US and Canada as well, exemption clauses permit health workers and even entire facilities to refuse to perform or assist in abortions if they claim it is against their religious or moral beliefs. In Italy, where abortions are permitted on broad grounds but must be performed in a hospital, *over half* of all hospital-based obstetricians/gynecologists and anesthesiologists have claimed conscience-based exemptions. (It is widely believed that many of them perform abortions privately, however.) In Poland, physicians at a national congress in 1991 adopted a Code of Medical Ethics that restricted abortion to a narrower range of grounds than that allowed by the law and threatened to expel from the profession any doctor who defied the new code. Rejecting even the possibility of severe fetal deformity as grounds for abortion, the association condemned all prenatal diagnostic tests as posing a threat to the life of the unborn. At least three Polish state hospitals had already announced their refusal to perform even those few abortions that *were* countenanced by the law.

> **"In 1989 a progressive woman became the mayor** of São Paulo and promulgated a law to allow abortion services in municipal hospitals. Feminist groups strongly influenced this decision. The first legal abortion service [for rape cases] was established at Jabaquara Hospital. Unfortunately, all of the doctors on staff refused to participate." Karen Stein and colleagues, *Abortion: Expanding Access and Improving Quality*

Second, where abortions are legal on some but not all grounds, opponents can restrict access by refusing to clarify the conditions under which they *are* allowed, holding to very narrow interpretations of the law, and making the qualification procedure so difficult that it becomes impossible for most women. By creating a chilling institutional environment, opponents discourage doctors who might otherwise be sympathetic from risking their careers to serve their patients' needs. In Brazil, for example, abortion is permitted when the pregnancy is a result of rape. But such cases are rarely processed because of the complicated legal requirements of proving that a rape has occurred. Although many private practitioners will perform the abortion for a fee, a woman petitioning for a legal abortion in a public hospital on these grounds—especially if she is young, unmarried, poor and with little formal schooling (in other words, a typical client)— will almost certainly be turned away.

A third restrictive tactic is to circumscribe what on the surface appears to be a liberal law with all sorts of qualifications such as waiting periods, quotas, permissions, limits on gestational age, residence requirements, mandatory counseling, and restrictions as to personnel and facilities that do not apply to other medical procedures. Belgium, France and the Netherlands, for example, as well as some states in the US, require a period of "reflection" of up to one week between a woman's first medical consultation that confirms the pregnancy and its termination. (This requirement is waived in the Netherlands for women requesting menstrual regulation whose period is less than sixteen days overdue.) The Netherlands and others also mandate counseling about alternatives to termination that emphasizes the woman's responsibility toward herself, her family, and the "unborn life."

Authorization rules may extend to the requirement of written consent of the woman's husband (in Turkey, for example, where early abortion is otherwise available on request) or of the parents or guardians of an unmarried minor (Barbados, Denmark, France, Italy, and Norway, among many others). In the United States forty-three states have passed laws that require parental notification or consent or, in its absence, judicial approval of abortion for unmarried minors. This is clearly not abortion "on request," nor does it recognize an adolescent's right to privacy in making the decision.

Consent requirements can also involve quite unrealistic demands of the medical profession itself. The government of Zambia, which in 1972 approved abortions up to twelve weeks on broad health and socioeconomic grounds, requires the approval of three medical practitioners, including one specialist. This in an African country with one physician to serve every ten thousand inhabitants, and almost none in the rural areas where most people live.

"**Making services dependent upon patient access to physicians** who are in fact unavailable denies in practice what legislative reform offers in principle . . . . Burdensome requirements of access to health personnel and facilities may be counter therapeutic in obstructing and delaying services."

Rebecca J. Cook, in *Women's Health in the Third World: The Impact of Unwanted Pregnancy*

Setting unnecessarily high qualifications for abortion providers and facilities presents another obstacle to service delivery under otherwise liberal laws. Although high standards of medical care are as appropriate for abortion as they are for all medical interventions, the question is whether those for abortion are stricter than for comparable medical procedures. In other words, are they intended primarily to protect clients or to make it harder for practitioners to offer services?

The requirement that abortions be performed only by physicians or by specialists in obstetrics and gynecology poses an almost insurmountable barrier in some countries, especially those with shortages of medical personnel. India is an oft-cited case. As mentioned previously, legal abortions can be performed only by ob/gyns in facilities especially licensed for this purpose. Because these are concentrated in the largest cities of certain states, the majority of rural women have no chance of obtaining services. As a result, the death rate from unsafe abortion has scarcely diminished in the thirty years since the Medical Termination of Pregnancy Act was passed. Yet in neighboring Bangladesh, trained female paramedics (Family Welfare Visitors) who perform the majority of menstrual regulation procedures in the country have an excellent record of safety and extend services to rural women throughout the country.

The question of special restrictions applying to abortion that do not apply to other medical procedures, called Targeted Regulation of Abortion Providers (TRAP), received a great deal of attention in the United States when a government agency gave final marketing approval to mifepristone (RU 486) in September 2000. Physicians who thought they could quietly dispense the new drug in their own offices and clinics were startled to discover how many regulations might apply. The requirements described in the box below are an example of TRAP legislation that has been passed in thirty-five states.

In the state of North Carolina, abortion providers must have a clinic with halls at least 60 inches wide, hot water between 100 and 116 degrees Fahrenheit, life-support equipment, and an ultra-sound machine. In North and South Carolina and Alabama, providers must examine the fetal remains; in North Dakota they must make sure that such remains (which for an early medical abortion are indistinguishable from menstrual blood) are buried, incinerated or cremated. *The New York Times,* 30 September 2000

The trump card in the hands of the obstructionists, if all else fails, is that of funding. Who pays for health care, and who pays for abortions?

Most European countries with national health insurance plans pay for abortions as a matter of course as long as they are in conformity with the terms of national legislation. In Great Britain the National Health Service pays for all abortions performed in NHS hospitals, although the procedure must be certified by two physicians on grounds of protecting the woman's health, for socioeconomic reasons, or in case of fetal deformity. Clients who are not eligible or willing to go through this process may pay a physician privately or turn to a clinic for reasonably priced services. Some European governments require nominal payments for elective abortions, however, or do not cover them at all. But virtually all of them reimburse the costs of medically mandated procedures or provide them in public hospitals at no cost.

"In the early period of reform [in Western Europe], when doctors often had to take risks to perform abortions, fees were high and only more affluent women were able to obtain a medically safe abortion . . . . Once abortion became legalized, it also became possible to regulate abortion fees and put a rein on doctors' tendencies to use their monopoly to set prices at a profitable level." Joyce Outshoorn, in *Abortion Politics: Public Policy in Cross-Cultural Perspective*

In Canada, provincial governments set their own policies on the funding of abortions in provincial health plans. Some pay for all abortions, others pay for those performed in hospitals but not in private clinics. Some provinces pay part of the costs of clinic services such as doctors' fees or laboratory tests while others pay all or none.

In the United States, which has no national health insurance system, the federal Medicaid program reimbursed states for the costs of abortions for low-income women otherwise eligible for medical assistance for four years following *Roe v. Wade*. But in 1977 a hostile Congress passed legislation prohibiting the use of federal funds for abortion except in cases of life endangerment. Exceptions for rape and incest were added in 1993. Because such cases are rare due to the complex reporting requirements, this means that the federal government now pays for virtually no abortions. To close the gap, sixteen states decided to use their own funds for this purpose. As in Canada, these geographical inequalities create another two-tiered system in which poor women who live in states or provinces that pay for abortions can obtain the services they need, but those living in more restrictive states or provinces cannot. For the better off who are more likely to be enrolled in private medical insurance plans, the majority of American plans and Health Maintenance Organizations do pay for abortion services. But one-third of private plans don't cover abortion services at all or else pay only for medically mandated procedures.

We opened this chapter with the question "When is abortion against the law and what difference does it make?" The answer is that the law has a complex, multilayered effect that is not always clear. On the one hand, safe abortion is widely available in some countries with very restrictive laws for women who can afford to pay. On the other hand, in some countries with liberal laws the imposition of regulations at the state and local levels entangles providers and clients alike in a maze of uncertainties and dead-ends.

Laws that apply criminal sanctions to abortion are often ignored or circumvented. Prosecutions for abortion are rare in those countries with strict criminal codes; convictions even rarer. The laws don't work because the demand to terminate unwanted pregnancies is typically so intense that women will go to any lengths, legal or illegal, to do so. Abortion providers (whether trained or untrained) are ready to provide; enforcers are often reluctant to enforce or do so very selectively. The major result of punitive laws is thus not an overall reduction in the number of abortions but a selective and wholly unnecessary increase in injuries and deaths to women from unsafe, clandestine, and self-induced procedures.

CHAPTER SIX

Inside the Medical Profession

"**My position on abortion evolved.** I had been taught that abortion was immoral. I gradually came to change, I came to feel that the law was immoral. There were all these young women whose health was being ruined, whose lives were being ruined . . . . From my point of view, it was poor medicine, it was poor public health policy." Jane Hodgson talks about her practice before *Roe v. Wade*, quoted in Carole Joffe, *Doctors of Conscience: The Struggle to Provide Abortion Before and After Roe v. Wade*

"**I hate doing them, but I do them every once in a while.** But the real reason we try to avoid them is that I don't want to be known in the community as a local abortionist. I want to be known as a doctor who loves mommies and their babies. I don't care what is said, there's a stigma attached to doing abortions." American physician practicing after *Roe v. Wade*, quoted in Jonathan B. Imber, *Abortion and the Private Practice of Medicine*

Physicians and other health professionals in Canada and the United States have had a long and complicated relationship to abortion that continues to this day. The political divisiveness and downright nastiness that characterizes the abortion debate in some communities does not help. The result is that a simple, legal procedure that should be a routine element of reproductive health care is not available on an outpatient basis in most hospitals. The majority of counties in both countries have no providers of abortion care. The majority of specialists do not even learn its techniques.

This untenable situation persists despite the fact that the leading medical groups in the US and Canada now stand on record as supporting *Roe v. Wade* and opposing legal and administrative obstacles that impede access or prevent health practitioners from advising their patients about all reproductive options. The American Medical Association (AMA), for example, which represents almost 300,000 members, points out that parental consent laws "appear to increase the health risks to the adolescent by delaying medical treatment or forcing the adolescent into an unwanted childbirth." The American College of Obstetricians and Gynecologists (ACOG) labels such requirements "unduly restrictive," overly deferential to parents given the health risks to adolescents of delaying abortion or delivering an unwanted child, and "in need of revision as a matter of public policy."

The American Medical Women's Association, with 12,000 members, has been particularly supportive of reproductive choice as good health policy. In its 1989 declaration, the AMWA affirms "a woman's right to choose abortion without governmental intervention and without restrictions placed on her physician's medical judgment." The AMWA also supports access to abortion without regard to economic status as well as minor's access to abortion and contraceptive services without the requirement of parental notification or consent. Prochoice professional groups such as the American Public Health Association, the National Association of Nurse Practitioners in Reproductive Health, the American College of Nurse Midwives, Physicians for Reproductive Choice and Health, and Medical Students for Choice are campaigning to reform the medical curricula, extend provider training to certain mid-level health professionals, and guarantee equitable access to safe and humane services.

This chapter tells the story of how the attitudes of medical professionals in Canada and the US have affected the delivery of abortion services in both positive and negative ways. It is a human story and also an intensely political story. We begin with a brief account of the clandestine years before the highest courts of both countries removed the criminal sanctions from abortion. We then turn to the period following the decisions in *Roe v. Wade* (1973) in the United States and *Morgentaler v. the Queen* (1988) in Canada, both of which created a system of abortion "on request," one deliberately, one by default. But is abortion on request really the case today? Why do so many hospitals refuse to provide them? Why are so few obstetrician/gynecologists learning how to perform them? What happens when governments recognize a woman's legal right to *have* an abortion, but health care personnel and institutions are placed under no obligation to *perform* them?

Ambivalence and contradictions:

medical practice before *Roe v. Wade*

As early as the mid-nineteenth century, the newly formed American Medical Association (AMA) spoke out against the evils of abortion and called for its criminalization. But what was so "evil" about abortion in their view?

Some researchers argue that the opposition of the medical establishment to abortion was motivated by a concern for women's safety. Women were snapping up quack remedies and flocking to lay practitioners, both skilled and unskilled, in their determination to interrupt unwanted pregnancies. Others insist that medical opposition was based on moral (although not narrowly religious) grounds. After all, the medical establishment was equally vehement in its opposition to artificial methods of contraception, declaring douches, pessaries, cervical caps, and condoms to be "unnatural" and "injurious to women." These were not religious claims about the sins of contraception or abortion. Rather, they reflected deep anxieties about what was happening to the *ideal of womanhood*. In the dominant medical view of the time, birth control signified an alarming decline in family values (to use a current phrase), that is, a willful desire among women to abandon their proper female roles. Such defiant behavior posed a fundamental threat to the social and moral order.

"Nowhere was the moralizing tendency of regular physicians more striking than in their relentless campaign against contraception and abortion. Medical school curricula and teachers were silent on these subjects; an address by the president of the American Gynecological Society in 1890 implied that 'physicians should have nothing to do with the nasty business.' Both contraception and abortion were associated . . . [in the] medical profession with obscenity, lewdness, sex, and, worst of all, rebellious women." Rosalind Pollack Petchesky, *Abortion and Woman's Choice: The State, Sexuality, and Reproductive Freedom*

It was not until 1937 that the AMA, at the relentless urging of birth control crusader Margaret Sanger, finally endorsed the use of contraception. But only as a therapeutic measure when further pregnancies were to be avoided for health reasons. Yet, as early as 1888, a physician writing in *The Medical and Surgical Reporter* suggested that the medical profession ought formally to consider what grounds were appropriate for the provision of contraceptive information to patients. "The demand upon the practitioner to prevent conception is an unquestionable fact," the author wrote.

"Under these circumstances, it is the duty of the profession to define more clearly what conditions justify and what do not justify interference, and then to settle upon some safe, efficient measures to meet the demand."

What were the conditions that might justify "interference" to prevent pregnancy? According to the author, the practitioner must distinguish between valid *medical reasons* (in cases where the physician confirmed that "evil results" would follow conception, for example if the wife had a history of life-threatening pregnancies), and mere *social or economic reasons* (that is, avoiding pregnancy for the woman's own "convenience," which could never be sanctioned). Although the argument as applied to contraception may sound quaint to us now, it has sustained the abortion debate to this day.

Following the criminalization of abortion throughout the US and Canada in the late nineteenth century, only extreme medical emergencies such as a threat to the pregnant woman's life constituted legal grounds for termination. Yet as medical practice evolved and physicians came to understand better how serious health conditions, dysfunctions, and diseases could be exacerbated by pregnancy, the list of medically approved contraindications to continuing a pregnancy grew longer. Many hospitals in the US routinely performed legal terminations on medical grounds in the first half of the twentieth century, although these procedures constituted only a small proportion of all abortions in the country. Privileged clients were typically drawn from white, middle- and upper-class families known personally to the hospitals' affiliated physicians. Less privileged women lacking such sponsorship, low-income and minority women, those living in rural areas, and the young and unmarried were forced to look elsewhere.

By the 1950s, advances in medical technology and obstetrical care were making it harder for physicians to claim that a woman might die if her pregnancy continued. Fewer and fewer hospital procedures were being approved. Yet, as was the case with divorce laws in which adultery (real or staged) was the only legal ground for termination, the law still required that the fiction of life-saving measures be maintained.

In the twenty-five years between 1940 and 1965 the number of hospital-approved abortions in the US dropped from an estimated thirty thousand to only eight thousand per year. During the 1950s, long before *Roe v. Wade* decriminalized abortion in all states, an estimated one million illegal abortions were performed every year. Carole Joffe, *Doctors of Conscience: The Struggle to Provide Abortion Before and After Roe v. Wade*; Boston Women's Health Book Collective, *The New Our Bodies Ourselves*

Meanwhile, the illegal abortion trade was thriving. Providers of every background—some skilled, some not—set themselves up in business. Women passed along home remedies and techniques to their daughters, sisters, and friends. A number of qualified ob/gyns and general practitioners risked their careers to provide safe services to women in need; others referred patients to their practicing colleagues or to skilled lay practitioners. Feminist groups in some states organized their own networks of referrals. In Chicago the Jane collective, which trained its own lay practitioners, performed about fifty procedures a week in the early 1970s. In the four years preceding *Roe v. Wade* they did over eleven thousand abortions with no deaths. Even some members of the clergy became involved. In New York in 1967 the Clergy Consultation Service on Abortion announced its willingness to counsel and refer women to doctors (whom they had screened) who would perform safe abortions. The network grew to include approximately 1,400 church people in twenty-four states. In the space of a few years these "gentle lawbreakers" referred about 100,000 American women to trusted providers both within and outside the country.

In 1962, the American Law Institute (ALI) sought to eliminate the fictions and inequities of the prevailing system by proposing a Model Criminal Code that would rationalize and standardize abortion laws across all of the states. Similar reform efforts were addressed to the patchwork of divorce laws and other civil and criminal statutes. Based in part on policies that had been adopted in Europe, the model code would permit abortion on therapeutic grounds, that is, if the continuation of the pregnancy would seriously impair the woman's physical or mental health, if the child was likely to be born with severe physical or mental defects, or if the pregnancy resulted from rape or incest.

Cautious support:
physicians and the move for reform

The American Law Institute's proposal attracted the support of many physicians and public health professionals, some legislators, the family planning establishment (Planned Parenthood Federation of America and others), and numerous civic and church groups such as the Young Women's Christian Association (YWCA) and the Episcopalian, Presbyterian, and Methodist churches. An outbreak of rubella (German measles) in the early 1960s that resulted in the birth of thousands of deformed babies, together with the publicity surrounding nine San Francisco ob/gyns charged with professional misconduct for terminating the pregnancies of women exposed to rubella early in their pregnancies, intensified the national drive for reform. The newly organized National Association for Humane Abortion, which included many reform-minded physicians, was also agitating for a reworking of the law. In 1965, however, the AMA refused to act on a recommendation by its Committee on Human Reproduction to support the reforms.

The AMA voted to adopt the model code as official policy in 1967. But it expressed reservations. Supportive in principal, the leadership nevertheless warned that "sound clinical judgment" rather than "mere acquiescence to the patient's demand" must prevail. Moreover, they insisted, abortions should be performed only by a licensed physician in an accredited hospital with the approval of at least two other doctors. In other words, the procedure should stay under strict medical jurisdiction. Only physicians could decide how, where, when, and whether it was appropriate to "intervene."

The problematic history of the Therapeutic Abortion Committees

There was a time when an individual doctor might have made a therapeutic abortion decision without consultation. In a difficult case, the opinion of one or two others might be sought. But by the 1950s the approval process was becoming more complicated. Doctors were getting nervous. Hospitals were setting up review boards to screen all petitions for termination. Not only did the group format protect individual practitioners, it also presented an appearance of respectability, objectivity, and professional solidarity.

Consisting of ob/gyns together with representatives from other departments, a three- or five-person board might meet once a week (or less frequently) to review petitions presented by doctors seeking authorization to perform a therapeutic operation. In Canada, at least, some hospital committees would not take referrals from physicians who were not affiliated with the hospital or even from affiliated but non-specialized family practitioners. Instead, a referral would have to go through a gynecologist on the hospital staff. Other experts such as a psychiatrist or heart specialist might also be consulted. A committee might interview the woman or not; excluding her was a means of ensuring that her emotional state would not sway committee members. Whereas some hospital committees operated by majority rule, others demanded unanimous approval for authorization. If even one member objected, the request was denied.

"It would seem that a few abortions were brought about
through the combined influence of economic pressure, social
factors, and convenience," observed two concerned ob/gyns
after reviewing a series of therapeutic abortion decisions in
1952. "To deny that these forces had not influenced us
would be incorrect; to accept them would be unwise; and
the best course would be to view future indications in the
light of strict medical principles directed toward preserving
the life and health of the mother." Physicians quoted by Rickie
Solinger in the journal *Feminist Studies*

Although the American Law Institute's Model Code did not
legislate prior approval by physicians or hospital therapeutic
abortion committees, many states that reformed their abortion
laws between 1967 and 1973 did so. When Canada broadened
the grounds for abortion in 1969 to include the protection of a
woman's physical health the committee structure was mandated.
The new legal requirements simply institutionalized a system that
was already in place in most hospitals where therapeutic abortions
were being performed.

The passage of the 1967 Therapeutic Abortion Act in California,
which added mental health grounds to the list of permissible indications
for abortion, meant that psychiatrists, psychologists, and social workers
would now play a major role on the committees. This represented a
major (and to some doctors, alarming) shift of emphasis within the
medical community. In the early days, not only was psychiatry viewed
as suspect by many members of the medical establishment but its
practitioners were thought to be unscientific and improperly influenced
by their patients' overwrought state. The strictest medical gatekeepers
charged that psychiatrists were "easily hoodwinked" into becoming
their patients' "unwitting accomplices" in the termination of
pregnancies that should have been carried to term. What would happen
now that the floodgates were open?

Plenty, it seems. Psychiatrists had always been involved to some extent in hospital abortion decisions, even in states with the most restrictive laws. But the introduction of mental health grounds opened the door for very broad interpretations of the law. They proved so popular that by 1968 an estimated 95 percent of all legal abortions in the US were performed on psychiatric grounds, most of them in California. According to sociologist Kristin Luker, California therapeutic abortion committees in 1970 approved over 90 percent of all requests for termination. Most of the remaining petitions were withdrawn by the pregnant woman.

The legal requirement of a psychiatric evaluation offered a lucrative business for specialists who were called to testify. Not only did psychiatrists learn to say (or write) what the committees needed to hear but women learned how to say what the psychiatrists needed to hear. A rash of quickly diagnosed "transient situational disturbances," "personality disorders," and "depressive neuroses" (some with suicide threats) among otherwise mentally healthy women was the unsurprising result.

"It was a joke, a charade," explains a California doctor recalling the committee's consideration of mental health grounds. "The patient would call, want an abortion, and we would tell her she had to see two psychiatrists . . . . We found three or four sympathetic doctors in the area that agreed to see these patients immediately and always agreed that the patient needed an abortion. All had the same diagnosis: '*situational anxiety.*' These were all normal women . . . but these were the hoops they had to go through." Quoted in Carole Joffe, *Doctors of Conscience: The Struggle to Provide Abortion Before and After Roe v. Wade*

As well intended as the reform movement was, then, it was

fundamentally flawed. Reforms were adopted state by state, tentatively and unevenly. Most states made no changes in their restrictive laws at all. What was legal in one state was illegal in another. The big problem, however, was with the committees charged with their implementation. No matter how dedicated they were, there was simply no way that individuals with very different outlooks could act in a fair and consistent manner.

For one thing, the committees often acted in haste. Pressed for time, their members had to deal with the cases in front of them with no clear criteria. Most were not experts, others were not interested. Some viewed their committee assignments as an administrative nuisance that they had to put up with.

Second, the personal attitudes of influential members played a powerful role. Physicians differed strongly among themselves both on the general principles involved and on the validity of individual indications. Conservative committees and individuals would hold to the strictest requirements of eligibility whereas more liberal committees found or invented reasons to approve almost every request. Some hospitals maintained quotas; once these were filled for the month the list was closed. A resourceful woman might find another physician and hospital willing to approve her case. Or she might travel to another state or find an illegal provider. All this at the cost of time, money, emotional distress, and a pregnancy that was advancing week by week.

"**Abortion commissions or individuals in a position to approve** or deny a request for termination of an unwanted pregnancy are seldom aware of, sensitive to, or even interested in the psychological rationale which is often the basis of the woman's decision." Henry P. David and colleagues, *Born Unwanted: Developmental Effects of Denied Abortion*

Third, personal favoritism and systematic class, race, and geographical bias pervaded the approval process. Whole categories of women in need were either excluded entirely from consideration because they lacked access or else were considered and turned away. Charges of unequal access and treatment fueled widespread challenges to the committee system and, indeed, to the still restrictive model of legal reform itself.

"A complete disaster," declared one American physician as early as 1958, writing in the journal *Obstetrics and Gynecology* about the idiosyncratic interpretations of the law. "Unworkable," concluded the Canadian Medical Association in 1971, only two years after the committee approval requirement was inserted into Canada's abortion law reform. "Unconstitutional," decreed the California Supreme Court in 1972 and the United States Supreme Court in 1973 in *Doe v. Bolton*, the companion case to *Roe v. Wade*. Whether mandated by law or imposed by hospitals, the courts concluded, the committee system served no useful medical purpose. Instead, it was an unjust intervention that both generally and selectively delayed, impeded, or blocked women's ability to obtain safe services.

The growing movement
for repeal of criminal laws

By the late 1960s many groups throughout the US were calling for repeal rather than reform of the abortion laws. The ALI's model criminal code had too many strings attached. It was still *criminal*. Not only were the grounds for termination still restricted, but the decision remained in medical (and state legislative) hands. Feminist groups argued that every woman has the right to control her own body and to make her own sexual and reproductive decisions without the interference of the state. Pro-repeal physicians and organizations such as the American Public Health Association argued that abortion is a private matter that should be decided between a woman and her doctor.

The repeal movement found a powerful advocate in the newly formed National Association to Repeal Abortion Laws (NARAL) which coordinated legal efforts and mobilized popular support across the country. In 1970 the Canadian Psychiatric Association became the first medical body in Canada to urge the removal of abortion from the criminal code. When a group called Doctors for Repeal of the Abortion Law petitioned members of the Senate to this effect in 1975, the Canadian Association to Repeal Abortion Laws (CARAL) was already mobilized to act.

When the Supreme Court decision in *Roe v. Wade* decriminalized abortion in the United States, two-thirds of the states still allowed abortion only to save a woman's life.

In 1970, New York, Hawaii, Alaska, and the District of Columbia removed abortion from their criminal codes entirely. The effect was electric. Women flocked to New York state from the eastern US and Canada. Services were offered in over one hundred facilities, including twenty-four free-standing clinics. In the first two years following repeal, two-thirds of all procedures in the state were performed on nonresidents and the number of abortions almost reached the number of live births. By 1972, half of all legal abortions in the country were performed in New York State, one-quarter in California, and the rest elsewhere.

In January of 1973, the US Supreme Court announced its historic decision in the case of *Roe v. Wade*. Overnight, hospitals in every state would be permitted to do elective abortions. Remember that the AMA had insisted all along that abortions should be performed only by a licensed physician in an accredited hospital. Now that abortion was legal for any reason, women in need of services had every reason to expect that hospitals would perform them.

But did they?

Whatever happened to hospital-based abortions?

To say that most hospitals in the United States responded slowly to the challenge of *Roe v. Wade* is an understatement. For some, a siege mentality set in. Influenced by the ambivalent or negative values of their affiliated ob/gyns and the growing backlash of an increasingly active antiabortion movement, few hospitals moved to add elective abortion to their health services. Indeed, in the conservative environment that characterized many medical facilities and/or the communities in which they were based, it would have required a determined effort on the part of prochoice physicians to make that happen.

Just how conservative were they? A national poll of physicians taken a month after *Roe v. Wade* found that whereas 52 percent favored the Supreme Court decision, 41 percent opposed it and 7 percent were not sure. Four years earlier, a similar poll reported that 40 percent of general practitioners and ob/gyns approved the idea of abortion on request as did over 70 percent of psychiatrists. The rest did not.

Whereas in 1973 hospitals performed more than half of all abortions in the US, by 1992 the figure had dropped to 7 percent. Only one-sixth of all general hospitals in the US in 1992 offered abortion services at all, and one-third of hospitals in Canada. From Stanley Henshaw and Jennifer Van Vort, in *Family Planning Perspectives*; Donley Studlar and Raymond Tatalovich, in *Abortion Politics: Public Policy in Cross-Cultural Perspective*

Most physicians in the early 1970s, including ob/gyns, were men. With the advance of the women's movement, mobilized in large part by the newly-formed National Organization for Women (NOW) and other feminist groups, and with threats of lawsuits for sex discrimination hovering over admissions boards, women applied and were accepted into medical schools (and the law) in unprecedented numbers. Between 1975 and 1985 the proportions female among ob/gyn residents (the period of in-hospital training following the completion of medical school) in the US rose from 15 to 42 percent.

We would expect that the entry of women into the profession would have an impact on the attitudes and practices of its members, and it did. A 1984 survey by Carole Weisman and associates of practicing ob/gyns who had graduated from medical school in the six years following *Roe v. Wade* found that female ob/gyns were far more likely than their male counterparts to agree strongly that women should have the legal right to abortion (90 percent did so, compared with 76 percent of men) and to disagree strongly with the imposition of restrictions such as mandatory waiting periods, parental consent for unmarried minors, and the exclusion of abortion from public funding such as Medicaid. Moreover, female ob/gyns were more likely than males to say they would have "no ethical reservations" about performing first-trimester abortions for every type of indication, ranging from saving the woman's life (91 percent) to "the mother is married and does not want more children" (63 percent). ("Having ethical reservations" does not necessarily mean that the physician would not do them, however.)

Does this mean that female ob/gyns are more likely to perform abortions? Yes. But do they perform more procedures on average than men do? No. This is because female ob/gyns are less likely to practice in partnerships or alone, where more abortions are performed, and more likely to work in multi-specialty group practices, hospitals, and medical schools where fewer abortions are performed. Although women in solo practice or partnerships perform more abortions on average than men in the same type of practice, the professional tracking system tends to steer women into salaried employment in institutional settings. At the time of the survey, equal proportions of female and male ob/gyns—about 12 percent—were working part time in a family planning or abortion clinic in addition to their regular routines.

"Opinion polls may indicate a public willingness to tolerate abortion as well as a willingness on the part of the medical profession to permit abortion, but the specialty that has assumed the responsibility for providing the service has not easily accommodated it to the practice of medicine. The abortion clinic, either free-standing or hospital-affiliated, symbolizes this lack of accommodation." Jonathan B. Imber, *Abortion and the Private Practice of Medicine*

What about the attitudes of other health professionals and support staff? A national survey of students and faculty in schools of medicine, nursing, and social work found that nurses were the most conservative of the three groups with respect to abortion and social workers the most liberal. It is important to realize that in hospitals where abortions *are* performed, the behavior of nurses, nurses' assistants, and receptionists can be quite negative toward abortion clients, with chilling effect. The opposite is true of free-standing clinics where staff are selected, and select themselves, for their positive views.

Providing safe abortions: private conscience or public responsibility?

Federal and state laws have made it very easy for hospitals and for people on their staffs to refuse to perform or assist in legal abortion procedures if they have personal or "institutional" reservations. Within weeks of *Roe v. Wade* the US Congress passed a law exempting federally funded institutions, agencies, and individuals from having to participate in abortions or sterilizations. State legislatures quickly followed suit. All but five states have since adopted "conscience clauses" that exempt medical personnel and even entire medical facilities, whether public or private, from performing or participating in abortion procedures if they do not wish to do so. Exemptions are also found in Canada.

The number of US hospitals performing abortions has dropped steadily from over 1,600 in 1975 to 855 in 1992. In the same period in Canada the number of hospital providers dropped from 274 to 191. Stanley Henshaw and Jennifer Van Vort, in *Family Planning Perspectives*; Donley Studlar and Raymond Tatalovich, in *Abortion Politics: Public Policy in Cross-Cultural Perspective*

The law of the state of Missouri, for example, specifies that "No physician, nurse, midwife, or hospital may be required to admit or treat a woman for the purpose of an abortion if admission or treatment is contrary to moral, ethical, or religious beliefs or established policy." A hospital may refuse to provide services without any justification. Moreover, according to the Missouri law and that of thirty-eight other states, no person or institution may be held liable for any damages (for example, a woman's death or the birth of a severely deformed infant) resulting from their refusal to perform an abortion.

Not surprisingly, the situation in which a medical practitioner or facility is allowed to withhold a routine or even life-saving procedure for reasons of personal or "institutional" conscience has triggered strong reactions from advocates of comprehensive reproductive health care. Not only does it interfere with the patient's ability to make medical choices according to her own moral or religious beliefs, it also denies her the full array of health care information and options to which she is entitled. In the case of institutional exemptions such as those for Catholic hospitals, all medical staff will be bound by them regardless of their private consciences.

In the United States, Catholic medical facilities account for one-tenth of all hospitals but one-sixth of all hospital admissions nationwide. The Ethical and Religious Directives under which they operate specifically prohibit the delivery to patients of services such as contraception, sterilization, abortion, artificial insemination and *in vitro* fertilization.
Rachel Benson Gold, in *The Guttmacher Report*

For Catholic facilities the prohibition of abortion is consistent with their religious ban on contraception, sterilization, and artificially assisted fertility treatments. Mergers of Catholic facilities with non-sectarian institutions have extended these policies, however, even to forbidding the latters' medical staff from referring patients to alternative sources of care. Yet it must be said that the majority of non-Catholic private facilities as well as most public and military hospitals do not offer abortion services either. Indeed, almost all abortions in the US are now performed in individual or group practices or in free-standing clinics. The hospitals have opted out.

The situation is somewhat different in Canada. Two-thirds of abortions are still done in hospitals even though only a small percentage of hospitals actually do them. Access and government funding vary from province to province, however, and from facility to facility. A few urban hospitals handle a large volume of cases. Others set strict residency requirements, arbitrary quotas on the numbers of procedures, and unrealistically low gestational limits such as eight or ten weeks. Some require general anesthesia even for early terminations or insist on a minimum of three consultations before the procedure. The shortage of providers has led to a wait of three to five weeks for services in some areas. Hospital cutbacks have added to the burden of overbooked clinics that struggle to keep pace with the demand.

Who learns to perform abortions?

If hospitals do not offer abortion services at all or else perform them only occasionally on therapeutic grounds, how do residents specializing in obstetrics and gynecology (or in family practice, if they are interested) learn the techniques of abortion care? The answer is that many don't.

In the early 1990s, *nearly half* of all graduating hospital residents in four-year obstetrics and gynecology programs in the US completed their studies without ever having performed a first-trimester abortion. By the late 1990s, the proportion never having performed a single abortion was still as high as one-third. Rene Almeling and colleagues, in *Family Planning Perspectives*

In 1991 a national survey found that only 12 percent of all US ob/gyn programs routinely offered training in first-trimester abortion techniques and only 6 percent in second-trimester techniques. Although others offered elective training (often off-site, that is, not on hospital premises), one-third made no provisions for abortion training at all. In Canada, too, training in techniques of surgical pregnancy termination for ob/gyn residents is largely optional; perhaps one-third receive it.

Responding to this lack of preparedness of specialists for performing even emergency procedures and to pressure from concerned physicians and advocacy groups, the Accreditation Council for

Graduate Medical Education in 1995 voted unanimously to require all residents in US ob/gyn hospital training programs to learn how to perform first- and second-trimester abortions. No sooner was the ruling announced than antiabortion legislators in the US Congress threatened to withdraw federal funding from any institution that complied. In a compromise measure, exemption clauses were introduced for residents or their institutions who claimed moral or religious objections.

Interestingly, the Council's ruling may have stopped the downward trend despite the compromise. A 1998 survey of the same programs reported by Rene Almeling and colleagues found that 46 percent claimed to offer routine training in first-trimester techniques and 34 percent elective training. *Routine* does not mean *required*, however. In only 26 percent of the programs are all of the ob/gyn residents trained. Abortion skills are most likely to be taught in public and non-religious private hospitals and least likely in military programs and, as one would expect, in church-operated facilities.

"**Abortion is the most common surgical procedure that women undergo**, and it seems reasonable to expect a graduate of an obstetrics and gynecology program to understand the procedure thoroughly. [Yet] our findings indicate that training opportunities for abortion are declining, and they will undoubtedly continue to do so unless changes are made in hospital services and training settings." P. D. Darney and colleagues, in *Family Planning Perspectives*

If abortion training is not offered in the hospital, where can a resident go? Most likely to a free-standing abortion clinic if there is one nearby and if the resident is willing to add to an eighty-hour work week plus several nights on call. It is in these clinics that one in every three abortions in Canada and the vast majority of abortions in the United States—seven of every ten procedures or almost one million every year—are now performed.

The rise of the free-standing clinic

The slow response of hospitals to the legalization of abortion in both Canada and the United States, combined with their tendency to maintain tight restrictions on patient eligibility, created new opportunities for practitioners willing to offer services in a different milieu. Advances in techniques of early termination such as uterine aspiration and the paracervical block (which made general anesthesia unnecessary) also meant that providers had no need of hospital facilities except as a backup for emergencies. A properly equipped medical office or clinic would do.

Women's health advocates in the early 1970s were eager to humanize abortion by creating more responsive, woman-centered clinics for sexual and reproductive health care. Physicians who had previously been doing unauthorized abortions could now do them openly. Some started their own clinics; others were recruited by colleagues because of their compassion and expertise. This was also a time when many health services were being decentralized nationwide in an effort to control escalating medical costs. The integrated community health center looked like a viable option.

New clinics, new approaches

Some of the earliest abortion clinics started up in the handful of liberal states before *Roe v. Wade*. In New York City, Women's Services opened its doors immediately following repeal of the state's abortion law in July 1970. In Washington DC, Preterm began services in 1971. As was the case with the first Morgentaler clinic in Montreal, the new centers attracted clients from all over the country. Many were referred by doctors relieved to know that they could finally send their patients to a good legal provider, assuming, that is, that the women could afford to pay. The new clinics also attracted physicians from the US, Canada, and overseas who were eager to acquire advanced surgical and counseling techniques.

"**The clinic was just inundated**," recalls a physician about the chaotic early months of Women's Services. "There were lines of patients around the block every single morning when we opened. From 7:00 A.M. to 11:00 P.M., we did two eight-hour shifts of all the staff and personnel. Usually one hundred or more people a day. Seven days a week." Quoted in Carole Joffe, *Doctors of Conscience: The Struggle to Provide Abortion Before and After Roe v. Wade*

The free-standing clinic model of service delivery, which has by now been so widely adopted following its early experimental years, offers a number of advantages to clients. Whether run by physicians, private corporations, family planning agencies, community health services, or women's health organizations, most try hard to create a comfortable physical and social environment that is as unlike the traditional hospital setting as possible. The decor may be homey or upscale. Staff members wear casual clothes rather than uniforms. Counselors may be selected more for their personal experience with abortion and their interaction style than for their formal educational qualifications. The client—the suburban housewife equally with the troubled teenager or the inner city mother of three—is supposed to feel relaxed and "at home."

With an emphasis on serving the client rather than catering to the medical culture of the physician-provider, relations among staff members and between staff and clients tend to be more informal and egalitarian. Physicians are part of the team. Individual or group counseling is supportive rather than judgmental. An assistant usually accompanies the client throughout the procedure to allay her fears and comfort her. Some clinics advertise an all-female staff. Confidentiality is easier to maintain, especially if the client travels to the clinic from another place. Even her personal physician (if she has one) need not know she is terminating a pregnancy.

Many free-standing clinics offer a range of women's health services such as tubal ligations, IUD insertion, emergency contraception, contraceptive injections, pills, PAP smears, HIV tests, and diagnosis and treatment of sexually transmitted diseases and other reproductive tract infections, along with pregnancy tests, prenatal advice, ultrasound, and medical and surgical abortions. Some provide general anesthesia if requested; others offer only local anesthesia or "twilight sleep" (IV sedation). Evening and weekend appointments, no waiting period, toll-free 24-hour telephone lines, *se habla español*, convenient locations in downtown office buildings or suburban shopping malls, low fees, all major credit cards and personal checks accepted, most health plans and Medicaid (where state law permits). Given the comfort and convenience it is not surprising that such clinics have become the providers of choice, if not of necessity, for many women.

Most free-standing clinics in Canada and the US are affiliated with the National Abortion Federation which sets very high medical standards. Because of the high volume of clients and the corresponding skills of the providers—many of whom have been doing abortions for years—complication rates in clinics tend to be lower on the whole than for most hospitals. Some of the busiest clinics perform more than five thousand procedures a year. Not only is abortion increasingly concentrated in clinics, but among clinics it is increasingly concentrated in the forty or fifty largest ones nationwide. Although staff physicians do not necessarily work full time, it would not be unusual for a doctor to do twenty procedures a day. Practice does not always make perfect, but there is a correlation. What becomes routine for the doctor—a negative, perhaps—is a positive for the client with respect to the quality of abortion care.

In addition, the cost of a clinic abortion is typically considerably lower than one done in a hospital and may be subsidized or charged on a sliding scale basis for those who cannot pay the full fee. Recent estimates for the US put the average cost of a clinic abortion in the first trimester at about $300 to $450, including all medical tests, counseling, treatment of complications (if any) and a followup visit. Unlike most other medical procedures, the cost has actually fallen over the past two decades after inflation is taken into account. Second-trimester procedures may range from $400 to as high as $2,500, depending on gestation and whether a general anesthesia is used (which requires a specialist), among other factors. Hospital services can cost twice as much.

> "The reality is that the clinics have provided more and better abortion services, with significantly lower complication rates, more attention to counseling and birth control, and at much lower cost, than have the nation's hospitals." Rosalind Pollack Petchesky, *Abortion and Woman's Choice: The State, Sexuality, and Reproductive Freedom*

The marginalization of abortion providers

Although free-standing clinics offer substantial advantages, especially for clients, there are disadvantages as well, especially for providers. Some but not all of these drawbacks accrue as well to physicians who do elective abortions in hospitals or as a regular part of their private practice. Twenty-five percent of all known providers are physicians who perform abortions in their own offices, yet private practice accounts for only 3 to 5 percent of all known procedures in the United States because it is illegal in some states and thus undoubtedly underreported.

The first disadvantage of being identified as an abortion provider is the sleaze factor. Decriminalization in the US and Canada could not obliterate overnight the aura of disrepute that surrounded the work of the formerly clandestine abortionist, no matter how skilled he or she might have been. Some physician-providers were highly appreciated by their colleagues who referred patients to them through the years. This does not mean that those pioneers who risked their careers were ever publicly acknowledged or rewarded, however. Instead they were often marginalized by the medical community and treated as somewhat less that fully professional (sometimes, even, as outcasts) by their colleagues and institutions. Some were refused hospital affiliation or teaching positions if they were known to perform abortions even on therapeutic grounds.

In the early days of the legal clinics, some physicians worked in them part time under false names to avoid the loss of hospital privileges that their activities might entail. After *Roe v. Wade* they were no longer fearful of being arrested or losing their licenses. But routine elective care has not been mainstreamed into gynecological/obstetrical training or hospital services, as we have seen. Thus, physicians who choose to do them with any frequency still find it difficult to reap the professional rewards that their specialization should offer. These rewards extend to the financial as well. Because clinics try to keep costs low and because private physicians who charge high fees for abortions are accused of profiteering, most providers earn far less in this practice than they would in almost any other.

"**Social stigma, professional isolation, peer pressure**, inadequate economic and other incentives, antiabortion harassment and violence, and the perception of abortion as an unrewarding field of medicine all adversely affect physicians' willingness to participate in abortion practice." National Abortion Federation, *Who Will Provide Abortions? Ensuring the Availability of Qualified Practitioners*

A second problem for the regular provider is the repetitive nature of high-volume clinic work. Despite the initial challenges of learning new techniques, performing early abortions can quickly become routine. For many skilled professionals it lacks the challenge that a more varied medical practice would entail. For this and other reasons, many are reluctant to train in this field. Clinic providers thus tend to be physicians working on a part-time basis, younger women doctors who are committed to providing safe services, or older (mostly male) physicians nearing or past retirement age who have been doing abortions for years, often in remembrance of the old days when it was still against the law.

Some clinics have attempted to overcome the problem of attracting and keeping medical staff by arranging for regular rotations of ob/gyns and family practice physicians from nearby hospitals. Some affiliates of the Planned Parenthood Federation of America as well as other reproductive health agencies also offer clinic-based training options for medical residents and physicians in pregnancy prevention and termination. Reproductive health advocates point out that if younger ob/gyns or family practitioners are to be attracted to the field to compensate for the "graying" of the current providers they will have to find the work both professionally and financially rewarding. But this would require radical changes in the attitudes of the medical profession at large as well as in the institutional arrangements between hospitals and clinics so that doctors could participate on a regular or rotating basis with no loss of income, prestige, or opportunities for administration, teaching, and research.

"**The shortage of physicians** [in the United States] trained and qualified and willing to offer abortion services, especially in rural areas, is acute and forces many women to travel long distances to find a provider. Nationwide, 84 percent of counties have no abortion provider." Stanley Henshaw and Jennifer Van Vort, in *Family Planning Perspectives*

The pool of skilled providers could be expanded significantly if mid-level personnel such as physicians' assistants, nurse practitioners, and nurse-midwives were legally permitted to perform first-trimester procedures. Many are already qualified to perform similar procedures such as taking uterine biopsies or inserting IUDs. Professional associations representing these workers, together with the American College of Obstetricians and Gynecologists and the American Public Health Association (among others), have all spoken out in favor of expanding the pool of providers in this way.

A third problem is that the isolation of abortion providers and the concentration of services in free-standing clinics exposes providers, staff, and clients alike to harassment and violence from antiabortion protesters. Demonstrators can also picket hospitals, of course, and they do. But it is difficult to pick out an abortion client or staff member from the crowds of employees, patients, and visitors entering and leaving a hospital on a typical day. In contrast, it is easy to blockade a clinic or the office of a known provider and target everyone who approaches. During the four years from 1987 to 1990, illegal blockades of reproductive health and family planning clinics in which abortions were performed resulted in the arrest of more than twenty-six thousand protesters in the US nationwide.

Of nonhospital facilities performing 400 or more abortions in 1992, 83 percent reported clinic picketing, 42 percent vandalism of their facilities, 34 percent demonstrations resulting in arrests, 28 percent picketing of the homes of staff members, 24 percent tracing of patients' license plates, 24 percent bomb threats, and 12 percent chemical attacks (with acid). Reported by Stanley K. Henshaw, in *Family Planning Perspectives*

Physician-providers together with their clinic associates and family members who live in some high-risk states or provinces and communities are routinely subjected to threats and acts of terrorism once their identity is known. Some have been murdered, in Canada as well as in the US. Many clinics and some hospitals have been forced to install tight security measures that make them look more like armed camps than health centers. Laws intended to guarantee freedom of access to clinic and hospital entrances by creating picket-free areas ("bubble zones") and forbidding specific acts of intimidation offer some protection if adequately enforced. But they cannot reduce the atmosphere of fear that surrounds the work and lives of so many health care providers whose conscience dictates that the needs of their patients come first, even before their own safety.

Physicians take a Hippocratic Oath in which they promise to do no harm. Some take this to mean that they should do no harm to the embryo or the fetus, whatever the cost to the pregnant woman. As a human being in need of care, she remains invisible in this calculus. Others maintain that by refusing to provide services to a woman in need, or by not referring her to a safe provider, they are in fact doing *her* harm. The possible harm done by providing a treatment must be balanced against the possible harm of withholding it. Who, then, can in good conscience unilaterally refuse?

It is reasonable to assume that all health practitioners (including general practitioners, physicians' assistants, nurses, midwives, and others) have a professional and humanitarian obligation to acquire the information and skills that they may be called upon to use. If this is the case, then the mastery of early and late abortion techniques and the treatment of complications from unsafe procedures should be a condition of certification in obstetrics and gynecology and, ideally, in general family practice as well. Ob/gyn students who claim moral reservations to performing abortions or sterilizations, or who find exemption clauses a convenient way to avoid performing a "distasteful chore," should choose a different medical specialty. And health practitioners who are unable or unwilling to provide safe legal services ought, as a legal and ethical obligation, to be *required* to refer patients promptly to someone who will.

"Regrettably, many aspects of medicine are both distasteful and a chore; these personal considerations, however, must never influence one's decision about doing what is best for the patient . . . . [T]he medical profession must be educated to the fact that abortion is no longer a favor to bestow but, rather, an obligation to perform." David A. Grimes, in *Obstetrics and Gynecology*

A sensible public health policy would ensure that all health facilities that offer obstetrical or gynecological services would have on their staff at least some trained practitioners, either physicians or mid-level professionals, who are willing to perform legal abortions. Exemptions to some staff (if granted) for reasons of personal conscience would never be extended to the institution as a whole. In particular, publicly funded hospitals, community health centers, and family planning clinics serving predominantly low-income populations would have a fundamental obligation to provide a full range of reproductive health services to their patients. Similarly, governments (federal, state or provincial, local) would have a fundamental obligation to guarantee that public institutions *do* provide safe services.

We have seen in this chapter that the legal freedom to choose to terminate a pregnancy means nothing without skilled providers. In the next chapter we turn to the issue of choice itself. As we shall see, the principles established in *Roe v. Wade* are by no means invulnerable. Instead, they are falling away piece by piece like chunks of glacial ice into the sea. What is the battle about? Who is winning? What's going on?

CHAPTER SEVEN

Private Opinion and Public Debate: Who Decides Who Decides?

"Three moral principles provide an ethical basis for the management of unwanted pregnancy. The principle of liberty guarantees a right to freedom of action; the utilitarian principle defines moral rightness by the greatest good for the greatest number; and justice requires that everyone have equitable access to necessary goods and services. Applied to unwanted pregnancy, these principles yield the conclusion that women have a natural right to reproductive freedom, and a social right to family planning and abortion services." Ruth Macklin, in *Women's Health in the Third World: The Impact of Unwanted Pregnancy*

"Abortion is a direct violation of the fundamental right to life of the human being . . . . Laws which authorize and promote abortion and euthanasia are therefore radically opposed not only to the good of the individual but also to the common good; as such they are completely lacking in authentic juridical validity. Abortion and euthanasia are thus crimes which no human law can claim to legitimize. There is no obligation in conscience to obey such laws; instead there is a grave and clear obligation to oppose them by conscientious objection." Pope John Paul II, *Evangelium Vitae*

A ppeals to the moral, the ethical, the right: the answers seem so obvious, so clear, so invincibly *true*. Each appeal contains some fundamental principle from which the argument flows. "Given this, then that follows." We have convinced ourselves; we try to convince others. Yet as the statements quoted above from a medical ethicist with a doctorate in philosophy and a religious leader with over nine hundred million followers illustrate rather nicely, some "self-evident" truths are mutually exclusive.

The debate about abortion has elicited its share and more of these truths. In this chapter we look more closely at some of the arguments for and against the voluntary termination of unwanted pregnancies. We look at the range of opinion among Canadians and Americans on the issue of when they believe abortion is immoral and when it should be illegal (the two are not necessarily the same). And we look at the clash of opinions in the courts and in federal, state, and provincial legislatures as representatives of prochoice and antichoice positions struggle to keep the other side at bay.

What the people think:
the large middle/pro and the very small no

Most of us are quite happy to oblige if someone asks us for our opinion about some issue of the day, even if we have given it little thought or have no strong feelings one way or another. Our off-the-top response may or may not reflect an underlying set of values. Some experts think it does. "Since abortion is an issue on which most Americans appear to have well-formed, stable opinions, it seems that public attitudes could be important sources of abortion policy" concludes one. Disagreeing with this assessment, others point out that the subject of abortion ranks low relative to most things about which people are concerned in their everyday lives such as job security, the cost of living, education, health care, and crime. Nor are opinions about abortion likely, *for most people*, to affect how they vote, or even how they behave when it comes to terminating a problem pregnancy.

One problem is that surveys sometimes ask questions that assume a level of information that the respondent simply does not have. For example, a question such as "In your opinion should abortion be more easily available than it is now, about the same, or more difficult to get?" assumes that the respondent is aware of the laws and policies currently in place and the availability of providers. Yet most people have no particular reason to know these things, just as they don't know things such as how much the US government gives in foreign aid each year, say, or how that compares with other countries, and thus whether we should be contributing more or less than we do now. How accessible *is* abortion? What *do* the federal and state or provincial laws permit? What regulations are in effect in hospitals and clinics? *Who knows?*

"**People's attitudes [to abortion] tend to be complex and ambivalent.** Answers to survey questions are notoriously sensitive to the wording of the questions." Donald Granberg and Beth Wellman Granberg, in *Family Planning Perspectives*

Another problem is that the sequence in which questions are asked and the way they are phrased will affect how people respond. For example, the statement "Abortion is a private matter that should be decided between a woman and her doctor" elicits high levels of agreement because "private" and "doctor" give positive signals. In contrast, the question "Do you believe that any woman who wants an abortion for any reason should be able to get it?" turns most people off. ("Wants?" "*Any* reason?") As, of course, does the phrase "abortion on demand." (Demand! Who does she think she *is*?!)

Too, surveys often elicit inconsistencies. Most people in Canada and the US believe that abortion should be legal and agree that the government should not interfere. ("The government" and "interfere" give negative signals.) Yet if asked about the conditions under which a woman should be permitted to terminate a pregnancy—she is unmarried, for instance, or she already has all the children she wants—people start setting limits. Yet who is going to enforce these limits if not "the government"?

Surveys show that about 70 percent of Americans typically agree that a pregnant woman should be allowed to terminate a pregnancy with her doctor's advice, and that the government should not interfere. Yet half also say that it should be illegal for doctors to prescribe RU 486, or for an unmarried woman to have an abortion just because she does not want the baby. These are typical contradictions. From *The Polling Report, Inc.*, *www.caral.ca*, and Stanley K. Henshaw and Greg Martire in *Studies in Family Planning*

Despite the ambiguities and inconsistencies, however, public opinion surveys over the years reveal some interesting results.

What the polls show: most people support legal abortion

First, the level of outright opposition to abortion for any reason—the Unconditional No—has dropped over the past thirty years even though the media coverage of this sector has ratcheted up considerably. In most polls in the US and Canada *only one person in ten is opposed to abortion for any reason.* At the other end of the spectrum, the proportion of people who believe that a woman should be able to obtain a legal abortion regardless of reason—the Unconditional Yes—fluctuates between about 30 and 40 percent (but sometimes more or less) depending on the survey. These are the supporters of abortion on request, although some will accept certain restrictions such as waiting periods. The remainder, about 50 to 60 percent, give a Conditional Yes response. Yes, they say, abortion should be legal, but only if . . .

If what? Most polls find that between 80 to 90 percent of all respondents agree that abortion should be legal for a woman whose life or health is endangered by the pregnancy, in cases where the pregnancy resulted from rape or incest, or if the fetus is severely deformed. These are the *therapeutic* or so-called "hard" reasons in which a pregnant woman is faced with a predicament not of her own making.

The Conditional Yes is less likely to tolerate the so-called "soft" reasons, however, such as being single or experiencing personal difficulties or conflicting responsibilities between school, work, marriage, and children. Yet these reasons account for almost all abortions nowadays. People tend to be more judgmental about these situations, believing that the girl or woman should accept the pregnancy and try to solve her problems in some other way. Only 40 to 50 percent of survey respondents in Canada and the US typically agree that abortion should be legal if the woman is unmarried, for example, or if she is still in school and would have to drop out, if she used contraception but it failed, or if she is married but the couple can't afford to have another child. The remainder say that abortion should *not* be legal for these reasons although they are willing to allow it for the "hard" reasons noted above.

Second, surveys show that for many Americans, *abortion is not a moral issue.* This was the view of over one-third of respondents to a 1998 Newsweek poll as well as a 1981 survey by Stanley Henshaw and Greg Martire that explored the issue in depth. Of those who said in 1981 that they believed that abortion *is* morally wrong in some or most cases, half nevertheless agreed that any woman who wants an abortion should legally be able to obtain one. This distinction between personal moralities and legal rights for everyone is important not only for the general public but also for gatekeepers such as physicians and legislators. It reflects an understanding of the need for basic legal protections and a tolerance of other points of view. Many people have moral or religious reservations about divorce, for example, or about premarital or extramarital sex, yet few would argue these days that such acts should be against the law.

It is one thing to talk about "the public," however, and quite another to talk about particular social groups. Age, sex, marital status, race and ethnicity, income, educational background, religious and political affiliation, place of residence, and a host of other social characteristics differentiate us one from another, individually and collectively. Within these distinctions, who is more likely to favor liberal access to abortion and who is most likely to resist?

Supporters and opponents: who are they?

"One of the important functions served by public opinion polls has been to demonstrate the absence of alignment on abortion by race, religion, gender and political party affiliation and to bring these findings to the attention of political leaders. This is important because politicians are exposed far more to the official views of sharply opposed interest groups and to the equally polarized depictions reported in the media than they are to the general views of their constituents." Alice S. Rossi and Bhavani Sitaraman, in *Studies in Family Planning*

Surprisingly, most polls show no significant differences between women and men in their support for abortion. Where gender gaps do appear, they may favor either sex. The strongest predictors of liberal abortion attitudes tend to be having a higher education and higher household income; being employed full time (for women) rather than part time or not at all; reporting one's religious affiliation as non-evangelical Protestant (especially Episcopalian), Jewish, other, or none, rather than Baptist, other evangelical Protestant, or Roman Catholic; living in a metropolitan area; living in the Northeastern, Northwestern and Western parts of the US rather than in the Midwest or South; being single, separated or divorced rather than currently married; defining oneself as politically liberal or moderate rather than conservative; and being a Democrat or independent rather than a Republican. (The majority of voters of both parties take qualified or unqualified prochoice positions, however.)

All things considered, the best single indicator of people's opinions about abortion is the frequency of reported church attendance. This is a sign of *religiosity*—that is, of the strength of a person's religious beliefs—rather than of religion *per se*. Calling oneself a Mormon or a Catholic, for example, doesn't mean much in the surveys unless one also attends church regularly. Some social scientists suggest that the influence of religion on people's personal behavior has been declining in the past few decades, even among those who call themselves evangelicals or born-again Christians.

Four of every five Catholics in the US believe it is possible to disagree with the pope on official positions such as abortion and contraception and still be a good Catholic. In the US, 82 percent of Catholics say abortion should be permitted under at least some circumstances, and 39 percent for *any* reason. The proportions of Catholics holding this view in Canada are almost as high: 77 and 36 percent, respectively. Survey results reported in Catholics for a Free Choice, *Catholics and Reproduction: A World View*

If we look for pockets of the most extreme antiabortion sentiment, we can find them among people of any religion who attend services more than once a week. In a 1998 survey authored by David M. Adamson and others of Americans' attitudes about domestic and international population issues, 30 percent of respondents who said they attended church more than once a week were opposed to abortion *on all grounds*, even to save a woman's life. No other identifiable group reached even half this level of opposition. In contrast, the strongest support for abortion on request is found among those who attend services less than once a week or report no religious affiliation.

People's attitudes toward abortion are related to other moral positions, of course. For example, abortion opponents are more likely to support mandatory prayer in the schools, to condemn homosexuality and nonmarital sexual relations, to disapprove of sex education and birth control for teenagers, to consider large families ideal, to hold more authoritarian values with regard to child rearing, to believe that divorce should be more difficult to get, and to oppose equal rights for women. A 1981 survey found that whereas more than nine of every ten members of the National Abortion Rights Action League (NARAL) supported the proposed Equal Rights Amendment to the US constitution, only one of every ten members of the National Right to Life Committee (NRLC) did so.

Crusaders: how they see the world

We have been talking so far about the general public But what about the abortion activists and movement leaders? Compared with their prochoice counterparts, studies show that activists in the antiabortion movement typically devote more time and energy to the cause and vote only for political candidates who share their conservative views. And although male activists on both sides tend to share quite similar socioeconomic backgrounds (most are professionals such as doctors, lawyers, or theologians), female activists differ sharply from one another not only in their values and beliefs but also in their personal life situations.

"The two sides have very little in common in the way they look at the world, and this is particularly true with regard to the critical issues of gender, sex and parenthood. The views on abortion of each side are intimately tied to, and deeply reinforced by, their views on these other areas of life." Kristin Luker, in *Family Planning Perspectives*

At the risk of oversimplification, let's consider some typical profiles. According to interviews conducted by Kristin Luker and by Donald Granberg, prochoice women leaders in the US tend to be highly educated (many have postgraduate degrees) and employed full time, married (late) to a man in the professions, have one or two children and a comfortable income. They rarely if ever attend church and typically say that religion is not important to them personally. In their support for gender equality they tend to view women's reproductive roles not as natural or God-given but as socially imposed barriers to full equality. Making love is an expression of affection and intimacy, an end in itself and not necessarily a means to having children. Prochoice activists tend to use effective contraception and to consider an accidental pregnancy "correctable."

And their antichoice counterparts? These activist women typically married when they were teenagers and their husbands are white collar workers or small businessmen with modest incomes. The women have graduated from high school and perhaps completed some college, have three or more children, and are not employed outside the home apart from their volunteer work. Whether Catholic or evangelical Protestant, they attend church at least once a week and say that family and religion are the most fulfilling aspects of their lives. They believe that women and men are inherently very different and that each has a natural, gendered role to play; that mothering is a full-time job; that women should not work outside the home; that the "liberation" of women represents a loss to womanhood, not a gain; and that the primary purpose of the sex act (indeed, its very beauty) is opening oneself to the possibility of the gift of life. A movement such as feminism that appears to devalue marriage, pregnancy, or motherhood devalues all women, in their view, and threatens everything they so deeply believe in.

Only one in ten Americans and Canadians say they are opposed to all abortions. Among these are some who may, when pressed, make exceptions to save a woman's life. How, then, has such a small minority achieved such a loud public voice? How has the extreme antiabortion position come to occupy—or *claimed* to occupy— the moral high ground compared with other views? How has the movement achieved so much political power? To answer these questions, we turn now to the rhetoric of the abortion debate.

The war of words: Whose rights? Who's right?

The "clash of absolutes" is the apt expression chosen by Harvard law professor Laurence Tribe in his analysis of the moral divisions of the abortion debate. After all, what belief could be more absolute than the right to life? Unless it is the right to liberty?

"**Our national institutions are braced for a seemingly endless clash of absolutes.** The political stage is already dominated by the well-rehearsed and deeply felt arguments, on either side of the abortion issue, that we have come to know so well. The debate is unending. None of its participants ever seems even mildly persuaded by the arguments of the other side." Laurence H. Tribe, *Abortion: The Clash of Absolutes*

The right to life of the unborn child; the right to liberty of the living woman. Both sides have their passionate adherents. But the struggle over rights does not end there. It is not just the rights of the fetus versus the rights of the woman, but the rights of the woman versus the rights of the State, of the man who inseminated her, of her parents if she is an unmarried minor, and of the physician and the clinic or hospital who have the power to decide her fate. No matter the circumstances of the conception, its product may be contested by any who lay claim to its future. An accidental pregnancy? Who can say yes or no to its continuation or termination? *Who owns the baby?*

In its attempt to negotiate this land-mined territory of competing rights and set the limits of state regulatory authority, the US Supreme Court in *Roe v. Wade* came up with what many believe to be a brilliant (although itself highly contested) solution. It did this, as we have seen, by shifting the balance of rights according to the length of gestation.

During the first six months, declares *Roe*, the woman's "right of privacy" to terminate a pregnancy is paramount. The individual states cannot interfere except to require that abortions be performed by a licensed physician and, in the second trimester, to impose regulations that "reasonably relate to the preservation and protection of maternal health." "With respect to the State's important and legitimate interest in potential life," however, the Court declares that the "compelling" point is at viability when the fetus presumably has "the capability of meaningful life outside the mother's womb." Thus, beginning in the third trimester, or somewhere around twenty-four to twenty-six weeks, the states can intervene even to the point of proscribing abortion entirely except when the procedure is necessary to preserve the woman's health or life.

Placing a marker such as the beginning of the third trimester beyond which the individual states have the authority to limit abortions to those that are medically advised is a useful way of balancing the interests of the pregnant woman and the fetus. It recognizes that pregnancy is an incremental process by which a tiny cluster of cells embedded in the walls of the uterus gradually becomes a fully formed human being that is ready to be born. It also recognizes that there is a significant transition in this process during which the fetus becomes capable of surviving outside the womb. *Roe* says nothing about a fetus's "right to life," however, nor does it refer to the fetus as a person or say when life begins.

"We need not resolve the difficult question of when life begins. When those trained in the respective disciplines of medicine, philosophy and theology are unable to arrive at any consensus, the judiciary, at this point in the development of man's knowledge, is not in a position to speculate as to the answer." US Supreme Court decision in *Roe v. Wade,* 1973

When does life begin?

The idea that life begins at conception and must be protected at all costs from that point forward is the most absolute of positions in the clash of absolutes. In its preoccupation with the "unborn person" it completely ignores the living person who is carrying the pregnancy. Moreover, such a view has no medical or scientific justification. First, there is no "moment" of conception: fertilization is a process that lasts up to twenty-four hours or more. Second, the fertilized ovum may take five or six days to move down the fallopian tube and another six to eight days to bury itself in the uterine lining. As we saw earlier, according to accepted medical opinion it is only when an embryo is *successfully implanted* that a pregnancy has been achieved. Third, the rate of spontaneous abortion between fertilization and implantation is extremely high. In nature there is nothing sacrosanct about the moment of conception. Quite the contrary: the first few weeks are a time for correcting nature's mistakes.

But it is not really the scientific evidence that is at issue here. The argument that life begins at conception is essentially a religious one. Those who promote it as a justification for criminalizing all abortions speak with the conviction that they represent the word of God. Yet such a view is by no means universally shared even among those religions that are based on the Judeo-Christian Bible.

A survey of Catholic priests in New York State found that nearly four of every ten said that they disagreed with or had doubts about the Church's teaching on abortion. Such doubts and disagreement were most common among younger priests. Even among those who agreed fully with the Church's position, however, a substantial number believed that laws permitting at least some abortions are legitimate. Survey results reported by Frank J. Traina in *Studies in Family Planning*

There is a great deal of disagreement among theologians both across and within religions about when a fetus becomes "human" and when it acquires a "soul." The situation is not helped by the fact that neither the ancient writers of the Old Testament nor the "modern" writers of the New Testament have anything to say about it. This leaves the question up to religious scholars and church leaders, each of whom has his favorite view.

Some of the ancient and medieval arguments about how and when the soul enters the fetus may seem rather arcane to us now. For example, it was commonly argued that a male fetus, being naturally favored, acquires a soul earlier than the female does. But these are not just historical relics equivalent to fussing about how many angels can dance on the head of a pin. For if it can be *decreed* that "life" begins at conception, then abortion even before the fertilized ovum is implanted in the womb (and thus even before a pregnancy has "scientifically" begun) involves the taking of human life and is an offense against God. And if the pre-embryo or embryo or fetus is legally defined as a person with a right to life and to equal protection of the laws, we're talking murder.

But the antichoice argument goes beyond the question of when human life begins. It is linked with the belief that abortion, perhaps more than any other single act, symbolizes a fundamental decline of moral values in an unrelentingly secular society. Together with contraception, it marks an alarming trend toward individualism, materialism, and the decline of religion and the family. Allow abortion on demand and you encourage personal irresponsibility. The sexual ingredient is powerful in this view. The preoccupation with protecting the "innocent life" of the unborn implies that the "other"—the carrier of this innocent life—is tainted with sexual guilt.

Perhaps, then, one reason why the very small minority of people who believe that abortion should be prohibited hold influence far beyond their numbers is because they, and they alone, claim to speak for God. For Life against Death. Good against Evil. They have framed the debate in such a way that those who hold different views are accused, individually and collectively, of terrible things.

"We in the prolife community are now beyond the point of talking. . . . We're putting our time . . . our energy . . . our prayers . . . and our money where our mouths have been. We're at the point of action, and our unified action is going to shut down the abortion industry in America." Baptist church pastor speaking of the need for direct action at a right-to-life conference in Fort Lauderdale, Florida, quoted by Patricia Donovan in *Family Planning Perspectives*

Add to this absolutist position the organizational and political power of the Roman Catholic Church, which in the United States is represented by the National Conference of Catholic Bishops. Add also the leadership of the evangelical Protestant churches, the Mormon Church (Church of Jesus Christ of the Latter Day Saints), and Jewish orthodoxy. Add to this the mass faith-based organizations such as the Moral Majority (now faded) and the Christian Coalition with their radio and television crusades. Add the National Right to Life Committee and other single-issue antiabortion groups. Then add the so-called New Right, or Radical Right, whose political representatives define themselves by their ultra-conservative views. All of these groups, separately and together, have campaigned to elect antiabortion legislators at all levels of government and target for defeat those who support a woman's right to choose.

The question of choice

The strongly prochoice position in this clash of absolutes claims to be no less moral. But it appeals not to God but to a different set of principles: principles that are based on ideas about universal human rights, social justice, and tolerance for the rights of others. Many of these rights are spelled out in United Nations documents such as the Universal Declaration of Human Rights and the Convention on the Elimination of All Forms of Discrimination Against Women. A specific right of individuals and couples "to determine freely and responsibly the number and spacing of their children" and to have the information and means to do so was formally recognized by the UN many years ago. Feminist groups and other advocates of women's health and rights throughout the world have extended the idea of reproductive self-determination to include sexual self-determination as well. Incorporating positive expressions of a healthy sexuality as well as protection from harm, the concept of sexual rights includes the right to bodily integrity and security, equality, diversity, and personhood. In essence, it claims the right to make one's own decisions as long as they do not infringe on the rights or dignity of others.

"**The human rights of women** include their right to have control over and decide freely and responsibly on matters related to their sexuality, including sexual and reproductive health, free of coercion, discrimination and violence. Equal relationships between women and men in matters of sexual relations and reproduction, including full respect for the integrity of the person, require mutual respect, consent and shared responsibility for sexual behaviour and its consequences." Platform for Action of the Fourth World Conference on Women, Beijing, China, 1995, paragraph 96.

The notion of sexual rights means that, at a minimum, no person, male or female, should be made to enter into any sexual relationship (marital or nonmarital) or engage in any specific sexual act in the absence of his or her free and full consent. The prochoice position takes this one step farther by declaring that *no woman should be forced to become pregnant, to continue a pregnancy, or to bear a child against her will.*

In this view, consent to sexual intercourse does not imply consent to pregnancy. Sexual relations and pregnancy are distinct behaviors or events and must be separately agreed to. Because a pregnancy places a heavy physical burden on the woman, even a risk to her life if she carries it to term, and because she has a right to bodily integrity, that is, to protect herself from possible harm, then she also has the right to refuse to carry a pregnancy to term. This means that neither the State nor a physician, parent, husband, boyfriend, or anyone else should be granted the authority to veto her decision to terminate a pregnancy, although they may of course try to change her mind.

"Any serious discussion of the moral and ethical issues of abortion must be prefaced by a clear understanding that the status of the fetus and whether it shall be regarded as a 'person' or a 'human life' do not exhaust the bases for moral inquiry . . ." Rosalind Pollack Petchesky, *Abortion and Woman's Choice: The State, Sexuality, and Reproductive Freedom*

The fetus is not "nothing" in this view. A woman is responsible for deciding about her pregnancy as early as possible and to act on it if she can, either by seeking an early termination or by preparing herself for motherhood with good prenatal care. Nor do her rights of privacy or liberty or security of the person always trump the well-being of the fetus. NARAL, for example, fully supports the Supreme Court's decision in *Roe* that allows the individual states to prohibit abortions in the third trimester except where the woman's life or physical health are in jeopardy. What the prochoice position does insist on, however, is that the rights of the woman are paramount in the early months of a pregnancy.

Prochoice activists reject the claim that antiabortion groups occupy the moral high ground and that all truly religious and moral people disapprove of abortion. Public opinion polls show that many highly ethical people in the US and Canada, including some with deeply held religious convictions, believe that an offense graver than abortion is to force a woman to bear a child against her will or to bring an unwanted child into the world.

"Right is to care for your children, to give them what they need." A Dominican woman living in the US explains the meaning of a "right" to an interviewer, in Rosalind P. Petchesky and Karen Judd, *Negotiating Reproductive Rights: Women's Perspectives Across Countries and Cultures*

Advocates of choice claim to support families in all their diversity. They support children's rights, including the right of every child to be a wanted child. They are, they insist, *profamily, prochild, prochoice.* Like their antichoice counterparts they also engage in public education, electoral politics, and mass demonstrations in support of reproductive freedom. In alliance with organizations such as NARAL and CARAL, Planned Parenthood Federation of America, the National Family Planning and Reproductive Health Association, Catholics for a Free Choice, the Religious Coalition for Abortion Rights, the American Civil Liberties Union, the Fund for a Feminist Majority, and the National Organization for Women, they are working to defend the sexual and reproductive health and rights of girls and women in their own countries and throughout the world.

The politics of legislative confrontation

The clash of absolutes—of right against right and of rights against rights—is acted out in many places: in the streets surrounding women's health clinics and hospitals; in town halls and state or provincial legislatures; in federal parliaments and congresses; in the vast conference rooms of international assemblies; and in the courts. The results of these clashes can have a profound impact on the laws, policies and practices that determine whether people, regardless of their age and marital status or their social and economic circumstances, can obtain the reproductive health information and services they need.

For the small minority who believes in the *absolute* right to life of the fetus, the Supreme Court decision in January 1973 was of course a disaster. No sooner was *Roe v. Wade* announced than its political opponents sprang into action. The goal was to reverse the Court's decision and to make abortion illegal. Stacking the Court with antichoice judicial appointments was one option, but that would take time. Prochoice justices would have to die or retire and be replaced. It was easier and quicker to begin with the Congress, which within days was inundated with antiabortion bills.

Right-to-life initiatives in the US Congress

Sixty-eight proposed constitutional amendments were filed in the House of Representatives during the 1973 and 1974 sessions of the US Congress that would affirm the right to life of the fetus or else return to the states the authority to legislate against abortion. The first of many right-to-life amendments was submitted within *one week* of the Supreme Court decision in *Roe v. Wade*. Reported by Jeannie I. Rosoff in *Family Planning Perspectives*

Right-to-life initiatives took three forms. The major thrust was to write an amendment to the US constitution that would declare that human life begins at conception; that the fetus is entitled to equal protection of the laws from this "moment" forward; and that the word "person" as used in the Fourteenth Amendment includes the unborn at every stage of its development. (The *Roe* decision explicitly rejects this interpretation of personhood in the Constitution.) All factions of the antiabortion movement support the idea of a constitutional amendment, with one qualification: they cannot agree on making an exception to save the woman's life. Whereas some argue that exempting *bona fide* medical emergencies from a fetal protection clause is a necessary compromise, others insist that medical exceptions are nothing but a smokescreen for the continued practice of abortion. But these quibbles are moot, for none of the proposals so far has stood a chance of passing. Most have either failed to elicit sufficient sponsorship in the House or Senate or else died in committee.

Two other prolife approaches were intended to circumvent the unwieldy process of amending the Constitution. One, *The Human Life Statute*, would require a simple majority vote in both houses plus the signature of the President. Introduced in 1981, it did not win enough votes and would probably have been deemed unconstitutional in any case. The second try, in which the statute was resubmitted as an amendment to other legislation, was stopped by a filibuster. On the question of when life begins, however, its sponsors were not shy about stepping in where the Supreme Court justices had feared to tread.

"The Congress finds that . . . scientific evidence demonstrates that the life of each individual begins at conception . . . [and that] the Supreme Court . . . erred in not recognizing the humanity of the unborn child and the compelling interest of the several states in protecting the life of each person before birth, and . . . in excluding unborn children from the safeguards afforded by the equal protection provisions of the Constitution . . ." Amendment 2038 to debt ceiling legislation, proposed by Senator Jesse A. Helms in January 1981

Despite its adoption in the official platform of the Republican Party in 1976 (it's still there), neither the right-to-life constitutional amendments nor the equivalent legislation appeared to be going anywhere. In their place, opponents of *Roe* tried another tack. Introduced in 1981, the *Human Life Federalism Amendment* to the constitution would have granted to Congress and the states the authority to restrict or ban all abortions. If Congress failed to act, the states could pass their own criminal laws. This made a lot of antiabortion groups unhappy, though. True, the states would have the authority to outlaw all abortions. But would they do it? What would prevent them from doing what so many had done before *Roe v. Wade*, which was to liberalize or even repeal their restrictive laws?

"The right to abortion is not secured by this Constitution. The Congress and the several States shall have the concurrent power to restrict and prohibit abortions; *Provided,* That a law of a state more restrictive than a law of Congress shall govern." Human Life Federalism Amendment to the Constitution proposed by Sen. Orrin G. Hatch in 1981

Antiabortion groups in Canada were involved in their own struggles. How could they reverse the Supreme Court decision of 1988 in *Morgentaler v. The Queen* that removed the federal abortion law from the Criminal Code on grounds that it was unconstitutional? First, they could claim that the word "person" in existing Canadian human rights statutes extends to the unborn. But like its American counterpart, the Canadian Supreme Court also ruled that no federal or provincial statute, including the Canadian Charter of Rights, recognizes any rights of the unborn. (The Court also used this argument to deny a man's attempt to block his girlfriend's abortion.) Only when it has completely left its mother's body alive does the baby become a separate being with all the legal rights that personhood confers. Second, abortion opponents introduced a new federal law criminalizing all elective (but not medically mandated) procedures. Making abortion punishable by up to two years in jail unless a doctor determined that the pregnancy threatened a woman's physical or mental health, the bill was passed by the Canadian House of Commons in 1990. It was defeated in the Senate, however, and no other federal legislation has since been attempted.

Beyond the right to life: alternative tactics

These stories of the failure of the antiabortion forces to outlaw abortion entirely—that is, to win the war—do not mean that they did not win some very important battles. The flood of uncompromising right-to-life proposals in the United States immediately following *Roe* carried along with it hundreds of proposed riders, amendments, and bills that would limit access to abortion without banning it outright. Unsure of how to vote and intimidated by the accusations and pressure tactics of the antiabortion crusaders, many legislators found it more prudent to vote Yes rather than No on the new legislation.

"While a certain number of representatives must have opposed legalized abortion on the basis of their own religious or moral convictions, many—struck by the ferocity of the organized opposition and unable to gauge realistically the public temper—clearly acted in fear of political retaliation at the polls." Jeannie I. Rosoff describes the "blind panic" of members of Congress accused by antiabortion activists of being "murderers" if they refused to endorse right-to-life legislation, in *Family Planning Perspectives*

Landmark legislation allowing not only individuals but also private and public institutions to refuse to perform abortions under the so-called conscience clauses was passed almost immediately. Also passed was the first legislation prohibiting the use of federal funds for some abortion activities. Although the Hyde Amendment that disallowed the use of Medicaid funds for abortions for indigent women was not enacted until 1977, the Helms Amendment to the Foreign Assistance Act did pass. Prohibiting the use of foreign aid funds for abortion services or supplies, the passage of the Helms Amendment marked the beginning of an increasingly restrictive US policy directed at limiting the reproductive options of women in poor countries.

The most far-reaching of these restrictions derive from the Mexico City policy, which takes its name from the ultra-conservative position of the US delegation at the United Nations International Conference on Population that was held in Mexico City in 1984. Under Reagan administration guidelines, the US announced it would no longer fund family planning organizations in developing countries that offered abortion information, counseling, referrals, or services even if such organizations used their private funds to do so, and in countries where abortion is legal on most or all grounds. Referred to as the "global gag rule," the policy was in force from 1984 to January 1993 and rescinded during the first days of the Clinton presidency. It was reinstated in January 2001 by President George W. Bush on his first full day of office. Ironically, by withholding funds from those very organizations whose primary purpose is to *prevent* unwanted pregnancies but who refuse to abide by its terms, the policy makes it more likely that unwanted pregnancies *will* occur and that the demand for abortion will intensify. Moreover, the new version of the global gag rule prohibits the use of government aid money for organizations that speak out in favor of abortion law reform although antiabortion advocacy is allowed. Thus, not only does the policy violate our principles of democratic free speech and national sovereignty, it also imposes restrictions on organizations working in developing countries that would be considered intolerable (if not unconstitutional) in the United States.

A domestic gag rule barring family planning clinics receiving even small amounts of federal funding from counseling clients about abortion was instituted by the Secretary of Health and Human Services in 1987 during the Reagan years, upheld by the US Supreme Court in 1991 in the case of *Rust v. Sullivan*, and eliminated by President Clinton in 1993. Although not restricting public advocacy, it, too, placed family planning agencies in the position of having to choose between continuing to accept federal funding and advising their clients of their full legal rights.

In 2001, antiabortionists tried once again to make an end run around *Roe v. Wade* by conferring personhood on the fetus, this time as a potential victim of violence. *The Unborn Victims of Violence Act*, which passed the House of Representatives in April of that year, establishes separate penalties for individuals who knowingly or unknowingly harm an "unborn child" in the course of committing a federal crime. Although the victim of violence is of course the pregnant woman, it is the fetus that matters here.

Antichoice action at the state level

From the moment in January 1973 when the US Supreme Court voided those remaining state laws that criminalized abortion, the antichoice strategy at the state level was to see how quickly and drastically the presumed protections of *Roe* could be chipped away. If abortion was going to be legal for any reason, then it could at least be hard to get. Just how much could state initiatives accomplish?

Plenty. In 1999 alone, 439 antichoice measures were introduced in state legislatures of which seventy were enacted in thirty-four states. These numbers represent a tripling of antichoice proposals since 1995. Although the pace of new antichoice initiatives has slowed slightly since then, the total dipped only to 398 in 2001. Among the most frequently adopted over the years are state laws intended to:

- permit certain medical personnel and/or health facilities to refuse to perform or participate in abortions ("conscience clause") (forty-five states);

- restrict the performance of abortions to qualified physicians (forty-four states);

- require unmarried minors to notify one or both parents at least twenty-four hours before having an abortion, or to obtain the consent of at least one parent or, failing that, of a judge (forty-three states);

- regulate some aspects of abortion after fetal viability (forty-one states) and/or require "viability tests" for some pregnancies (five states);

- prohibit so-called "partial birth" abortions or the use of certain abortion procedures (thirty-one states);

- require that every woman seeking an abortion must give her "informed consent," usually after receiving state-mandated lectures on fetal development (thirty-one states);

- prohibit the use of state medical assistance funds for abortion services for low-income women who are otherwise eligible for subsidized medical care, except in cases of life endangerment or proven rape or incest (twenty-eight states);

- impose a mandatory waiting period between first contact with a physician (or the state-mandated lecture) and the performance of the procedure (twenty-one states);

- punish a nonparent who takes a minor across state lines for the purposes of obtaining an abortion (twenty states);

- prevent health care providers employed by the state or by institutions receiving state funds from counseling and/or referring women for legal abortion services under certain circumstances (state-imposed "gag rules") (sixteen states);

- prohibit public funds from paying for insurance that includes abortion coverage (twelve states);

- declare the intent of the state legislature to protect the life of the "unborn" (eleven states);

- require the husband's consent or notification (nine states); and

- prohibit private insurance coverage for abortion unless the woman pays an extra premium (six states).

Many states still have laws on their books prohibiting most abortions even though such laws have been ruled unconstitutional by state and federal courts. NARAL and NARAL Foundation, *Who Decides? A State-by-State Review of Abortion and Reproductive Rights*

Although not one of these state-imposed restrictions involves protecting the woman's health, the Supreme Court has upheld almost all of them on appeal except for spousal notification and the ban on "partial birth" abortions, which was ruled unconstitutionally vague and thus unenforceable in several state courts. In its 1989 decision in *Webster v. Reproductive Health Services* the Court went so far as to uphold the Missouri law that not only prohibits public employees and facilities from performing or assisting in abortions but also specifies that all abortions of at least sixteen weeks gestation be performed in a hospital (if you can find one that will do it), requires a "fetal viability test" if the woman appears to be at least twenty weeks pregnant, and declares that "the life of each human being begins at conception." In a five-to-four decision, the majority of justices argued in *Webster* that such restrictions do not impose an "undue burden" on a woman's legal right or personal ability to terminate a pregnancy. The minority, headed by Justice Harry A. Blackmun who had written the Court's majority decision in *Roe v. Wade*, strongly disagreed.

"The women of this Nation still retain the liberty to control their destinies. But the signs are evident and very ominous, and a chill wind blows." Justice Harry A. Blackmun, writing a dissenting opinion on the Court's acceptance of restrictions in *Webster v. Reproductive Health Services*, US Supreme Court, 1989

The Court's *Webster* decision sent shockwaves through the prochoice community. Was *Roe v. Wade* about to fall? Prochoice advocates seized the initiative. Like their antichoice counterparts, they wanted to reduce their dependence on the ideological and political makeup of the US Supreme Court.

Prochoice initiatives: can *Roe* be protected?

Drawing on many cosponsors in the House and the Senate, prochoice legislators drafted the *Freedom of Choice Act of 1989* to incorporate the protections of *Roe* into a federal statute. If it had passed, it would undoubtedly have been subjected to constant judicial review as antiabortion opponents tried to circumvent or reverse it. Yet this scenario, too, is moot. The unequivocally prochoice language of the Act could not win enough Congressional support. In any case, Republican President George Bush (senior), in a continuation of the conservative policies of his predecessor, Ronald Reagan, had promised a veto.

Ten years later, in the final years of the Clinton administration, family planning supporters introduced a bill that addressed a broad range of reproductive health concerns. Among other initiatives, *The Family Planning and Choice Protection Act of 1999* proposes to increase federal funding for family planning clinics, prohibit domestic gag rules that prevent health care providers from offering all options to their clients, repeal limitations on Medicaid funding of abortion services for poor women, and promote public awareness of emergency contraception and mifepristone (RU 486). Like *The Freedom of Choice Act*, it also codifies the principles of freedom of choice stated in *Roe v. Wade* while rejecting most subsequent limitations. And also like its predecessor, it shows little chance of passing.

A significant achievement during the eight-year Clinton administration, however, was the bipartisan majority support for a federal law to protect abortion providers' and clients' access to clinics and hospitals. Clinic confrontations had been intensifying and violence escalating to the point of bombings, arson, and murder. The *Freedom of Access to Clinic Entrances Act* was signed into law in 1994. Prohibiting all violent, obstructive, and threatening behaviors while protecting the constitutional rights of protesters to peaceful assembly and free speech, the Act has survived numerous constitutional challenges. At the state and provincial levels, too, prochoice action has been aimed at protecting clinic facilities, clients, and personnel so that state or provincial and local police and not just "the feds" can respond to a crisis. In the US, fifteen states plus the District of Columbia have enacted their own clinic access protection laws.

"The Freedom of Access to Clinic Entrances Act does not prohibit protesters from praying, chanting, counseling, carrying signs, distributing handbills or otherwise expressing opposition to abortion, so long as these activities are carried out in a non-violent, non-obstructive manner." Decision of the US Court of Appeals for the Fourth Circuit in *American Life League, Inc. v. Reno*, 1995

Advocates of choice are also working to protect public funding and private insurance coverage of abortion health care at the state level. In all, sixteen states now pay for services for indigent women from their own medical assistance programs to compensate for the unavailability of federal Medicaid funds. Advocates are also lobbying to protect Medicaid and Title X funding of contraceptive services for low-income women and to require private insurance companies to cover all costs of prescription contraceptives as they do other prescription drugs. In Congress, there are moves to extend the right to obtain an abortion in overseas base hospitals to women serving in the military and to overturn the global gag rule, among other initiatives. *The Global Democracy Promotion Act*, which would extend to groups in other countries the same rights to engage in legal activities and free speech that are recognized in the US, was introduced in Congress with bipartisan support early in 2001. Attached as an amendment to the *Foreign Relations Authorization Act* in May of that year, it was dropped because of intense lobbying from the Bush administration and the promise of a presidential veto.

In the clash of absolutes—of life versus liberty, of the rights of the pregnant woman versus the rights of the fetus—we lose sight of the rights of the living child. Yet surely this is paramount. No child asks to be born. By the accident (or double accident) of its conception and the social circumstances of its birth, the child *arrives*. Common sense would dictate that we focus our attention not on some abstract right of every fertilized egg to develop and be born, then, but on the very real right of every child, once it is born, to live a decent life.

"We are constantly asking ourselves the question—Is life only precious at 20 weeks [gestation]? What becomes of the living corpse that we call a 'child' who stands mute, helpless and resigned to fate, whom we constantly meet in the world around us?" Family planning administrators Alka Dhal and Ruba Mazumdar talk about the need for expanding women's access to safe abortion services in India, in *Planned Parenthood Challenges*

We might assume that people who claim to value all human life from the moment of conception would go out of their way to support programs that give disadvantaged children and parents a better chance. But this is not the case. Surveys show that, on average, respondents who are strongly opposed to abortion are also more likely to define themselves as political conservatives than are their prochoice counterparts. This stance typically translates into less support for domestic programs for poor families, single mothers, ethnic minorities, and immigrants—indeed, for anything that smacks of "socialism" or the "welfare state." The logic of this position is elusive, however. For if the conservative philosophy is intended to reward individual initiative and minimize governmental interference in our lives, then surely opposing individuals' efforts to regulate their own fertility is as inconsistent with this philosophy as are appeals to the government to make abortion a criminal offense.

The American survey by David Adamson and others that was mentioned earlier found that respondents who oppose US economic assistance for *both* contraception and legal abortion to poor countries that request it (15 percent of those interviewed) are also more opposed to development assistance in general and to specific programs for improving women's and children's health, reducing domestic violence, helping women to become more economically self-sufficient, and lowering infant mortality. On these and other counts, then, the antiabortion position appears to lack not only logic but also charity and compassion. Indeed, such findings suggest that those who declare that every embryo has a right to life may rarely concern themselves with the question, *What* life?

CHAPTER EIGHT

Why Safe Abortion is a Global Issue

"Couples and individuals have both a right and a responsibility to determine the number and spacing of their children. Individual choice is the ethical bedrock on which we must build, free from coercion and free from obstruction. Any interference with this right to choose, for whatever cause, is morally repugnant." Former Director-General of the World Health Organization, Halfdan Mahler, on receiving the United Nations Population Award in 1995

Throughout the world, religious conservatives and fundamentalists have seized on abortion as a symbol of a profound conflict between the sacred and the profane. Coalitions of antiabortion groups such as the International Right to Life Federation and Human Life International have mobilized allies in North America, Europe, and the developing world. Together with the Roman Catholic Church and its powerful organization of lay members, Opus Dei, they have been lobbying to impose new punitive abortion laws in Central and Eastern European countries (especially Poland) and to protect the old criminal laws that are still in force in Latin American, sub-Saharan African, and Asian countries such as Nigeria, the Philippines, and Brazil. They have also tried to insert fetal protection or "personhood" clauses into the constitutions of a number of countries, sometimes successfully, sometimes not.

The clash of absolutes has been particularly sharp at several United Nations conferences. At the International Conference on Population and Development held in Cairo in 1994 and the Fourth World Conference on Women held in Beijing in 1995, for example, representatives of civil and women's rights groups and family planning organizations together with like-minded government delegations went nose to nose with representatives of the Holy See (the Vatican) and its political allies over the language of a reproductive rights agenda that would promote women's equality and empowerment.

"We must begin with, and have as our ultimate objective, comprehensive, good quality reproductive and sexual health services, that foster women's rights and empowerment, while ensuring that men take responsibility for their own sexual behavior, fertility, and the well-being of their partners and children. Adrienne Germain and Rachel Kyte, *The Cairo Consensus: The Right Agenda for the Right Time*

The Canadian and US delegations to Cairo and Beijing together with most representatives from Europe and the developing world supported the language of women's rights. The Vatican, however, which has permanent observer status at the UN and participates in conference negotiations, forged an alliance with several conservative Islamic and Catholic governments to try to block the use of terms such as "reproductive health," "sexual rights," "family planning," and even "gender." They claimed these were codewords intended to undermine the sanctity of human life and the family.

The world views of the contenders could not have been farther apart.

Advocates of reproductive choice insisted that women everywhere have the right to manage their own sexuality and to have access to safe, effective, affordable, and acceptable methods of family planning. In response, Pope John Paul II wrote in a widely distributed 1995 encyclical letter *Evangelium Vita* that the "contraceptive mentality" is "evil" and that making abortion safe and legal creates a "culture of death." Similar alliances and divisions took shape during the five-year followup meetings to Cairo and Beijing held in New York in 1999 and 2000. The war of words was fought over the same concepts and even the same sentences as in the earlier meetings.

Given the depth of the ideological divisions, it is remarkable how much progress was made in defining safe abortion as a global issue for women's health. Although almost always qualified with the warning that "in no case should abortion be promoted as a method of family planning," several important principles were written into the documents. These include the recognition that in many countries unsafe abortion is a serious threat to women's lives and health; that governments should consider reviewing laws that punish women who have undergone illegal abortions; that research be supported on the causes and consequences of unsafe abortion; and that whether abortion is legal or not, women are entitled to humane medical treatment of injuries from unsafe procedures.

"In all cases, women should have access to quality services for the management of complications arising from abortion. Post-abortion counselling, education and family planning services should be offered promptly, which will also help to avoid repeat abortions." *Programme of Action*, International Conference on Population and Development, 1994

Delegates to the Cairo Plus-Five conference went even further. "In circumstances where abortion is not against the law," they declared, "health systems should train and equip health service providers and take other measures to ensure that such abortion is *safe and accessible.*" Introduced by the Brazilian delegation, this proposal triggered heated debate. In the end, the Islamic delegations who were initially opposed joined the majority consensus while the Holy See, Nicaragua, and Argentina submitted formal reservations. An attempt to insert an exemption clause to allow physicians to refuse to perform abortions, refuse training to perform them, or deny women information or referrals where abortion is legally permitted went down to defeat.

The ideological wars over sexuality and reproduction, over women's rights in the family and society, and over the place of religion in public policy show no signs of abating. Quite the contrary: the arguments are becoming increasingly sophisticated. Among those who have dug in their heels on one side or another, no one seems to be particularly persuaded by opposing points of view. But as the rhetoric continues, an estimated six hundred thousand of the world's women die annually from the complications of pregnancy (including unsafe abortion) and childbirth. Most of them live in poor countries. At least 150 million women worldwide who say they want no more children are not using contraception. Every year, 100 million unwanted pregnancies occur.

Yet, of all the social and health-related challenges facing humanity today, the problem of inaccessible, delayed, or unsafe abortion and unwanted childbearing is one that lends itself to a comparatively straightforward solution. In developing countries, although access to abortion is often highly restricted, it is legal almost everywhere in order to save a woman's life. It is legal in two-thirds of all developing countries to protect a woman's health. This means that the door is open for health professionals not only to press for legal reforms but also to provide good medical care within the existing legal framework if they choose to do so.

Medical experts estimate that about one-fourth of all maternal deaths worldwide could be avoided if women had access to safe abortion services. The relatively simple technology and skills needed for early pregnancy termination can be acquired by dedicated practitioners with fairly low levels of formal education, not just nurses or physicians. Safe services for treating unwanted pregnancies and the complications of miscarriage or badly performed (often self-induced) abortions can be integrated into a range of family planning and health programs, public and private, urban and rural. If basic sexual and reproductive health care were available for all and not just a privileged few, women living in poor countries would no longer incur the terrible risks resulting from unwanted pregnancies nor the burdens of raising children that they never intended to have.

In most industrialized countries, and particularly in the United States and Canada, the problem of inaccessibility (where it exists) results primarily from the refusal of many medical personnel and institutions to provide safe services and from the often arbitrary restrictions on abortion providers and clients that are imposed by legislators, health providers, and other gatekeepers. Again, the solution is comparatively straightforward. Given that abortion is a common and necessary medical procedure and a legal right, all relevant public health facilities should be required to offer pregnancy termination services as a condition of receiving public funds. The procedure ought to be routinely covered by provincial health plans, in the case of Canada, and by private insurance companies, health maintenance organizations, and state and federal programs in the United States. The supply of skilled providers can be augmented and their professional isolation reduced by the mandated training of all ob/gyns and family practitioners in the techniques of abortion care. Mid-level health professionals can also be trained to perform early medical abortions and vacuum aspiration procedures. Restrictions on providers or clients that are unrelated to the quality of care should be rescinded.

The temptation to establish a legal right and then to surround it with all sorts of qualifications and compromises—that is, to give it and then to take it away—is nowhere more evident than in the Canadian and American treatment of abortion. Yet it serves no useful purpose. Indeed, it causes harm. Not only do the various restrictions weigh most heavily on those who are least able to bear them—the young, the poor, the uneducated, the uninsured, the unmarried, the nonwhite—but the resulting delays add unnecessarily to the costs, the health risks, and the distress of the person who is seeking safe services. Unfair, punitive, and undemocratic, such restrictions are often unenforceable as well. As law professor Laurence Tribe points out in his book *Abortion: The Clash of Absolutes*, "The overarching problem with all these purported compromises is that they are not compromises at all. Many of the laws put forward to stake out what is supposedly a middle ground in the abortion debate, rather than meaningfully protecting either life or choice, randomly frustrate both and do not move us closer to a society of caring, responsible people."

In our opinion, we would do well as a society to be less obsessed about who gets or provides abortions, and more obsessed about ensuring that everyone (including young people) has the information and services they need to ensure a healthy and voluntary sexual and reproductive life. We would do well, too, to pay less attention to the small but vocal minority of antiabortionists who would deny all women the right to safe medical care on the grounds that they are protecting the life of the unborn, and more attention to those advocates of human rights who are working throughout the world to protect women's health and improve the lives of the children who live among us.

CHAPTER NOTES

Chapter One: Regulating Our Fertility: Ancient Customs, Current Practices

For information on how contraceptives work and on the specific advantages and disadvantages of each, the best source is the encyclopedic *Contraceptive Technology* (1998) edited by Robert A. Hatcher and colleagues, now in its seventeenth revised edition. A major resource on questions of reproductive health, the volume includes chapters on sexuality, sexually transmitted diseases and HIV/AIDS, genital cancers, the menstrual cycle and menopause, early stages of pregnancy, fertility impairments, adolescent sexuality and childbearing, and worldwide population trends in addition to the twelve chapters on contraceptive methods. Written primarily for clinicians and reporting on the latest research, the book is accessible to the general reader as well. Most of the technical information in Chapter One is drawn from this book, including contraceptive failure rates and the risks of conceiving from unprotected intercourse.

Other excellent sources of information on contraceptive choices for women are *The Whole Truth About Contraception: A Guide to Safe and Effective Choices* (1997) by Beverly Winikoff and Suzanne Wymelenberg, and *Our Bodies Ourselves for the New Century* (1998), the latest edition of this classic work produced by the Boston Women's Health Book Collective. Or, consult *The New Our Bodies, Ourselves: A Book by and for Women* (1992). These works explain the advantages and drawbacks of different contraceptive methods in great detail from the user's perspective.

On the fascinating variety of ancient and traditional methods of fertility regulation around the world, many of which are still practiced, sources include Wolfgang Jochle's article "Menses-inducing drugs: their role in antique, medieval, and renaissance gynecology and birth control" (1974); Norman E. Himes famous treatise on *The Medical History of Contraception* (1970, first published in 1936); *Eve's Herbs: A History of Contraception and Abortion in the West* (1997) by John M. Riddle; and *The History of Obstetrics and Gynecology* (1994) by Michael J. O'Dowd and Elliot E. Phillipp, which includes accounts of contraception and abortion drawn from ancient Hebrew, Islamic and Greek texts. A startling list of indigenous methods and patent medicines used by Nigerian adolescents today can be found in Valentine O. Otoide and colleagues, "Why Nigerian adolescents seek abortion rather than contraception" (2001).

Anthropological accounts of indigenous abortion methods include the extensive review by George Devereux (1955), *A Study of Abortion in Primitive Societies*. See also Lucile F. Newman's *Women's Medicine: A Cross-Cultural Study of Indigenous Fertility Regulation* (1985) and the scientific volume edited by Axel I. Mundigo and Cynthia Indriso, *Abortion in the Developing World* (1999). For descriptions of "passive infanticide" as an indirect method of postpartum fertility control, see Susan Scrimshaw, "Infanticide in human populations" (1984) and the volume edited by Nancy Scheper-Hughes on *Child Survival: Anthropological Perspectives on the Treatment and Maltreatment of Children* (1987). Additional information on the treatment of unwanted children can be found in Rosalind Pollack Petchesky's *Abortion and Woman's Choice: The State, Sexuality, and Reproductive Freedom* (1984); Peter Laslett, Karla Oosterveen and Richard M. Smith (ed.), *Bastardy and its Comparative History* (1980); and Barbara Miller, *The Endangered Sex: Neglect of Femlae Children in Rural North India* (1981).

International statistical data on topics such as nonmarital sexual activity, women's reproductive intentions and current contraceptive practices, the proportions of births that are unwanted at the time of conception, and the practice of abortion are available from fact sheets produced by the Population Reference Bureau in Washington, DC; by the United Nations Population Division; and by the International Planned Parenthood Federation, among others organizations. The best journal sources are *Studies in Family Planning* published by The Population Council in New York and *Family Planning Perspectives* and *International Family Planning Perspectives* published by The Alan Guttmacher Institute (AGI) in New York. An excellent brief overview of contraceptive practice and abortion law and practice internationally is AGI's *Sharing Responsibility: Women, Society & Abortion Worldwide* (1999). For detailed statistics on contraceptive practice and fertility desires worldwide consult *Levels and Trends of Contraceptive Use* published by the United Nations Population Division (1999).

The relative risks of dying from contraceptive use, safe and unsafe abortion and childbearing in developed and developing countries are described in the AGI report mentioned above; in *Reproductive Health in Developing Countries* (1997) edited by Amy O. Tsui, Judith Wasserheit and John G. Haaga; and in *Contraception and Reproduction: Health Consequences for Women and Children in the Developing World* (1989) edited by a Working Group of the National Research Council in Washington DC. See also Christopher Murray and Alan Lopez's *Health Dimensions of Sex and Reproduction* (1998) for a comprehensive international treatment of the health risks of certain sexual practices, sexually transmitted diseases, pregnancy, abortion and childbearing. Eileen L. McDonagh, arguing for the need to recognize a condition of "wrongful pregnancy" when the woman does not give her consent, discusses the legal implications of the heavy physical burden imposed by the fetus on the pregnant woman in *Breaking the Abortion Deadlock: From Choice to Consent* (1996). The dangers of childbirth in historical perspective and the medical profession's response are described in Michael J. O'Dowd and Elliot E. Phillipp, *The History of Obstetrics and Gynecology* (1994).

Changing patterns of sexual behavior, contraception, abortion, and childbearing among teenagers in developing countries are described in publications such as *Adolescent Reproductive Behavior in the Developing World* (1998) edited by John Bongaarts and Barney Cohen; the research guide *Learning About Sexuality* (1996) edited by Sondra Zeidenstein and Kirsten Moore; *Into a New World: Young Women's Sexual and Reproductive Lives* produced by the Alan Guttmacher Institute (1998); and *The Uncharted Passage: Girls' Adolescence in the Developing World* (1998) written by Barbara Mensch, Judith Bruce and M. E. Greene.

We refer to several specific studies in Chapter One. The US survey of sexual behavior, *Sex in America*, is by Robert Michael and colleagues (1994). References to Kinsey's findings on the frequency of intercourse are in Christopher Tietze, "Probabilities of pregnancy resulting from a single unprotected coitus" (1980). On women's attitudes about menstruation see the World Health Organization, "A cross-cultural study of menstruation: implications for contraceptive development and use" (1981). The study of women in Cali, Colombia by Carole Browner is described in "Abortion decision making: some findings from Colombia" (1979). On menstrual regulation see Ruth Dixon-Mueller, "Innovations in reproductive health care: menstrual regulation policies and programs in Bangladesh" (1988); Luke T. Lee and John M. Paxman, "Legal aspects of menstrual regulation" (1977); and comments by Sajeda Amin and Syeda Nahid Mukith Chowdhury in the report of a meeting at The Population Council, *Abortion: Expanding Access and Improving Quality* (1998) edited by Karen Stein and others. Additional interpretations of (and botanical recipes for) removing menstrual "blockages" in ancient Greece, in the US in the eighteenth to twentieth centuries, and in West Africa, Indonesia, Bangladesh, Bolivia, and Guatemala can be found in Etienne van de Walle and Elisha P Renne (eds.), *Regulating Menstruation: Beliefs, Practices, Interpretations* (2001). Anthropologist Nancy Scheper-Hughes describes the use of menstrual regulating preparations in Northeast Brazil in *Death Without Weeping: The Violence of Everyday Life in Brazil* (1992).

With regard to the costs of contraception, an excellent treatment of women's *perceptions* of the relative costs of contraception, pregnancy, and abortion can be found in Kristin Luker's insightful work, *Taking Chances: Abortion and the Decision Not to Contracept* (1975). This study is based on interviews with women in California who took contraceptive risks that resulted in abortion despite having used effective contraception in the past. An excellent overview of the impediments to contraceptive information and services in the US (including inadequate sexuality education programs in the schools) can be found in Sarah S. Brown and Leon Eisenberg (eds.), *The Best Intentions: Unintended Pregnancy and the Well-Being of Children and Families* (1995).

A survey of private insurance companies in the US conducted by the Alan Guttmacher Institute (1994) found that 85 percent pay for contraceptive sterilization and two-thirds for abortion. But not one of the five major reversible contraceptive methods (IUDs, diaphragms, and hormonal implants, injectables, and pills) was routinely reimbursed by more than 40 percent of typical plans. Half of the large-group plans covered no reversible contraceptive methods at all. Health Maintenance Organizations (HMOs) typically provide more comprehensive contraceptive coverage, but some require copayment. In Canada, contraceptives are not covered under most provincial health insurance plans, although some abortions are.

For low-income women in the US, Medicaid reimburses states for the costs of contraceptive services to clients eligible for state medical assistance, although restrictions on eligibility are tight. Few single adolescents have access unless they already have a baby and are eligible for Aid for Families with Dependent Children (AFDC). Title X funds of the Public Health Service Act go directly to a network of about four thousand public and private nonprofit family planning organizations that are required by law to offer free services to women and adolescents living below the poverty line while charging others on a sliding scale. In contrast, many European countries pay all or most of the costs of contraceptive counseling and supplies for everyone through their universal national health plans.

Chapter Two: Making the Abortion Decision

What makes a pregnancy unwanted? Among the earliest and most insightful analyses are those of E. M. and J. M. Pohlman in *Psychology of Birth Planning* (1969) and Paula Hollerbach Hass in "Wanted and unwanted pregnancies: a fertility decision-making model" (1974). Information on the numbers and the social and demographic characteristics of women having abortions in both developed and developing countries can be found in *Sharing Responsibility: Women, Society & Abortion Worldwide* (1999) published by The Alan Guttmacher Institute (AGI), and in many articles by AGI researchers. These include Stanley K. Henshaw and Jennifer Van Vort (1994) on abortion services in the US, Stanley K. Henshaw, Susheela Singh and Taylor Hass (1999) on the incidence of abortion worldwide, and Akinrinola Bankole, Susheela Singh and Taylor Hass (1999) on the characteristics of women who obtain abortion worldwide. This last reference also reports the percentage of women in a number of countries who say they want to delay or stop childbearing but are not using any method of contraception. The reference to proportions single among women hospitalized for complications in Nigeria is in E. I. Archibong (1991), and for Shanghai, China, in Z. C. Wu and colleagues (1992).

For more information about the demographic characteristics of abortion clients in Canada and the US, see Robert A. Hatcher and colleagues (1998) and Paul Sachdev (1993). The 1995 national survey of US women describing women's contraceptive behavior refers to the National Survey of Family Growth as reported in AGI's *Sharing Responsibility*, Appendix Table 1, which contains information on sexual behavior and contraceptive practice for dozens of countries.

On unwanted pregnancy and abortion among US teenagers see the Alan Guttmacher Institute, "Teen Sex and Pregnancy" (1999), and Kristin Luker's *Dubious Conceptions: The Politics of Teenage Pregnancy* (1996). Comparisons of unwanted pregnancies and their outcomes based on a 1987 national survey of married and unmarried US women according to their age and poverty status can be found in Sarah S. Brown and Leon Eisenberg (eds.), *The Best Intentions: Unintended Pregnancy and the Well-Being of Children and Families* (1995).

For a look at how women make decisions about sex, contraception, abortion, birth and adoption, several studies are particularly useful. Kristin Luker's *Taking Chances: Abortion and the Decision Not to Contracept* (1975) examines women's ambivalence about contraception and pregnancy in California after abortion was legalized in that state. Nancy Howell Lee's *The Search for an Abortionist* (1969) traces the process by which women identified clandestine providers and how they felt about their experiences in the late 1960s before *Roe v. Wade*. Mary Kay Zimmerman's *Passage Through Abortion: The Personal and Social Reality of Women's Experiences* (1977) is an excellent guide to the situation of women seeking abortion in a midwestern US city, as is Paul Sachdev's *Sex, Abortion, and Unmarried Women* (1993) for young women in Ontario, Canada. Sachdev's earlier book, *Unlocking the Adoption Files* (1989), has some interesting observations about how birth mothers feel about placing their infants for adoption. The more recent book by psychiatrist Nada L. Stotland, *Abortion: Facts and Feelings* (1998), is an excellent source for helping women decide whether to terminate or carry the pregnancy to term. It also includes guidelines for the professional counselor.

Other experience-based studies include Patricia Lunneborg's upbeat *Abortion: A Positive Decision* (1992) and Rita Townsend and Ann Perkins's downbeat *Bitter Fruit: Women's Experiences of Unplanned Pregnancy, Abortion, and Adoption* (1991). On women's experiences with criminal abortion in the US and Canada see Ellen Messer and Kathryn May, *Back Rooms: Voices from the Illegal Abortion Era* (1994); Carole Joffe, *Doctors of Conscience: The Struggle to Provide Abortion Before and After Roe v. Wade* (1995); and Childbirth by Choice Trust, *No Choice: Canadian Women Tell Their Stories of Illegal Abortion* (1998).

Why do women have abortions? All of the studies mentioned above have a great deal to say on this topic, as well as on women's feelings afterwards, for the samples of women interviewed. The national study of US women noted in the text that refers to multiple reasons is by Aida Torres and Jacqueline Forrest (1988). Selected international comparisons are drawn from Akinrinola Bankole and colleagues, "Reasons why women have induced abortions: evidence from 27 countries" (1998).

With regard to women's "personal moralities" as influenced by religious and moral values of their societies, we rely heavily on the richly interpreted international research volume edited by Rosalind P. Petchesky and Karen Judd, *Negotiating Reproductive Rights: Women's Perspectives Across Countries and Cultures* (1998). On Muslim attitudes toward contraception and abortion, see Abdel Rahim Omran, *Family Planning in the Legacy of Islam* (1992). The treatment of contraception and abortion in the Jewish tradition is described in David F. Feldman, *Birth Control in Jewish Law* (1968). For the many treatments of Catholic opinion see the references in

Chapter Seven. An interesting perspective on Catholic women's contraceptive and abortion attitudes and practices can be found in Catholics for a Free Choice, *Catholics and Reproduction: A World View* (1997). The reference to American women's moral reservations is in Stanley K. Henshaw and Greg Martire (1982) and to the apparent lack of such reservations among Chinese women in Sichuan province in Luo Lin and colleagues (see Luo, 1999).

Reports of women's escalating attempts to terminate an unwanted pregnancy (including the methods that *didn't* work) in eight developing countries can be found in Dale Huntington and colleagues, "Survey questions for the measurement of induced abortion" (1996). The women of Cali, Colombia are described by Carole Browner (1979), and the adolescent girls in Mexico City by N. Ehrenfeld (1999). The women hospitalized in north-eastern Brazil are in Chizuru Misago and Walter Fonseca (1999). The consequences of presenting late for menstrual regulation in Bangladesh are reported in Ruth Dixon-Mueller (1988). The study of American women having illegal abortions in the late 1960s and their search for an abortionist is by Nancy Howell Lee (1969).

Information on the attitudes of health care practitioners at various levels, ranging from untrained village midwives to market vendors to nurses and physicians, is drawn from the international volume edited by Axel I. Mundigo and Cynthia Indriso, *Abortion in the Developing World* (1999). We include specific references to the papers by E. Djohan and others (Indonesia), Susan Pick and others (Mexico City), Fred V. Cadelina (the Philippines), P. Hewage (Sri Lanka), and Zhou Wei-Jin and colleagues (China; see Zhou). Other perspectives, particularly on the conservative attitudes of many physicians in Latin America, can be found in the volume edited by Alan Rosenfield and colleagues, *Women's Health in the Third World: The Impact of Unwanted Pregnancy* (1989).

Chapter Three: The Procedure

For a practical and readable guide to abortion services and regulations in the US see *The Abortion Resource Handbook* by K Kaufmann (1997). This is especially useful for young women who need to know about parental notification and consent rules and how to get around them. The guide contains sample forms and a list of resources. Other consumer-friendly books with good advice include the Boston Women's Health Book Collective *Our Bodies Ourselves for the New Century* (1998) and *The Whole Truth About Contraception* by Beverly Winikoff and Suzanne Wymelenberg (1997).

For technical information and clinical guidelines for service providers see *Contraceptive Technology* by Robert A. Hatcher and colleagues (1998) and *Clinical Policy Guidelines 2000* published by the National Abortion Federation. Medical texts include *A Clinician's Guide to Medical and Surgical Abortion* by Maureen Paul and colleagues (1999); *Modern Methods of Inducing Abortion* edited by David T. Baird and colleagues (1995); and Warren M. Hern's *Abortion Practice* (1990). Texts for gynecologists and obstetricians such as *Williams Obstetrics* (1997) by F. Gary Cunningham and associates include information on the stages of fetal development. The discussion of pain management draws on Phillip G. Stubblefield's article in *Women's Health in the Third World: The Impact of Unwanted Pregnancy* edited by Alan Rosenfield and others (1989).

References to training curricula and guidelines for clinicians in the practice of abortion are on the website of the National Abortion Federation (www.prochoice.org). The websites of the Planned Parenthood Federation (www.plannedparenthood.org) and the National Abortion and Reproductive Rights Action League (www.naral.org) are also excellent sources of information on abortion safety.

Statistical information for the US, including estimates of deaths from unsafe abortion before *Roe v. Wade*, can be found in publications of The Alan Guttmacher Institute such as Rachel Benson Gold's *Abortion and Women's Health: A Turning Point for America?* (1990). Statistics on the number and distribution of abortions according to length of gestation in the US are compiled annually by the Centers for Disease Control and Prevention in Atlanta in their series on abortion surveillance. See Rachel Benson Gold (above) and Robert A. Hatcher's *Contraceptive Technology* (1998) for a summary. See also *Abortion Matters* (1996) by Stimezo Nederland (for The Netherlands), and *Sex, Abortion, and Unmarried Women* (1993) by Paul Sachdev (for Canada).

US-based organizations and agencies working to promote safe abortion in developing countries publish many research reviews and program guidelines. Of special help in the preparation of this chapter were reports published by The Population Council in New York, including *Abortion: Expanding Access and Improving Quality* (1998) by Karen Stein and others, and *Acceptability of First Trimester Medical Abortion* (1994) by Beverly Winikoff. See also the articles by Charlotte Ellertson, Batya Elul and Beverly Winikoff, "Can women use medical abortion without medical supervision?" in the journal *Reproductive Health Matters* (1997) and by Batya Elul and colleagues, "Can women in less-developed countries use a simplified medical abortion regimen?" (2001). International drug trials using lower doses of mifepristone are reported in Eric A. Schaff and colleagues (1999) and World Health Organisation Task Force on Post-ovulatory Methods of Fertility Regulation (2000), among other sources. An account of the science and politics surrounding the development of RU 486 can be found in Etienne-Emile Baulieu's *The 'Abortion Pill:' RU-486, A Woman's Choice* (1990).

New York-based Family Care International in association with IPAS, International Planned Parenthood Federation and the Population Council has produced an excellent practical guide for action in developing countries, *Prevention and Management of Unsafe Abortion* (1998), written by Ellen Brazier and others. In looseleaf binder format, it includes sections on the social and economic impact of unsafe abortion, techniques of safe abortion, emergency treatment of complications, community education, and law and policy, with excerpts from case studies around the world and extensive references. IPAS, in Carrboro, North Carolina, distributes manual vacuum aspiration kits worldwide along with guides such as *Manual Vacuum Aspiration: A Summary of Clinical & Programmatic Experience Worldwide* by Forrest C. Greenslade and colleagues (1993) and *Manual Vacuum Aspiration Guide for Clinicians* by Laura Yordy and others (1993). Pathfinder International has also produced a guide written by Cathy Solter and colleagues, *Manual Vacuum Aspiration: A Comprehensive Training Course* (1997). For emergency contraception see the Division of Reproductive Health of the World Health Organization, *Emergency Contraception: A Guide for Service Delivery* (1998).

On the management of complications from unsafe abortion in developing countries, see *Postabortion Care: Lessons from Operations Research* (1999) edited by Dale Huntington and Nancy J. Piet-Pelon for The Population Council and "Care for postabortion complications: saving women's lives" by Cathy Solter and colleagues (1997) in addition to the publications listed above.

Reports on the use of Cytotec in Brazil are from Regina Maria Barbosa and Margareth Arilha in *Planned Parenthood Challenges: Unsafe Abortion* (1993) published by the International Planned Parenthood Federation, and Chizuro Misago and Walter Fonseca in *Abortion in the Developing World* edited by Axel I. Mundigo and Cynthia Indriso (1999). The World Health Organization's warning about methotrexate, produced by the Special Programme of Research, Development and Research Training in Human Reproduction of the World Health Organization, the United Nations Development Programme, the United Nations Population

Fund and the World Bank, is reproduced in the journal *Reproductive Health Matters* (Number 9, May 1997). For evidence on the absence of negative effects of abortion on subsequent fertility see F. Gary Cunningham and associates, *Williams Obstetrics* (1997); Peter Frank and associates, "The effect of induced abortion on subsequent fertility" (1993); Rachel Benson Gold, *Abortion and Women's Health* (1990); and C. J. R. Hogue, Ward Cates and Christopher Tietze, "The effects of induced abortion on subsequent reproduction" (1982), among other sources.

Chapter Four: Psychological Consequences of Abortion and the Myth of Regret

On the scientific rejection of the concept of post-abortion syndrome, the best place to begin is Nada L. Stotland's article, "The myth of the abortion trauma syndrome" in the *Journal of the American Medical Association* (1992). The extensive literature on the psychological consequences of induced abortion includes many review articles that summarize major findings and identify flaws (if any) in the research methods. See, for example, the 1973 article on the psychological effects of abortion by Joy D. and Howard J. Osofksy and Renga Rajan, "Psychological effects of abortion: with emphasis upon immediate reactions and followup"; Nancy Adler and colleagues in *Science* (1990); Paul Dagg in the *American Journal of Psychiatry* (1991); Nada Stotland's edited volume, *Psychiatric Aspects of Abortion* (1991); Nancy F. Russo's "Psychological aspects of unwanted pregnancy and its resolution" (1992); Nancy F. Russo and Kristin I. Zierk's "Abortion, childbearing and women's well-being" (1992): and Nada Stotland's *Abortion: Facts and Feelings* (1998).

The list of case studies on which the reviews are based is a long one. It is best to consult the references listed in the review articles mentioned above and in the summary *Fact Sheet* on "The emotional effects of induced abortion" by Planned Parenthood Federation of

America on their website www.plannedparenthood.org (2000). The fact sheet includes an interesting discussion of the "so-called post-abortion syndrome."

Of particular usefulness in the preparation of Chapter Four were the studies by Harry Brody, Stewart Meikle and Richard Gerritse (1971) comparing the psychological consequences to Canadian women who terminate with those who deliver; Robert Athanasiou and colleagues (1973) comparing women at The Johns Hopkins University hospital who have early- and late-term procedures and term births; Joy D. and Howard J. Osofksy and Renga Rajan (1973) comparing women with early and late procedures in Philadelphia; and D. R. Urquhart and A. A. Templeton (1991), comparing medical and surgical inductions in Great Britain.

For general responses to abortion, see Howard J. Osofky and Joy D. Osofky's edited volume, *The Abortion Experience: Psychological and Medical Impact* (1973) and Nada L. Stotland's edited volume, *Psychiatric Aspects of Abortion* (1991). The studies of women's personal experiences noted in the bibliography for Chapter Two are also relevant here, such as those by Nancy Howell Lee, Paul Sachdev, and Mary Kay Zimmerman, among others. References to the discussion in the text of post-abortion denial and repression, and of the effects of social support on women's reactions, can be found in Paul K. B. Dagg (1991).

The painful and complex issues raised by the discovery of fetal abnormalities through amniocentesis and the subsequent decision to abort (or not) are discussed by authors such as Barbara Katz Rothman in *The Tentative Pregnancy* (1993); Aliza Kolker and B. Meredith Burke in *Prenatal Testing: A Sociological Perspective* (1998); and Rayna Rapp in *Testing Women, Testing the Fetus* (1999).

What happens to women who are denied permission to terminate?

Citations for many of these studies can be found in Paul K. B. Dagg's review article (1991), among other sources. The Canadian study of emotional outcomes of women granted and denied a therapeutic abortion is by Harry Brody and colleagues (1971) and the Scottish study by Gordon Horobin, *Experience with Abortion: A Case Study of North-East Scotland* (1973). These studies also comment on the proportions of women denied therapeutic abortion who terminate illegally or who carry the pregnancy to term and place the child for adoption. The classic Czechoslovakian (Matijcek, Dytrych, and Schuller) and Swedish (Forssman and Thuwe) studies of the effects on the child of being born unwanted following the mother's denied request to terminate the pregnancy are detailed in the volume edited by Henry P. David and colleagues, *Born Unwanted: Development Effects of Denied Abortion* (1988).

How do researchers ask about the "wantedness" status of a pregnancy? There are dozens of sources. For the US, survey questions can be found for the Survey of Family Growth in Sarah S. Brown and Leon Eisenberg (eds.), *The Best Intentions: Unintended Pregnancy and the Well-Being of Children and Families*, published by the Institute of Medicine of the National Academy of Sciences (1995). This volume also includes an excellent discussion of the methodological difficulties in sorting out the effects of "unwantedness" from the effects of disadvantaged economic and social circumstances in general. The questions cited in the text for the National Survey of Families and Households are from Jennifer S. Barber, "Unwanted childbearing, health and mother-child relationships" (1999) as is the extensive discussion of the effects of unwanted childbearing on mothers' depression and their interactions with young children. Sources for estimating the extent of unplanned and unwanted births in developing countries include Dale Huntington, Barbara Mensch, and Vincent C. Miller, "Survey questions for the measurement of induced abortion" (1996) and John Bongaarts, "Trends in unwanted childbearing in the developing world (1997). The Bongaarts article is the source of the worldwide information on unwanted childbearing reported here.

Finally, for a look at the phenomenon of postpartum depression see Peter J. Cooper and Lynne Murray, "Postnatal depression" in the *British Medical Journal* (1998) and Mary Boyle's reports in *Re-Thinking Abortion* (!997) that negative feelings following childbirth ("baby blues") are far more common than those following abortion. The comment in the text referring to up to 70 percent of women who have mild, transient symptoms of depression following "normal" childbirth is from the Planned Parenthood Federation of America, Fact Sheet, "Emotional effects of induced abortion," *www.plannedparenthood.org* (2000).

Chapter Five: When Is Abortion Against the Law and What Difference Does It Make?

The Population Division of the United Nations, The Alan Guttmacher Institute in New York, and the Reproductive Freedom Project of the American Civil Liberties Union (among other organizations) keep close tabs on the evolution of abortion laws and policies around the world. In 1992, 1993 and 1995, the UN published a three-volume series of country studies called *Abortion Policies: A Global Review,* Volumes I-III. The Alan Guttmacher Institute regularly publishes updated legal analyses. The AGI report *Sharing Responsibility: Women, Society and Abortion Worldwide* (1999) draws extensively on the UN data, on "A global review of laws on induced abortion, 1985-1997" by A. Rahman, L. Katzive and S. K. Henshaw (1998), and on the classic review by Christopher Tietze and Stanley Henshaw, *Induced Abortion: A World Review* (1986). Other sources include Paul Sachdev, *International Handbook on Abortion* (1988); Rita J. Simon, *Abortion: Statutes, Policies, and Public Attitudes the World Over* (1998); Axel Mundigo and Cynthia Indriso, *Abortion in the Developing World* (1999); and Henry P. David (ed.), *From Abortion to Contraception: A Resource to Public*

Policies and Reproductive Behavior in Central and Eastern Europe from 1917 to the Present (1999).

References to women imprisoned for abortion in Chile and Nepal are in AGI's *Sharing Responsibility*; see also Lidia Casas-Becerra (1997). On the legal definitions of pregnancy and abortion with special reference to the legal status of menstrual regulation see Luke T. Lee and John M. Paxman (1977). Rebecca Cook of the University of Toronto has written extensively on reproductive health laws and policies. A particularly interesting analysis of how laws regulating abortion can be strictly or liberally interpreted can be found in her article "Abortion laws and policies: challenges and opportunities" (1989) prepared for an international symposium on abortion and women's health organized by the International Women's Health Coalition in New York. The definition of when pregnancy begins by the International Federation of Gynecology and Obstetrics appears in the proceedings of this symposium, *Women's Health in the Third World: The Impact of Unwanted Pregnancy* (1989), edited by A. Rosenfield, M. F. Fathala, A. Germain and C. L. Indriso. On the timing of fertilization and implantation and the definition of when pregnancy begins by the American Association of Obstetricians and Gynecologists see Robert Hatcher and colleagues, *Contraceptive Technology* (1998).

On the history of abortion legislation and practices and the attitudes of the medical profession in the United States, Canada and Europe, see Peter Fryer, *The Birth Controllers* (1965); David Kennedy, *Birth Control in America: The Career of Margaret Sanger* (1970); Linda Gordon, *Woman's Body, Woman's Right: A Social History of Birth Control in America* (1976); Wendell W. Walters, *Compulsory Parenthood: The Truth About Abortion* [in Canada] (1976); James Mohr, *Abortion in America: The Origins and Evolution of National Policy, 1800-1900* (1978); Carl N. Degler, *At Odds: Women and the Family in America from the Revolution to the Present* (1980); Marilyn Jane Field, *The Comparative Politics of Birth Control:*

Determinants of Policy Variation and Change in the Developed Nations (1983); Rosalind Petchesky, *Abortion and Woman's Choice: The State, Sexuality, and Reproductive Freedom* (1984); Kristen Luker, *Abortion and the Politics of Motherhood* (1984); James Reed, *The Birth Control Movement and American Society: From Private Vice to Public Virtue* (1985); Mary Ann Glendon, *Abortion and Divorce in Western Law* (1987); Ellen Chesler, *Woman of Valor: Margaret Sanger and the Birth Control Movement in America* (1992); Marianne Githens and Dorothy Stetson, *Abortion Politics: Public Policy in Cross-Cultural Perspective* (1996); Donald T. Critchlow (ed.), *The Politics of Abortion and Birth Control in Historical Perspective* (1996); L. J. Reagan, *When Abortion Was a Crime: Women, Medicine, and Law in the United States, 1867-1973* (1997); Rickie Solinger (ed.), *Abortion Wars: A Half Century of Struggle, 1950-2000* (1997); and Donald T. Critchlow, *Intended Consequences: Birth Control, Abortion, and the Federal Government in Modern America* (1999). This is just a sampling!

The historical references to Lord Ellenborough's Act in Britain and its impact on Canadian abortion law are from B. M. McLachlin (1991). The court cases involving the careers of Henry Morgentaler and Jane Hodgson are described in Carole Joffe's *Doctors of Conscience: The Struggle to Provide Abortion Before and After Roe v. Wade* (1995). The story of Morgentaler is also told on the website of the Canadian Abortion Rights Action League, "Morgentaler Chronology," *www.caral.ca*, as well as in some of the references below.

For more on the 1973 US Supreme Court decision in *Roe v. Wade* see Kristin Luker, *Abortion and the Politics of Motherhood* (1984); Marian Faux, *Roe v. Wade: The Untold Story of the Landmark Supreme Court Decision that Made Abortion Legal* (1988); Sarah Weddington, *A Question of Choice* (1992); and D. J. Garrow, *Liberty and Sexuality: The Right to Privacy and the Making of Roe v. Wade* (1994). The 1988 Supreme Court decision in Canada in the case of Morgentaler

v. The Queen is described in Janine Brodie and colleagues, *The Politics of Abortion* (1992) which also contains the text of the 1882 and 1985 Criminal Codes; Paul Sachdev (1993); Janine Brodie's "Health vs. rights: comparative perspectives on abortion policy in Canada and the United States" (1994); and Ted G. Jelen and Marthe A. Chandler (eds.), *Abortion Politics in the United States and Canada* (1994); and Dorothy Studlar and Raymond Tatalovich (1996), among other sources. J. Douglas Butler and David F. Walbert's edited volume *Abortion, Medicine and the Law* (1992) is an invaluable guide through the thickets of the legal, medical and ethical aspects of abortion.

Regulatory and cost barriers to abortion in Canada and the United States are described in Sachdev (1993) and Studlar and Tatalovich (1996); Marlene Fried's "Abortion in the US: barriers to access" (1997); the AGI report *Sharing Responsibility*; and, most important for the United States, in the compilation of state laws and congressional actions published by NARAL called *Who Decides? A State-by-State Review of Abortion and Reproductive Rights* (2002). Additional information for the US can be found on NARAL's website www.prochoice.org and for Canada on the website of the Canadian Abortion Rights Action League www.caral.ca, which includes the report "Abortion in Canada Today: The Situation Province by Province." For abortion costs and information on negotiating state-imposed abortion restrictions, especially for minors, see K. Kaufman's *The Abortion Resource Handbook* (1997). The costs of abortion are also discussed in Beverly Winikoff and Suzanne Wymelenberg's *The Whole Truth About Contraception* (1997), among other sources. Insurance coverage of contraception and abortion by private companies and HMOs is reviewed in the Alan Guttmacher Institute's *Uneven and Unequal: Insurance Coverage and Reproductive Health Services* (1994). References for Europe are drawn from Marianne Githens and Dorothy McBride Stetson (1996) and Henry P. David (1999).

Chapter Six: Inside the Medical Profession

Policy statements from professional associations quoted in the introduction are from the NARAL website. Although positive in their overall tone, some statements from the medical establishment still stress the preservation of the physician's authority over abortion rather than the woman's right to have one. In 1996, for example, the American Medical Association declared that "It is the policy of the AMA . . . to strongly condemn any interference by the government or other third parties that causes a physician to compromise his or her medical judgment as to what information or treatment is in the best interest of the patient." The American College of Obstetricians and Gynecologists inserted a statement in the Congressional Record back in 1977 that made the point even more clearly. "The final decision as to performing the abortion must be left to the medical judgment of the pregnant woman's attending physician in consultation with the patient," they stated. "That responsibility is the physician's, both ethically and by reason of his experience" (quoted in Imber, 1986).

Historical material on medical practice before *Roe v. Wade* is drawn primarily from Rosalind Petchesky's *Abortion and Woman's Choice: The State, Sexuality and Reproductive Freedom* (1984) and Carole Joffe's *Doctors of Conscience: The Struggle to Provide Abortion Before and After Roe v. Wade* (1995). Other references can be found in the notes to Chapter Five on the history of medical atttitudes and practices in the US. For references to the Jane collective and the Clergy Consultation Service see Joffe (1995) and Laurence Tribe (1990). The 1888 article from *The Medical and Surgical Reporter* on medical indications for contraceptive "intervention" is cited in Petchesky (1984).

The work of the therapeutic abortion committees in Canada and the US is described in Doctors for the Repeal of the Abortion Law, "Survey of hospital abortion committees in Canada" (1975); Kristin

Luker, *Taking Chances: Abortion and the Decision Not to Contracept* (1975) [in California]; Wendell W. Walters, *Compulsory Parenthood* (1976) (in Canada); Janine Brodie, "Health v. rights: perspectives in abortion policy in Canada and the US" (1994); Carole Joffe, *Doctors of Conscience* (1995); and Donley Studlar and Raymond Tatalovich, "Abortion policy in the United States and Canada" (1996). For a detailed account and critique of the US experience and the early role of psychiatrists in abortion decision-making see Rickie Solinger, "'A complete disaster': abortion and the politics of hospital abortion committees, 1950-1970" (1993). Gordon Horobin (ed.), *Experience with Abortion* (1973) describes the medical and social indications likely to be rejected in Scotland and the behavioral differences between liberal and conservative "consultants."

With regard to physicians' attitudes, the 1973 and 1969 national polls and the study of ob/gyns at the Johns Hopkins University are cited in Jonathan B. Imber, *Abortion and the Private Practice of Medicine* (1986). Imber's own study of doctors in the Northeastern US also looks at the way in which hospitals and private practitioners instruct their staff to refer abortion requests to specialized clinics. For an analysis of physicians' attitudes and their impact on hospital decisions regarding elective abortion see Constance A. Nathanson and Marshall H. Becker, "Obstetricians' attitudes and hospital abortion services" (1980). The 1984 survey of recently graduated ob/gyns that compares male and female practitioners is by Carol S. Weisman and colleagues (1986). On the attitudes of students of medicine, nursing, and social work see Nada Stotland (ed.), *Psychiatric Aspects of Abortion* (1991). An interesting survey of attitudes of general practitioners in Britain toward the morality and legality of the current law is in Colin Francome and Edward Freeman's "British general practitioners' attitudes toward abortion" (2000).

On conscience clauses in the US see NARAL's compendium of

state laws in *Who Decides? A State-by-State Review of Abortion and Reproductive Rights* (2002). The Missouri law is from the 2000 edition. For Canada see Childbirth by Choice Trust, *Abortion in Canada Today: The Situation Province by Province* (1997). The effect of exemptions on the supply of providers in Europe is reported in Paul Sachdev (ed.), *International Handbook on Abortion* (1988). On the expansion of conscience-based exemptions into pharmacies and the insurance industry see AGI's "Conscience makes a comeback in the age of managed care" in *The Guttmacher Report on Public Policy* (1998).

The websites of NARAL (www.naral.org) and CARAL (www.caral.ca) are excellent sources of information on the supply of abortion providers in hospitals and clinics and on medical training. On the diminishing supply of abortion providers and their professional marginalization in the US, begin with AGI's "The unmet need for legal abortion services in the US" (1975) and move on to the report of a symposium sponsored by the National Abortion Federation and the American College of Obstetricians and Gynecologists, *Who Will Provide Abortions? Ensuring the Availability of Qualified Practitioners* (1991); David Grimes, "Clinicians who provide abortions: the thinning ranks" (1992); and Stanley Henshaw and Jennifer Van Vort, "Abortion services in the United States, 1991 and 1992;" (1994). See also the National Abortion Federation's *The Role of Physician Assistants, Nurse Practitioners, and Nurse-Midwives in Providing Abortions* (1997).

On a more general note are articles by Stanley Henshaw, "Factors hindering access to abortion services" (1995) and Marlene Gerber Fried, "Abortion in the US: barriers to access" (1997). The impact on services of mergers of Catholic and non-Catholic hospitals is described by Patricia Donovan, "Hospital mergers and reproductive health care" (1996); Rachel Benson Gold, "Advocates work to preserve reproductive health care access when hospitals merge" (2000); and Physicians for Reproductive Choice and Health,

Mergers and You: The Physicians Guide to Religious Hospital Mergers (2001). Patrician Donovan's article on "The restoration of abortion services at Cook County Hospital" (1993) offers a chilling account of how a municipal board decided not to provide services to poor women.

The hospital training of ob/gyn residents in abortion techniques has been tracked by Rene Almeling and colleagues (2000), including the 1998 survey cited in this chapter. For earlier surveys see Philip Darney and colleagues (1987); Carolyn Westhoff and colleagues (1993); H. Trent MacKay and Andrea Phillips MacKay (1995); and Carolyn Westhoff (1995). For a fascinating in-depth report of the training experience of physicians in an urban women's health care agency read Mary Ann Castle and Barbara Fisher's "Anatomy of a physician education programme" (1997). Planned Parenthood's activities in providing contraceptive and abortion training to physicians and residents and a summary of the current status of training nationwide are noted on its website (www.plannedparenthood.org).

The intense activity of some of the early abortion clinics is described in Carole Joffe (1995) and Mary Kay Zimmerman (1977). Sheryl Burt Ruzek's book on *The Women's Health Movement: Feminist Alternatives to Medical Control* (1978) offers an excellent guide to some of the early efforts at setting up women-centered services, including a report on the Jane collective. See Stimezo Nederland (1996) for the Dutch clinic experience. Descriptions of clinics listed in the Yellow Pages are from the District of Columbia, although almost any metropolitan telephone book will do. See also *The Abortion Resource Handbook* by K. Kaufmann (1997). Ob/gyns who perform office abortions in Los Angeles County are described in Lewis Wyatt and colleagues (1995).

The lower costs of abortion services in clinics than hospitals are mentioned in Rachel Benson Gold's *Abortion and Women's Health*

(1990); other cost estimates are in K. Kaufmann (1997) and Beverly Winikoff and Suzanne Wymelenberg (1997). The harassment of abortion providers and the extent of clinic violence are described on the CARAL and NARAL websites mentioned above; see additional references in the notes to Chapter Seven. National data for the US, including that quoted in this chapter, are presented in Stanley Henshaw (1995) and Jacqueline Darroch Forrest and Stanley Henshaw (1987).

Proposals for integrating practitioners into the professional mainstream and for training nonphysicians are in National Abortion Federation (1991 and 1997). On strategies for improving women's access to safe services in developing countries despite legal restrictions see Rebecca J. Cook, "Abortion laws and policies: challenges and opportunities" (1989); Karen Stein and colleagues, *Abortion: Expanding Access and Improving Quality* (1998); and Adrienne Germain and Theresa Kim, *Expanding Access to Safe Abortion: Strategies for Action* (1998), among other excellent sources.

Chapter Seven: Private Opinion and Public Debate: Who Decides Who Decides?

Among the many sources of data on public opinion on abortion in the US and Canada are the following: Donald Granberg and Beth Granberg, "Abortion attitudes 1965-1980" (1980); Stanley K. Henshaw and Greg Martire, "Abortion and the public opinion polls: morality and legality" (1982); Alice S. Rossi and Bhavani Sitaraman, "Abortion in context: historical trends and future changes" (1988); Paul Sachdev, *Sex, Abortion, and Unmarried Women* [in Canada] (1993); Donley T. Studlar and Raymond Tatalovich, "Abortion policy in the United States and Canada" (1996); Larry L. Bumpass, "Measurement of public opinion on abortion" (1997); and David L. Adamson and colleagues, *How Americans View World Population Issues: A Survey of Public Opinion* (2000). See also the chapters on early public opinion in Howard J. Osofksy and Joy D.

Osofsky, *The Abortion Experience* (1973) and the introduction to Carole Joffe, *Doctors of Conscience* (1995). The website *www.caral.ca* (see The Polling Report, Inc.) summarizes the results of more than 100 US public opinion polls on abortion attitudes and political preferences conducted since 1996 by Gallup, ABC/Washington Post, NBC/Wall Street Journal, CNN/Time, CBS/New York Times, and Newsweek.

A comparative look at public opinion polls in the US, Canada, Western and Eastern Europe and selected other countries between 1981-1984 and 1991-1994 conducted by Gallup organizations can be found in Rita J. Simon's *Abortion: Statutes, Policies, and Public Attitudes the World Over* (1998). In most European countries and in China, India, and Japan, for example, a higher percentage of the population than in the US or Canada (in the low to mid 90s) believes that abortion should be legal to protect a woman's health (but only 65 percent in Ireland). Yet support for the so-called soft reasons is lower in most European countries except Sweden, and higher in China, India, and Japan.

The contrasting characteristics of pro-life and pro-choice activists are drawn from Donald Granberg, "The abortion activists" (1981); Kristin Luker, *Abortion and the Politics of Motherhood* (1984); and Faye D. Ginsburg, *Contested Lives: The Abortion Debate in an American Community* (1989) which describes how the community divided when the first abortion clinic opened in Fargo, North Dakota in 1981. Ginsburg also includes personal narratives of prolife and prochoice women. For in-depth interviews with key public activists on both sides see Marian Faux, *Crusaders: Voices from the Abortion Front* (1990).

The quote on public attitudes as a source of abortion policy is from Elizabeth Adell Cook and colleagues, "Measuring public attitudes on abortion" (1993), but a much fuller analysis of the result of public opinion polls between 1972 and 1991 as they reflect prochoice and prolife positions can be found in Cook and colleagues, *Between Two Absolutes: Public Opinion and the Politics of Abortion* (1992). The discussion of abortion as a moral and legal issue is from Henshaw and Martire (above); of inconsistencies of survey responses from Cook (above, 1993); of the very high level of opposition to abortion from those who attend church more than once a week from Adamson (above);. and of the relationship between attitudes about abortion and other moral issues from Granberg and Granberg (above) and Cook (above, 1992). The Alan Guttmacher Institute has compiled a very useful volume of articles on abortion politics in the US from 1974 to 1999 called *Readings on Induced Abortion, Vol. 1: Politics and Policies* (2000).

The section on the war of words (and much of what follows in the legislative issues) relies extensively on Laurence H. Tribe's *Abortion: The Clash of Absolutes* (1990). This is a must-read book. Other excellent sources are J. Douglas Butler and David F. Walbert (eds.), *Abortion, Medicine and the Law* (1992); Donald P. Judges, *Hard Choices, Lost Voices: How the Abortion Conflict Has Divided America, Distorted Constitutional Rights, and Damaged the Courts* (1993); and D. J. Garrow, *Liberty and Sexuality: The Right to Privacy and the Making of Roe v. Wade* (1998). For more on the clash of absolutes and what she defines as the "failure" of rights-based arguments in general, and not just in regard to abortion, see Mary Ann Glendon's *Rights Talk: The Impoverishment of Political Discourse* (1991). The quotes from the *Roe v. Wade* decision in the introduction to this section are from The Center for Reproductive Law and Policy, *Roe v. Wade and the Right to Privacy* (2001). The full text of this decision is in 410 US 113 (1973) and on various websites, such as *www.findlaw.com*.

Legal implications of the "personhood" of the fetus are analyzed in Laurence Tribe (above); the political attempts to establish it in Patrician Donovan, "When does personhood begin?" (1983) and

Harriet F. Pilpel, "The fetus as person: possible legal consequences of the Hogan-Helms Amendment" (1974).

The literature on the moral and political position of the Catholic Church with respect to abortion is enormous. An excellent (and exhaustive) source is Hans Lotstra's *Abortion: The Catholic Debate in America* (1985); see also John T. Noonan's *The Morality of Abortion: Legal and Historical Perspectives* (1970) together with his famous treatise on *Contraception: A History of Its Treatment by the Catholic Theologians and Canonists* (1966). For a critical alternative to the establishment view see the various publications of Catholics for a Free Choice, including *A New Rite: Conservative Catholic Organizations and their Allies* (1994) and *Catholics and Reproduction: A World View* (1997). Gary Wills's book *Papal Sin: Structures of Deceit* (2000) offers some fascinating insights into the papal positions on contraception and abortion as well as on other controversial issues, as does Robert McClory's book *Turning Point: The Inside Story of the Papal Birth Control Commission* (1995).

On the divisive abortion politics of the New Right and the mix of fundamentalist religion and politics see Michele McKeegan, *Abortion Politics: Mutiny in the Ranks of the Right* (1992) and Dallas A. Blanchard, *The Anti-Abortion Movement and the Rise of the Religious Right: From Polite to Fiery Protest* (1994). Karen Armstrong's historical study of fundamentalisms in Islam, Judaism, and Protestantism, *The Battle for God* (2000), provides fascinating insights into the fears of the fundamentalists and the origins of what she calls "a theology of exclusion, rage, and hatred." In his book based on the American experience, Jim Wallis raises similar questions about the absence of civility and compassion among the more vocal of the fundamentalist groups in *Who Speaks for God?* (1996). Dallas Blanchard's *The Anti-Abortion Movement: References and Resources* (1996) includes invaluable descriptions and annotated source materials of thirty-nine major antiabortion movement organizations together with an analysis of their support services and coalitions.

Various aspects of the morality of abortion are discussed in Daniel Callahan, *Abortion: Law, Choice and Morality* (1970); in Frederick Jaffe and colleagues, *Abortion Politics: Private Morality and Public Policy* (1981); and in Ronald Dworkin, *Life's Dominion: An Argument About Abortion, Euthanasia, and Individual Freedom* (1993), among many other sources. Some of these, such as Lloyd Steffen's *Life/Choice: The Theory of Just Abortion* (1994) attempt to carve out an ethically acceptable "middle ground," but with questionable success. For selected feminist positions on abortion see Beverly Wildung Harrison, *Our Right to Choose: Toward a New Ethic of Abortion* (1983); Rosalind Pollack Petchesky, *Abortion and Woman's Choice* (1984); Marlene Gerber Fried, *From Abortion to Reproductive Freedom: Transforming a Movement* (1990); and Eileen L. McDonagh, *Breaking the Abortion Deadlock: From Choice to Consent* (1996), among other sources. The development of the idea of women's rights as human rights is traced in many studies, including Julie Peters and Andrea Wolper's volume, *Women's Rights, Human Rights: International Feminist Perspectives* (1995).

Public policies in Canada and the United States viewed in the context of those of other Western countries are analyzed in Mary Ann Glendon, *Abortion and Divorce in Western Law* (1987) and Marianne Githens and Dorothy McBride Stetson (eds.), *Abortion Politics: Public Policy in Cross-Cultural Perspective* (1996). On state restrictions in the US see NARAL and Naral Foundation, *Who Decides? A State-by-State Review of Abortion and Reproductive Rights* (2002); for Canada see Childbirth by Choice Trust, *Abortion in Canada Today: The Situation Province by Province* (1997). Donald Judges (cited above) has more on the Freedom of Choice Act and its legal basis.

For data on clinic violence and the motives of pro-life extremists in the 1980s, such as the activities of Randall Terry's Operation Rescue, see the references in the previous chapter plus those noted above in the discussion of fundamentalist religion and right-wing politics. An excellent source on the tactics of protesters and the experiences of clinic personnel in the US and Canada is Patricia Baird-Windle and Eleanor J. Bader's *Targets of Hatred: Anti-Abortion Terrorism* (2001). The federal clinic protection law is explained in NARAL, "Freedom of Access to Clinic Entrances Act (FACE)" (2000). This is available on the Website *www.naral.org* along with a description of the Family Planning and Choice Protection Act of 1999 (2000).

The Mexico City policy and global gag rule are described in the Alan Guttmacher Institute, "Endangered: US aid for family planning overseas (1996) and Susan A. Cohen, "Implementing the global gag rule" (2000) and "Global gag rule: exporting antiabortion ideology at the expense of American values" (2001) as well as on the relevant websites.

Chapter Eight: Why Safe Abortion is a Global Issue

On the international scene, the struggles between women's rights groups and antiabortion forces in Brazil, Nigeria, and the Philippines are described in Ruth Dixon-Mueller's *Population Policy and Women's Rights* (1993) and the activities of Opus Dei in Steve Askin's *A New Rite: Conservative Catholic Organizations and their Allies* (1994).

For analysis and commentary on the ideological conflicts, governmental alliances, and role of the Holy See (the Vatican) at two critically important UN conferences in the 1990s, the following publications are useful: Adrienne Germain and Rachel Kyte, *The Cairo Consensus: The Right Agenda for the Right Time* (1995); C. Alison McIntosh and Jason L. Finkle, "The Cairo Conference on Population and Development: a new paradigm?" (1995); Francoise

Girard, "Cairo + Five: reviewing progress for women five years after the International Conference on Population and Development (1999); United Nations Department of Public Information, *The Beijing Declaration and The Platform for Action* (1996); and International Women's Health Coalition, "Beijing Plus Five: analysis of negotiations and final 'further actions' document" (2000). This is just a sampling of what is available. The prochoice comment of Halfdan Mahler quoted in the box is reprinted in the journal *Population and Development Review* 21 (3), 1995, as is the reaction of Pope John Paul II who calls the "contraceptive mentality" evil and abortion a "culture of death." The statistics cited on maternal mortality and the nonuse of contraception are from Girard (above).

For a selection of the (then) new perspectives on women and population leading up to the UN conferences and in the international field of family planning, see Ruth Dixon-Mueller, *Population Policy and Women's Rights: Transforming Reproductive Choice* (1993); Gita Sen, Adrienne Germain, and Lincoln C. Chen (eds.), *Population Policies Reconsidered: Health, Empowerment, and Rights* (1994); and Sonia Correa, *Population and Reproductive Rights: Feminist Perspectives from the South* (1994). The edited volume by Harriet B. Presser and Gita Sen, *Women's Empowerment and Demographic Processes: Moving Beyond Cairo* (2000) offers an excellent followup for researchers.

A SAMPLING OF PROCHOICE ORGANIZATIONS IN THE UNITED STATES AND CANADA

A good source of information and referrals for high quality abortion care is **Planned Parenthood** (call 1-800-230-PLAN for the nearest clinic). Call the hotline of the **National Abortion Federation** to ask about providers in your area, state or provincial regulations, and financial help (1-800-772-9100 in the US and 1-800-424-2280 in Canada). **The National Women's Health Network** is another good source of information and support (202-347-1140). See **Abortion Clinics On-Line** at *www.gynpages.com* or call 770-993-0772 to find out about public and private clinics, physicians' offices, and hospital providers by state and city in the US and for selected providers in Canada, Austria, Australia, Belgium, England, Netherlands, and Spain. For emergency contraception consult *www.not-2-late.com.*

ACLU Reproductive Freedom Project

American Civil Liberties Union
125 Broad Street, 18th floor, New York, NY 10004 tel 212-549-2500; fax 212-549-2652; email *aclu@aclu.org*

Website *www.aclu.org.* News bulletins on US Supreme Court cases, federal and state legislative and court actions, pending bills on all aspects of contraception and abortion access, services for adolescents and low-income women, conscience clauses, etc.

Alan Guttmacher Institute

120 Wall Street, New York, NY 10005 tel 212-248-1111; fax 212-248-1952; email *info@agi-usa.org*
Website *www.agi-usa.org* includes research findings on abortion in the US and other countries; data bases; policy analyses; articles and reports; news releases. Publications include *Family Planning Perspectives, International Family Planning Perspectives, The Guttmacher Report on Public Policy,* and numerous special reports and factsheets.

Canadian Abortion Rights Action League (CARAL)

616-880 Wellington Street, Ottawa, Ontario K1R 6K7 tel 1-888-642-2725; fax 613-789-9960; email *caral@caral.ca*
Website *www.caral.ca* includes factsheets on contraception and abortion in Canada, teenage pregnancy, prenatal development, costs of unintended pregnancy; information on counseling, anti-choice and pro-choice organizations, public opinion, politics; clinics by province with waiting times, funding policies, etc. Newsletter, videos, publications.

Catholics for a Free Choice (CFFC)

1436 U Street NW, Suite 301, Washington, DC 20009-3997 tel 202-986-6093; fax 202-332-7995; email *cffc@catholicsforchoice.org*
Website *www.catholicsforchoice.org* has information on Catholic organizations and Catholic opinion about contraception and abortion, statements of US Bishops, Vatican politics.

Publications include fact sheets, a newsjournal *Conscience*, special reports.

Center for Reproductive Law and Policy (CRLP)

120 Wall Street, 14th floor, New York, NY 10005
1146 19th Street NW, Washington DC 20036
NY tel 917-637-3600; fax 917-637-3666; DC tel 202-530-2975; fax 202-530-2976
Website *www.crlp.org* addresses reproductive rights as human rights, legal issues, international laws, US global gag rule, contraception, abortion, adolescent rights, female genital mutilation. Publications include factsheets and briefing papers, action kits, media resources; videos. Newsletter *Of Counsel*.

Childbirth by Choice Trust

344 Bloor Street West, Suite 502, Toronto, Ontario M5S 3A7 tel 416-961-7812; fax 416-961-5771; email *info@cbctrust.com*
Website *www.cbctrust.com* contains information on abortion statistics and medical procedures in Canada, where to go for abortion counseling and services; special information for teens, chronology of court cases in Canada, prenatal development, etc. Publications include *No Choice: Canadian Women Tell Their Stories of Illegal Abortion*.

Choice USA

1010 Wisconsin Avenue NW, Suite 410, Washington, DC 20007 tel 1-888-784-4494, 202-965-7700; fax 202-965-7701; email *info@choiceusa.org*
Website *www.choiceusa.org*. Abortion facts plus advocacy activities, including campus organizing, student fellowships and internships for students, prochoice leadership training, information campaigns for emergency contraception and RU 486.

Family Care International

588 Broadway, Suite 503, New York, NY 10012 tel 212-941-
5300; fax 212-941-5563; email *resources@familycareintl.org*
Website *www.familycareintl.org*. Technical and policy guidelines
for safe pregnancy, delivery, and the management of unsafe
abortion in developing countries. Publications include research
and training manuals (e.g., *Prevention and Management of
Unsafe Abortion: A Guide for Action*), presentation materials,
slide shows, country reports.

Feminist Majority Foundation

1600 Wilson Blvd., Suite 801, Arlington VA tel 703-522-2214;
fax 703-522-2219; email *femmaj@feminist.org*
Website *www.feminist.org* describes a wide range of feminist
activities and issues; newsletter. Abortion rights section includes
information on resources, clinic access and violence, STDs/
AIDS; campaign for RU 486, lobbying efforts.

International Women's Health Coalition

24 East 21st Street, New York, NY 10010 tel 212-979-8500; fax
212-979-9009; email *iwhc@iwhc.org*
Website *www.iwhc.org* describes the Coalition's work in Africa, Asia
and Latin America; special reproductive health concerns
(adolescent health and rights, sexual rights, access to safe
abortion); international policy issues and activities (including
UN conferences); publications on abortion, contraceptive
research, sexuality and gender, STDs, etc.

IPAS

300 Market Street, Suite 200, Chapel Hill, NC 27516 tel 919-
967-7052; fax 919-929-0258; email *ipas@ipas.org*
Website *www.ipas.org*. Special interest in applied aspects of abortion
technology (vacuum aspiration) and post-abortion care and

training programs in developing countries. Publications include training manuals in the use of vacuum aspiration.

Medical Students for Choice

PO Box 70190, Oakland, CA 94612 tel 510-238-5210; fax 510-238-5213 Website *www.ms4c.org*. Represents students at 100 medical schools in US and Canada; focus on abortion training and medical curricula; advocacy to increase trained providers and improve abortion services. Reference materials, bibliographies, conferences, etc.

National Abortion and Reproductive Rights Action League (NARAL)

1156 15th Street NW, Suite 700, Washington, DC 20005 tel 202-973-3000; fax 202-973-3096; email *naral@naral.org*

Websites *www.naral.org* and *www.fight4choice.com* include news bulletins, legislative updates for state and federal bills, Supreme Court; press releases; factsheets on all aspects of abortion; list of state affiliates. Publications include an annual compilation of legislation: *Who Decides? A State-by-State Review of Abortion and Reproductive Rights*

National Abortion Federation (NAF)

1755 Massachucetts Avenue NW, Suite 600, Washington, DC 20031 tel 202-667-5881; fax 292-667-5890; email *naf@prochoice.org*

Website *www.prochoice.org*. NAF maintains a list of affiliated providers; fact sheets on pregnancy, clinic violence, legal issues; media materials and press releases; legislative action; conferences and workshops. Publications include clinical guidelines for abortion providers; guide to abortion decision-making; conference proceedings.

National Coalition of Abortion Providers

206 King Street, Alexandria, VA 22314 tel 703-684-0055; fax
    703-684-5051; email *ron@ncap.com*
Website *www.ncap.com* contains lists of clinics by state. NCAP
    represents 150 independent abortion providers, not including
    Planned Parenthood clinics, and engages in political action
    and other activities on behalf of providers.

NOW Legal Defense and Education Fund

395 Hudson Street, New York, NY 10014 tel 212-925-6635; fax
    212-226-1066; email *lir@nowldef.org*
Washington policy office: 1522 K St. NW, Suite 550, Washington
    DC 20005 tel 202-326-0040; fax 202-589-0511; email
    policy@nowldef.org
Website *www.nowldef.org* explains LDEF's legal work in the areas
    of pregnancy, sexual harassment, sex discrimination, divorce,
    domestic violence, and reproductive rights. Legal actions
    include litigation against antiabortion clinic violence by
    Operation Rescue, the Army of God, and the American
    Coalition of Life Activists.

Pathfinder International

9 Galen Street, Suite 217, Watertown, MA 02472 tel 617-924-
    7200; fax 617-924-3833; email *information@pathfind.org*
Website *www.pathfind.org* includes Pathfinder's reproductive health
    and family planning programs in developing countries;
    contraception, abortion, adolescent services, HIV/AIDS, etc.
    Training guides in vacuum aspiration and emergency
    contraception.

Physicians for Reproductive Choice and Health

55 West 39th Street, 10th floor, New York, NY 10018 tel
    646-366-1890; fax 646-366-1897; *info@prch.org*

Webset *www.PRCH.org* lists medical education resources for abortion probiders, profiles of physician providers, speaker program for medical abortion (RU 486), slide shows, physician-medical student support network; advocacy activities; newsletter.

Planned Parenthood Federation of America (PPFA)

810 Seventh Avenue, New York, NY 10019 tel for medical questions and services 1-800-230-PLAN tel 212-541-7800; fax 212-245-1845; email *communications@ppfa.org*

Website *www.plannedparenthood.org*. Factsheets, answers to frequently asked questions about sex, contraception, abortion, STDs; affiliated providers; adoption referrals; state laws; international programs; press releases and newsletters; publications, books for sale.

Planned Parenthood Federation of Canada

1 Nicholas Street, Suite 430, Ottawa, Ontario K1N 7B7 tel 613-241-4474

Website *www.ppfc.ca* has fact sheets on contraception and abortion in Canada; information about clinic services and counseling; pregnancy advice; information for teens; awards and scholarships; guides on sexuality and reproductive health for youth and teachers; publications and reports; international programs.

Population Action International (PAI)

1300 19th Street NW, 2nd floor, Washington, DC 20036 tel 202-557-3400; fax 202-728-4177; email *pai@popact.org*

Website *www.populationaction.org* includes fact sheets on sexual and reproductive health issues in developing countries;

community-based programs; adolescent services; HIV/AIDS; international family planning legislation; publications on policy issues, reproductive health risks, contraceptive choice, country programs, etc.

The Population Council

One Dag Hammarskjold Plaza, New York, NY 10017 tel 212-339-0500; fax 212-755-6052; email *pubinfo@popcouncil.org*. Website *www.popcouncil.org* describes the Council's activities in international population and social policy, reproductive health and family planning, biomedical research; quality of care; unwanted pregnancy and unsafe abortion. Publishes *Studies in Family Planning* plus many special reports and working papers on contraception, abortion, STDs, biomedical technology, adolescents, and women.

The Religious Coalition for Reproductive Choice (RCRC)

1025 Vermont Avenue NW, Suite 1130, Washington, DC 20005 tel 202-628-7700; fax 202-628-7716; email *info@rcrc.org* Website *www.rcrc.org* describes RCRC' mission; organizational membership; campaigns for choice and against clinic violence; surveys; media ads, sermons, prayers; public education activities with clergy, church members, legislators.

Sexuality Information and Education Council of the United States (SIECUS)

130 West 42nd Street, Suite 350, New York, NY 10036-7802 tel 212-819-9770; fax 212-819-9776; email *siecus@siecus.org* Website *www.siecus.org* covers an enormous range of activities and issues: domestic and international public policy, media, school health programs, sexuality education and health guidelines, international conferences, training and advocacy programs,

information for teens and parents, adolescent pregancy prevention, HIV/AIDs.

REFERENCES

Adamson, David M., Nancy Belden, Julie DaVanzo and Sally Patterson. 2000. *How Americans View World Population Issues: A Survey of Public Opinion*. Santa Monica, CA: RAND.

Adler, Nancy E., Henry P. David, Brenda N. Major, Susan H. Roth, Nancy F. Russo and Gail E. Wyatt. 1990. "Psychological responses after abortion." *Science* 248 (April), 41-44.

Alan Guttmacher Institute. 1975. "The unmet need for legal abortion services in the U.S." *Family Planning Perspectives* 7 (5), 224-230.

_____. 1994. *Uneven and Unequal: Insurance Coverage and Reproductive Health Services*. New York: The Alan Guttmacher Institute.

_____. 1996. "Endangered: U.S. Aid for family planning overseas." *Issues in Brief*. New York: The Alan Guttmacher Institute.

_____. 1998. "Conscience makes a comeback in the age of managed care." *The Guttmacher Report on Public Policy* 1 (1).

_____. 1998. *Into a New World: Young Women's Sexual and Reproductive Lives*. New York: The Alan Guttmacher Institute.

_____. 1999. *Sharing Responsibility: Women, Society and Abortion Worldwide*. New York: The Alan Guttmacher Institute.

_____. 1999. "Teen sex and pregnancy." *Facts in Brief*. New York: The Alan Guttmacher Institute.

_____. 2000. *Readings on Induced Abortion. Volume 1: Politics and Policies*. New York: The Alan Guttmacher Institute.

Almeling, Rene, Laureen Tews and Susan Dudley. 2000. "Abortion training in U.S. obstetrics and gynecology residency programs, 1998." *Family Planning Perspectives* 32 (6), 268-271, 320.

Archibong, E. I. 1991. "Illegal induced abortion—a continuing problem in Nigeria." *International Journal of Obstetrics and Gynecology* 34 (3), 261-265.

Armstrong, Karen. 2000. *The Battle for God.* New York: Ballantine.

Athanasiou, Robert, Wallace Oppel, Leslie Michelson, Thomas Unger and Mary Yager. 1973. "Psychiatric sequelae to term birth and induced early and late abortion: a longitudinal study." *Family Planning Perspectives* 5 (4), 227-231.

Azize-Vargas, Yamila and Luis A. Avilés. 1997. "Abortion in Puerto Rico: the limits of colonial legality." *Reproductive Health Matters* 9 (May), 56-65.

Baird, David T., David A. Grimes, and Paul F. A. Van Look (eds.). 1995. *Modern Methods of Inducing Abortion.* London: Blackwell Science Ltd.

Baird-Windle, Patricia, and Eleanor J. Bader. 2001. *Targets of Hatred: Anti-Abortion Terrorism.* New York: Palgrave.

Bankole, Akinrinola, Susheela Singh, and Taylor Haas. 1998. "Reasons why women have induced abortions: evidence from 27 countries." *International Family Planning Perspectives* 24 (3), 117-127.

_____. 1999. "Characteristics of women who obtain induced abortion: a worldwide review." *International Family Planning Perspectives* 25 (2), 68-77.

Barber, Jennifer S. 1999. "Unwanted childbearing, health and mother-child relationships." *Journal of Health and Social Behavior* 40 (3), 231-257.

Barbosa, Regina Maria, and Margareth Arilha. 1993. "Is Cytotec an answer?" *Planned Parenthood Challenges* 1. London: International Planned Parenthood Federation, 20-22.

Baulieu, Etienne-Emile with Mort Rosenblum. 1990. *The 'Abortion Pill:' RU-486, A Woman's Choice*. New York: Simon and Schuster.

Blanchard, Dallas A. 1994. *The Anti-Abortion Movement and the Rise of the Religious Right: From Polite to Fiery Protest*. New York: Twayne.

_____. 1996. *The Anti-Abortion Movement: References and Resources*. New York: G. K. Hall.

Bongaarts, John. 1997. "Trends in unwanted childbearing in the developing world." *Studies in Family Planning* 28 (4), 267-277.

_____, and Barney Cohen (eds.). 1998. *Adolescent Reproductive Behavior in the Developing World*. Special issue of *Studies in Family Planning* 29 (2).

Boston Women's Health Book Collective. 1998. *Our Bodies Ourselves for the New Century*. New York: Simon and Schuster.

_____. 1992. *The New Our Bodies, Ourselves: A Book by and for Women*. New York: Simon and Schuster.

Boyle, Mary. 1997. *Re-Thinking Abortion: Psychology, Gender, Power and the Law*. London and New York: Routledge.

Brazier, Ellen, Rahna Rizzuto, and Merrill Wolf. 1998. *Prevention and Management of Unsafe Abortion: A Guide for Action*. New York: Family Care International.

Brodie, Janine. 1994. "Health vs. rights: comparative perspectives on abortion policy in Canada and the United States." In Gita Sen and Rachel Snow (eds.), *Power and Decision: The Social Control of Reproduction*. Cambridge, MA: Harvard School of Public Health, 123-146.

Brodie, Janine, Shelley A. M. Gavigan, and Jane Jenson. 1992. *The Politics of Abortion*. Toronto: Oxford University Press.

Brody, Harry, Stewart Meikle and Richard Gerritse. 1971.

"Therapeutic abortion: a prospective study." *American Journal of Obstetrics and Gynecology* 109, 347-353.

Brown, Sarah S. and Leon Eisenberg (eds.). 1995. *The Best Intentions: Unintended Pregnancy and the Well-being of Children and Families.* Washington, DC: National Academy Press.

Browner, Carole. 1979. "Abortion decision making: some findings from Colombia." *Studies in Family Planning* 10 (3), 96-106.

Bumpass, Larry L. 1997. "The measurement of public opinion on abortion: the effects of survey design." *Family Planning Perspectives* 29 (4), 177-180.

Butler, J. Douglas and David F. Walbert (eds.). 1992. *Abortion, Medicine and the Law.* 4th ed. New York: Facts on File.

Callahan, Daniel. 1970. *Abortion: Law, Choice and Morality.* New York: Macmillan.

Casas-Becerra, Lidia. 1997. "Women prosecuted and imprisoned for abortion in Chile." *Reproductive Health Matters* 9 (May), 29-36.

Castle, Mary Ann and Barbara Fisher. 1997. "Anatomy of a physician education programme." *Reproductive Health Matters* 9 (May), 46-55.

Cadelina, Fred V. 1999. "Induced abortion in a province in the Philippines: the opinion, role and experience of traditional birth attendants and government midwives." In Axel I. Mundigo and Cynthia Indriso (eds.), *Abortion in the Developing World.* New Delhi: Vistaar Publications, 311-320.

Catholics for a Free Choice. 1994. *A New Rite: Conservative Catholic Organizations and their Allies.* Washington, DC: Catholics for a Free Choice.

_____. 1997. *Catholics and Reproduction: A World View.* Washington, DC: Catholics for a Free Choice.

Center for Reproductive Law and Policy. 2001. *Roe v. Wade and the Right to Privacy*. New York: Center for Reproductive Law and Policy.

Chesler, Ellen. 1992. *Woman of Valor: Margaret Sanger and the Birth Control Movement in America*. New York: Simon and Schuster.

Childbirth by Choice Trust. 1997. *Abortion in Canada Today: The Situation Province by Province*. Toronto: Childbirth by Choice Trust.

_____. 1998. *No Choice: Canadian Women Tell their Stories of Illegal Abortion*. Toronto: Childbirth by Choice Trust.

Cohen, Susan A. 2000. "Implementing the global gag rule." *The Guttmacher Report* 3 (2), 5-7.

_____. 2001. "Global gag rule: Exporting antiabortion ideology at the expense of American values." *The Guttmacher Report* 4 (3), 1-3.

Cook, Elizabeth Adell, Ted G. Jelen and Clyde Wilcox. 1992. *Between Two Absolutes: Public Opinion and the Politics of Abortion*. Boulder, CO: Westview.

_____. 1993. "Measuring public attitudes on abortion: methodological and substantive considerations." *Family Planning Perspectives* 25 (3), 118-121 & 145.

Cook, Rebecca J. 1989. "Abortion laws and policies: challenges and opportunities." In A. Rosenfield, M. F. Fathalla, A. Germain and C. L. Indriso (eds.), *Women's Health in the Third World: The Impact of Unwanted Pregnancy*. *International Journal of Gynecology & Obstetrics* Supplement 3, 61-87.

Cooper, Peter J. and Lynne Murray. 1998. "Postnatal depression." *British Medical Journal* 316, 1884-86.

Correa, Sonia, in collaboration with R. Reichmann. 1994. *Population and Reproductive Rights: Feminist Perspectives from the South*. London: Zed Books.

Critchlow, Donald T. (ed.) 1996. *The Politics of Abortion and Birth Control in Historical Perspective.* University Park, PA: Pennsylvania State University Press.

――――. 1999. *Intended Consequences: Birth Control, Abortion, and the Federal Government in Modern America.* New York: Oxford University Press.

Cunningham, F. Gary and others. 1997. *Williams Obstetrics,* 20th ed. Stamford, CT: Appleton and Lange.

Dagg, Paul K. B. 1991. "The psychological sequelae of therapeutic abortion, denied and completed." *American Journal of Psychiatry* 148 (5), 578-585.

Darney, P. D, U. Landry, S. MacPherson, and R. L. Sweet. 1987. "Abortion training in U.S. obstetrics and gynecology residency programs." *Family Planning Perspectives* 19 (4), 161-2.

David, Henry P. 1992. "Abortion in Europe, 1920-91: a public health perspective." *Studies in Family Planning* 23 (1), 1-22.

David, Henry P., Z. Dytrych, Z. Matejcek, and V. Schuller (eds.) 1988. *Born Unwanted: Developmental Effects of Denied Abortion.* New York: Springer.

David, Henry P. and Jany Rademakers. 1996. "Lessons from the Dutch abortion experience." *Studies in Family Planning* 27 (6), 341-343.

David, Henry P. (ed.) 1999. *From Abortion to Contraception: A Resource to Public Policies and Reproductive Behavior in Central and Eastern Europe from 1917 to the Present.* Westport, CT: Greenwood Press.

Degler, Carl N. 1980. *At Odds: Women and the Family in America from the Revolution to the Present.* Oxford: Oxford University Press.

Devereux, George. 1976. *A Study of Abortion in Primitive Societies.* Rev. ed. New York: International Universities Press.

Dixon-Mueller, Ruth. 1988. "Innovations in reproductive health care: menstrual regulation policies and programs in Bangladesh." *Studies in Family Planning* 19 (3), 129-140.

_____. *Population Policy and Women's Rights: Transforming Reproductive Choice*. Westport, CT: Praeger, 1993.

Djohan, E., R. Indrawasih, M. Adenan, H. Yudomustopo, and M. G. Tan. 1999. "The attitudes of health care providers towards abortion in Indonesia." In Axel I. Mundigo and Cynthia Indriso (eds.), *Abortion in the Developing World*. New Delhi: Vistaar Publications, 281-292.

Doctors for Repeal of the Abortion Law. 1975. "Survey of hospital abortion committees in Canada." Dundas, Ontario: Doctors for Repeal of the Abortion Law. (On file in the Library of Parliament)

Donovan, Patricia. 1983. "When does personhood begin?" *Family Planning Perspectives* 15 (1), 40-44.

_____. 1985. "The Holy War." *Family Planning Perspectives* 17 (1), 5-9.

_____. 1993. "The restoration of abortion services at Cook County Hospital." *Family Planning Perspectives* 25 (5), 227-231.

_____. 1996. "Hospital mergers and reproductive health care." *Family Planning Perspectives* 28 (6), 281-284.

_____. 1998. "Falling teen pregnancy, birthrates: what's behind the declines?" *The Guttmacher Report on Public Policy* 1 (5), 6-8.

Dworkin, Ronald M. 1993. *Life's Dominion: An Argument about Abortion, Euthanasia, and Individual Freedom*. New York: Knopf.

Ehrenfeld, N. 1999. "Female adolescents at the crossroads: sexuality, contraception and abortion in Mexico." In Axel I. Mundigo and Cynthia Indriso (eds.), *Abortion in the Developing World*. New Delhi: Vistaar Publications, 368-386.

Ellertson, Charlotte, Batya Elul and Beverly Winikoff. 1997. "Can women use medical abortion without medical supervision?" *Reproductive Health Matters* 9 (May), 149-161.

Elul, Batya, Selma Hajri, Nguyen thi Nhu Ngoc, Charlotte Ellertson, Claude Ben Slama, Elizabeth Pearlman, and Beverly Winokoff. 2001. "Can women in less-developed countries use a simplified medical abortion regimen?" *The Lancet* 357 (May), 1402-1405.

Faux, Marian. 1988. *Roe v. Wade: The Untold Story of the Landmark Supreme Court Decision that Made Abortion Legal.* New York: Macmillan.

_____. 1990. *Crusaders: Voices from the Abortion Front.* New York: Birch Lane Press.

Feldman, David M. 1968. *Birth Control in Jewish Law.* New York: New York University Press.

Forrest, Jacqueline Darroch and Stanley K. Henshaw. 1987. "The harrassment of U.S. abortion providers." *Family Planning Perspectives* 19 (1), 9-13.

Forrest, Jacqueline Darroch. 1988. "Contraceptive needs through stages of women's reproductive lives." *Contemporary Obstetrics and Gynecology* 32, 12-16 and 21-22.

_____. 1994. "Epidemiology of unintended pregnancy and contraceptive use." *American Journal of Obstetrics and Gynecology,* 170, 1485-1488.

Francome, Colin and Edward Freeman. 2000. "British general practitioners' attitudes toward abortion." *Family Planning Perspectives* 32 (4), 189-191.

Frank, Peter, Roseanne McNamee, Philip C. Hannaford, Clifford R. Kay and Sybil Hersch. 1993. "The effect of induced abortion on subsequent fertility." *British Journal of Obstetrics and Gynaecology* 100 (June), 575-580.

Frejka, Tomas. 1985. "Induced abortion and fertility." *International Family Planning Perspectives* 11 (4), 125-129.

Fried, Marlene Gerber. 1990. *From Abortion to Reproductive Freedom: Transforming a Movement.* Boston: South End Press.

———. 1997. "Abortion in the US: barriers to access." *Reproductive Health Matters* 9 (May), 37-45.

Fryer, Peter. 1965. *The Birth Controllers.* London: Secker and Warburg.

Garrow, D. J. 1998. *Liberty and Sexuality: The Right to Privacy and the Making of Roe v. Wade.* Berkeley: University of California Press.

Germain Adrienne, and Rachel Kyte. 1995. *The Cairo Consensus: The Right Agenda for the Right Time.* New York: International Women's Health Coalition.

Germain, Adrienne, and Theresa Kim. 1998. *Expanding Access to Safe Abortion: Strategies for Action.* New York: International Women's Health Coalition.

Girvin, Brian. 1996. "Ireland and the European Union: the impact of integration and social change on abortion policy." In Marianne Githens and Dorothy McBride Stetson (eds.), *Abortion Politics: Public Policy in Cross-Cultural Perspective.* New York: Routledge, 165-186.

Ginsberg, Faye D. 1989. *Contested Lives: The Abortion Debate in an American Community.* Berkeley: University of California Press.

Girard, Francoise. 1999. "Cairo + Five: reviewing progress for women five years after the International Conference on Population and Development." *Journal of Women's Health and Law* 1 (1), 1-14.

Githens, Marianne and Dorothy McBride Stetson (eds.). 1996. *Abortion Politics: Public Policy in Cross-Cultural Perspective.* New York: Routledge.

Glendon, Mary Ann. 1987. *Abortion and Divorce in Western Law.* Cambridge, MA: Harvard University Press.

_____. 1991. *Rights Talk: The Impoverishment of Political Discourse.* New York: Free Press.

Gold, Rachel Benson. 1990. *Abortion and Women's Health: A Turning Point for America?* New York: Alan Guttmacher Institute.

_____. 2000. "Advocates work to preserve reproductive health care access when hospitals merge." *The Guttmacher Report* 3 (2), 3-4 & 12.

Gordon, Linda. 1976. *Woman's Body, Woman's Right: A Social History of Birth Control in America.* New York: Grossman.

Granberg, Donald, and Beth Wellman Granberg. 1980. "Abortion attitudes, 1965-1980: Trends and determinants." *Family Planning Perspectives* 12 (5), 250-261.

Granberg, Donald. 1981. "The abortion activists." *Family Planning Perspectives* 13 (4), 157-163.

Greenslade, Forrest D., Ann H. Leonard, Janie Benson, Judith Winkler, and Victoria L. Henderson. 1993. *Manual Vacuum Aspiration: A Summary of Clinical and Programmatic Experience Worldwide.* Carborro, NC: Ipas.

Grimes, David A. 1992. "Clinicians who provide abortions: the thinning ranks." *Obstetrics and Gynecology* 80 (4), 719-23.

Harrison, Beverly Wildung. 1983. *Our Right to Choose: Toward a New Ethic of Abortion.* Boston: Beacon Press.

Hass, Paula Hollerbach. 1974. "Wanted and unwanted pregnancies: a fertility decision making model." *Journal of Social Issues* 30 (4), 125-164.

Hatcher, Robert A., James Trussell, Felicia Stewart, Willard Cates Jr., Gary K. Stewart, Felicia Guest, and Deborah

Kowal. 1998. *Contraceptive Technology*. 17th rev. ed. New York: Ardent Media.

Henshaw, Stanley K., and Greg Martire. 1982. "Abortion and the public opinion polls: morality and legality." *Family Planning Perspectives* 14 (2), 53-55 & 59-60.

Henshaw, Stanley K., and Jennifer Van Vort. 1994. "Abortion services in the United States, 1991 and 1992." *Family Planning Perspectives* 26 (3), 100-106.

Henshaw, Stanley K. 1995. "Factors hindering access to abortion services." *Family Planning Perspectives* 27 (2), 54-59, 87.

_____, Susheela Singh, and Taylor Haas. 1999. "The incidence of abortion worldwide." *International Family Planning Perspectives* 25 Supplement, S30-S37.

Hern, Warren M. 1990. *Abortion Practice*. Philadelphia: Lippincott.

Hewage, P. 1999. "Induced abortion in Sri Lanka: opinions of reproductive health care providers." In Axel I. Mundigo and Cynthia Indriso (eds.), *Abortion in the Developing World*. New Delhi: Vistaar Publications, 321-336.

Himes, Norman E. 1970 [first published 1936]. *The Medical History of Contraception*. New York: Schocken.

Hogue, C. J. R., Ward Cates, and Christopher Tietze. 1982. "The effects of induced abortion on subsequent reproduction." *Epidemiologic Review* 4, 66-94.

Horobin, Gordon (ed.). 1973. *Experience with Abortion: A Case Study of North-East Scotland*. Cambridge: Cambridge University Press.

Huntington, Dale, Barbara Mensch, and Vincent C. Miller. 1996. "Survey questions for the measurement of induced abortion." *Studies in Family Planning* 27 (3), 155-161.

Huntington, Dale, and Nancy J. Piet-Pelon (eds.). 1999.

Postabortion Care: Lessons from Operations Research. New York: The Population Council.

Ilumoka, Adetoun Olabisi. 1992. "Reproductive rights: a critical appraisal of the law relating to abortion." In Mere N. Kisekka (ed.), *Women's Health Issues in Nigeria.* Zaria: Tamaza Publishing, 87-104.

Imber, Jonathan B. 1986. *Abortion and the Private Practice of Medicine.* New Haven: Yale University Press.

Institute of Medicine, National Academy of Sciences. 1975. *Legalized Abortion and the Public Health.* Washington, DC: National Academy of Sciences.

International Planned Parenthood Federation. 1993.

Overview, Responses, Action. *Planned Parenthood Challenges* 1. London: International Planned Parenthood Federation.

International Women's Health Coalition. 2000. "Beijing Plus Five: analysis of negotiations and final 'further actions' document." New York: International Women's Health Coalition.

Jaffe, Frederick, Barbara Lindheim, and Philip Lee. 1981. *Abortion Politics: Private Morality and Public Policy.* New York: McGraw Hill.

Jelen, Ted G. and Marthe A. Chandler (eds.) 1994. *Abortion Politics in the United States and Canada: Studies in Public Opinion.* Westport, CT: Praeger.

Jochle, Wolfgang. 1974. "Menses-inducing drugs: their role in antique, medieval, and renaissance gynecology and birth control." *Contraception* 10 (4), 428-436.

Joffe, Carole. 1995. *Doctors of Conscience: The Struggle to Provide Abortion Before and After Roe v. Wade.* Boston: Beacon Press.

Judges, Donald P. 1993. *Hard Choices, Lost Voices: How the Abortion Conflict Has Divided America, Distorted Constitutional Rights, and Damaged the Courts.* Chicago: Ivan R. Dee.

Kaufmann, K. 1997. *The Abortion Resource Handbook.* New York: Simon and Schuster.

Kolker, Aliza and B. Meredith Burke. 1998. *Prenatal Testing: A Sociological Perspective.* Westport, Conn.: Bergin and Garvey.

Laslett, Peter, Karla Oosterveen, and Richard M. Smith (eds.). 1980. *Bastardy and its Comparative History.* Cambridge, MA: Harvard University Press.

Lee, Luke T., and John M. Paxman. 1977. "Legal aspects of menstrual regulation." *Studies in Family Planning* 8 (10), 273-278.

Lee, Nancy Howell. 1969. *The Search for an Abortionist.* Chicago: University of Chicago Press.

Londoño E., Maria Ladi. 1989. "Abortion counseling: attention to the whole woman." In A. Rosenfield, M. F. Fathalla, A. Germain and C. L. Indriso (eds.), *Women's Health in the Third World: The Impact of Unwanted Pregnancy. International Journal of Gynecology & Obstetrics* Supplement 3, 169-174.

Lotstra, Hans. 1985. *Abortion: The Catholic Debate in America.* New York: Irvington.

Luker, Kristin. 1975. *Taking Chances: Abortion and the Decision Not to Contracept.* Berkeley: University of California Press.

_____. 1984. *Abortion and the Politics of Motherhood.* Berkeley: University of California Press.

_____. 1984. "The war between the women." *Family Planning Perspectives* 16 (3), 105-110.

_____. 1996. *Dubious Conceptions: The Politics of Teenage Pregnancy.* Cambridge, MA: Harvard University Press.

Lunneborg, Patricia. 1992. *Abortion: A Positive Decision.* New York: Bergin and Garvey.

Luo, Lin, Wu Shi-zhong, Chen Ziao-qing and Li Min-xiang. 1999. "Induced abortion among unmarried women in Sichuan

Province, China: a survey." In Axel I. Mundigo and Cynthia Indriso (eds.), *Abortion in the Developing World*. New Delhi: Vistaar Publications, 337-345.

MacKay, H. Trent, and Andrea Philllips MacKay. 1995. "Abortion training in obstetrics and gynecology residency programs in the United States, 1991-1992." *Family Planning Perspectives* 27 (3), 112-115.

Macklin, Ruth. 1989. "Liberty, utility, and justice: an ethical approach to unwanted pregnancy." In A. Rosenfield, M. F. Fathalla, A. Germain and C. L. Indriso (eds.), *Women's Health in the Third World: The Impact of Unwanted Pregnancy*. *International Journal of Gynecology & Obstetrics* Supplement 3, 27-50.

McClory, Robert. 1995. *Turning Point: The Inside Story of the Papal Birth Control Commission*. New York: Crossroads Press.

McDonagh, Eileen L. 1996. *Breaking the Abortion Deadlock: From Choice to Consent*. New York: Oxford University Press.

McIntosh, C. Alison and Jason L. Finkle. 1995. "The Cairo Conference on Population and Development: a new paradigm?" *Population and Development Review* 21 (2), 223—260.

McKeegan, Michele. 1992. *Abortion Politics: Mutiny in the Ranks of the Right*. New York: Free Press.

McLachlin, B. M. 1991. "Crime and women: feminine equality and the criminal law." Paper presented to the Elizabeth Fry Society, Calgary, Alberta. The Supreme Court of Canada. Unpublished.

Mensch, Barbara S., Judith Bruce, and M. E. Greene. 1998. *The Uncharted Passage: Girls' Adolescence in the Developing World*. New York: The Population Council.

Messer, Ellen and Kathryn E. May. 1994. *Back Rooms: Voices from the Illegal Abortion Era*. Buffalo, NY: Prometheus Books.

Michael, Robert T., John H. Gagnon, Edward O. Laumann, and

Gina Kolata. 1994. *Sex in America: A Definitive Survey.* Boston: Little Brown.

Miller, Barbara D. 1981. *The Endangered Sex: Neglect of Female Children in Rural North India.* Ithica NY: Cornell University Press.

Misago, Chizuru, and Walter Fonseca. 1999. "Determinants and medical characteristics of induced abortion among poor urban women in North-East Brazil." In Axel I. Mundigo and Cynthia Indriso (eds.), *Abortion in the Developing World.* New Delhi: Vistaar Publications, 217-227.

Mohr, James C. 1978. *Abortion in America: The Origins and Evolution of National Policy, 1800-1900.* New York: Oxford University Press.

Mundigo, Axel I., and Cynthia Indriso (eds.). 1999. *Abortion in the Developing World.* Published for the World Health Organization. New Delhi: Vistaar Publications.

Murray, Christopher J. L. and Alan D. Lopez (eds.). 1998. *Health Dimensions of Sex and Reproduction.* Published by the Harvard School of Public Health for WHO and the World Bank. Cambridge, MA: Harvard Univesity Press.

Naamane—Guessous, Soumaya. 1993. "Traditional methods still widely used." *Planned Parenthood Challenges* 1. London: International Planned Parenthood Federation, 14-16.

NARAL & NARAL Foundation. 2002. *Who Decides? A State-by-State Review of Abortion and Reproductive Rights.* Washington, DC: NARAL

Nathanson, Constance A. and Marshall H. Becker. 1980. "Obstetricians' attitudes and hospital abortion services." *Family Planning Perspectives* 12 (1), 26-32.

National Abortion Federation and the American College of Obstetricians and Gynecologists. 1991. *Who Will Provide*

Abortions? Ensuring the Availability of Qualified Practitioners.
Washington DC: National Abortion Federation.

National Abortion Federation. 1997. *The Role of Physician Assistants, Nurse Practitioners, and Nurse-Midwives in Providing Abortions: Strategies for Expanding Abortion Access.* Washington, DC: National Abortion Federation.

_____. 2000. *Clinical Policy Guidelines.* Washington, DC: National Abortion Federation.

Newman, Lucile F. (ed). 1985. *Women's Medicine: A Cross-Cultural Study of Indigenous Fertility Regulation.* New Brunswick: Rutgers University Press.

Noonan, John T. 1966. *Contraception: A History of Its Treatment by the Catholic Theologians and Canonists.* Cambridge: Harvard University Press.

_____. (ed.) 1970. *The Morality of Abortion: Legal and Historical Perspectives.* Cambridge: Harvard University Press.

O'Dowd, Michael J. and Elliot E. Phillipp. 1994. *The History of Obstetrics and Gynecology.* New York: Parthenon.

Omran, Abdel Rahim. 1992. *Family Planning in the Legacy of Islam.* New York: Routledge.

Osofsky, Howard J., and Joy D. Osofsky (eds.). 1973. *The Abortion Experience: Psychological and Medical Impact.* New York: Harper and Row.

Osofky, Joy D., Howard J. Osofsky, and Renga Rajan. 1973. "Psychological effects of abortion: with emphasis upon immediate reactions and followup." In Howard J. Osofky and Joy D. Osofsky (eds.), *The Abortion Experience: Psychological and Medical Impact.* New York: Harper and Row, 188-205.

Otoide, Valentine O., Frank Oronsaye and Friday E. Okonofua. 2001. "Why Nigerian adolescents seek abortion rather than contraception: evidence from focus-group discussions." *International Family Planning Perspectives* 27 (2), 77-81.

Outshoorn, Joyce. 1996. "The stability of compromise: abortion politics in Western Europe." In Marianne Githens and Dorothy McBride Stetson (eds.), *Abortion Politics: Public Policy in Cross-Cultural Perspective*. New York: Routledge, 145-165.

Paul, Maureen, E. Steve Lichtenberg, Lynn Borgatta, David Grimes and Phillip Stubblefields (eds.). 1999. *A Clinician's Guide to Medical and Surgical Abortion*. New York: W. B. Saunders.

Petchesky, Rosalind Pollack. 1984. *Abortion and Woman's Choice: The State, Sexuality, and Reproductive Freedom*. Boston: Northeastern University Press.

_____, and Karen Judd (eds.). 1998. *Negotiating Reproductive Rights: Women's Perspectives Across Countries and Cultures*. London and New York: Zed Books.

Peters, Julie, and Andrea Wolper (eds). 1995. *Women's Rights, Human Rights: International Feminist Perspectives*. New York: Routledge.

Physicians for Reproductive Choice and Health. 2001. *Mergers and You: The Physicians' Guide to Religious Hospital Mergers*. New York: Physicians for Reproductive Choice and Health.

Pick, Susan, Martha Givuadan, Suzanne Cohen, Marsela Alvarez, and Maria Elena Collado. 1999. "Pharmacists and market herb vendors: abortifacient providers in Mexico City." In Axel I. Mundigo and Cynthia Indriso (eds.), *Abortion in the Developing World*. New Delhi: Vistaar Publications, 293-310.

Pilpel, Harriet F. 1974. "The fetus as person: possible legal consequences of the Hogan-Helms amendment." *Family Planning Perspectives* 6 (1), 6-7.

Pinotti, José Aristodemo, and Anibal Faúndes. 1989. "Unwanted pregnancy: challenges for health policy." In A. Rosenfield, M. F. Fathalla, A. Germain and C. L. Indriso (eds.), *Women's Health in the Third World: The Impact of Unwanted Pregnancy*.

International Journal of Gynecology & Obstetrics Supplement 3, 97-102.

Pohlman, E, M., and J. M. Pohlman. 1969. *Psychology of Birth Planning.* Cambridge, MA: Schenkman.

Potts, Malcolm, Peter Diggory, and John Peel. 1977. *Abortion.* Cambridge: Cambridge University Press.

Rahman, Anika, Laura Katzive and Stanley K. Henshaw. 1998. "A global review of laws on induced abortion, 1985-1997." *International Family Planning Perspectives* 24 (2), 56-64.

Rapp, Rayna. 1999. *Testing Women, Testing the Fetus: The Social Impact of Amniocentesis in America.* New York: Routledge.

Reagan, L. J. 1997. *When Abortion Was a Crime: Women, Medicine, and Law in the United States, 1867-1973.* Berkeley, CA: University of California Press.

Reed, James. 1985. *The Birth Control Movement and American Society: From Private Vice to Public Virtue.* Princeton: Princteon University Press.

Riddle, John M. 1997. *Eve's Herbs: A History of Contraception and Abortion in the West.* Cambridge: Harvard University Press.

Rosenfield, A., M. F. Fathalla, A. Germain and C. L. Indriso (eds.). 1989. *Women's Health in the Third World: The Impact of Unwanted Pregnancy. International Journal of Gynecology & Obstetrics* Supplement 3.

Rossi, Alice S. and Bhavani Sitaraman. 1988. "Abortion in context: historical trends and future changes." *Family Planning Perspectives* 20 (6), 273-282.

Rossof, Jeannie I. 1975. "Is support of abortion political suicide?" *Family Planning Perspectives* 7 (1), 13-22.

Rothman, Barbara Katz. 1993. *The Tentative Pregnancy: How Amniocentesis Changes the Experience of Motherhood.* New York: Norton.

Russo, Nancy F. 1992. "Psychological aspects of unwanted pregnancy and its resolution." In J. Douglas Butler and David. F. Walbert (eds.), *Abortion, Medicine, and the Law* (4th ed.). New York: Facts on File, 593-626.

_____, and Kristin L. Zierk. 1992. "Abortion, childbearing and women's well-being." *Professional Psychology: Research and Practice* 23 (4), 269-280.

Ruzek, Sheryl Burt. 1978. *The Women's Health Movement: Feminist Alternatives to Medical Control.* New York: Praeger.

Sachdev, Paul (ed.). 1988. *International Handbook on Abortion.* New York: Greenwood Press.

_____. 1989. *Unlocking the Adoption Files.* Lexington, MA: Lexington Books.

_____. 1993. *Sex, Abortion, and Unmarried Women.* Westport: CT: Greenwood.

Sai, Fred T. 1993. "Unsafe abortion must be tackled now." *Planned Parenthood Challenges* 1. London: International Planned Parenthood Federation, 2-3.

Schaff, Eric A., Steyel H. Eisinger, Lisa S. Stadalius, Peter Franks, Bernard Z. Gore, and Suzanne Poppema. 1999. "Low-dose mifepristone 200 mg and vaginal misoprostol for abortion." *Contraception* 59, 1-6.

Scheper-Hughes, Nancy (ed.). 1987. *Child Survival: Anthropological Perspectives on the Treatment and Maltreatment of Children.* Boston: D. Reidel.

_____. 1992. *Death Without Weeping: The Violence of Everyday Life in Brazil.* Berkeley: University of California Press.

Scrimshaw, Susan C. M. 1984. "Infanticide in human populations: societal and individual concerns." In Glenn Hausfater and Sarah Blaffer Hrdy (eds.), *Infanticide: Comparative and Evolutionary Perspectives.* New York: Aldine, 439-462.

Sen, Gita, Adrienne Germain, and Lincoln C. Chen (eds.). 1994. *Population Policies Reconsidered: Health, Empowerment, and Rights.* Cambridge, MA: Harvard School of Public Health, distributed by Harvard University Press.

Simon, Rita J. 1998. *Abortion: Statutes, Policies, and Public Attitudes the World Over.* Westport, CT: Praeger.

Solinger, Rickie. 1993. "'A complete disaster': abortion and the politics of hospital abortion committees, 1950-1970." *Feminist Studies* 19 (2), 241-268.

_____ (ed.). 1997. *Abortion Wars: A Half Century of Struggle, 1950-2000.* Berkeley, CA: University of California Press.

Solter, Cathy., H. B. Johnston, and N. Hengen. 1997. "Care for postabortion complications: saving women's lives." *Population Reports*, Series L, No. 10. Baltimore, MD: Johns Hopkins School of Public Health, Population Information Program.

Solter, Cathy, Betty Farrell, and Miguel Gutierrez. 1997. *Manual Vacuum Aspiration: A Comprehensive Training Course.* New York: Pathfinder International.

Steffen, Lloyd. 1994. *Life/Choice: The Theory of Just Abortion.* Cleveland, OH: The Pilgrim Press.

Stein, Karen, Beverly Winikoff, and Virginia Kallianes. 1998. *Abortion: Expanding Access and Improving Quality.* New York: The Population Council.

Stern, Daniel N. *Diary of a Baby.* New York: Basic Books.

Stimezo Nederland. 1996. *Abortion Matters: 25 Years Experience in the Netherlands.* Maastricht: Stimezo Nederland.

Stotland, Nada L. (ed). 1991. *Psychiatric Aspects of Abortion.* Washington, DC: American Psychiatric Press.

_____. 1992. "The myth of the abortion trauma syndrome." *Journal of the American Medical Association* 268 (15), 2078-2079.

————. 1998. *Abortion: Facts and Feelings*. Washington, DC: American Psychiatric Press.

Studlar, Donley T. and Raymond Tatalovich. 1996. "Abortion policy in the United States and Canada: do institutions matter?" In Marianne Githens and Dorothy McBride Stetson (eds.), *Abortion Politics: Public Policy in Cross-Cultural Perspective*. New York and London: Routledge, 73-95.

Stubblefield, Phillip G. 1989. "Control of pain for women undergoing abortion." In A. Rosenfield, M. F. Fathalla, A. Germain and C. L. Indriso (eds.), *Women's Health in the Third World: The Impact of Unwanted Pregnancy*. *International Journal of Gynecology & Obstetrics* Supplement 3, 131-140.

Tadiar, Alfredo Flores. 1989. "Commentary on the law and abortion in the Philippines." In A. Rosenfield, M. F. Fathalla, A. Germain and C. L. Indriso (eds.), *Women's Health in the Third World: The Impact of Unwanted Pregnancy*. *International Journal of Gynecology & Obstetrics* Supplement 3, 89-92.

Tietze, Christopher. 1960. "Probabilities of pregnancy resulting from a single unprotected coitus." *Fertility and Sterility*, 11, 485-488.

———— and Stanley K. Henshaw. 1986. *Induced Abortion: A World Review*. New York: The Alan Guttmacher Institute.

Torres, Aida and Jacqueline Darroch Forrest. 1988. "Why do women have abortions?" *Family Planning Perspectives* 20 (4), 169-176.

Townsend, Rita, and Ann Perkins. 1991. *Bitter Fruit: Women's Experience of Unplanned Pregnancy, Abortion, and Adoption*. Alameda, CA: Hunter House.

Traina, Frank J. 1974. "Catholic clergy on abortion: preliminary findings of a New York state survey." *Family Planning Perspectives* 6 (3), 151-156.

Tribe, Laurence H. 1990. *Abortion: The Clash of Absolutes.* New York: W. W. Norton.

Tsui, Amy O., Judith Wasserheit, and John G. Haaga (eds.). 1997. *Reproductive Health in Developing Countries: Expanding Dimensions, Building Solutions.* Washington: National Academy Press.

United Nations, Department of Economic and Social Affairs. 1975. *Status of Women and Family Planning.* New York: United Nations.

_____, Population Division. 1992, 1993, 1995. *Abortion Policies: A Global Review.* Vols. I-III. New York: United Nations.

_____. 1999. *Levels and Trends of Contraceptive Use as Assessed in 1998.* New York: United Nations.

_____, Dept. of Public Information. 1996. *The Beijing Declaration and The Platform for Action.* New York: United Nations.

United States Census Bureau. 2001. *Fertility of American Women: Population Characteristics, June 1998.* Washington, DC: U.S. Department of Commerce.

Urquhart, D. R. and A. A. Templeton. 1991. "Psychiatric morbidity and acceptability following medical and surgical methods of induced abortion." *British Journal of Obstetrics and Gynecology* 98, 396-399.

van de Walle, Etienne, and Elisha P. Renne (eds.). 2001. *Regulating Menstruation: Beliefs, Practices, Interpretations.* Chicago: University of Chicago Press.

Varkey, Sanjani Jane. 2000. "Abortion services in South Africa: available yet not accessible to all." *Family Planning Perspectives* 26 (2), 87-88.

Villareal, Jorge. 1989. "Commentary on unwanted pregnancy, induced abortion, and professional ethics: a concerned physician's point of view." In A. Rosenfield, M. F. Fathalla, A. Germain and C. L. Indriso (eds.), *Women's Health in the Third*

World: The Impact of Unwanted Pregnancy. International Journal of Gynecology & Obstetrics Supplement 3, 51-56.

Wallis, Jim. 1996. *Who Speaks for God? An Alternative to the Religious Right—A New Politics of Compassion, Community, and Civility.* New York: Dell.

Walters, Wendell W. 1976. *Compulsory Parenthood: The Truth About Abortion.* Toronto: McClelland and Stewart.

Weddington, Sarah. 1992. *A Question of Choice.* New York: G. P. Putnam's Sons.

Weisman, Carol S., Constance A. Nathanson, Martha Ann Teitelbaum, Gary A. Chase and Theodore M. King. 1986. "Abortion attitudes and performance among male and female obstetrician-gynecologists." *Family Planning Perspectives* 18 (2), 67-73.

Westhoff, Carolyn, Frances Marks and Allan Rosenfield. 1993. "Residency training in contraception, sterilization, and abortion." *Obstetrics and Gynecology* 81 (2), 311-314.

Westhoff, Carolyn. 1995. "Abortion training in residency programs." *Journal of the American Medical Women's Association* 49 (5), 150-152 & 164.

Wills, Gary. 2000. *Papal Sin: Structures of Deceit.* New York: Doubleday.

Winikoff, Beverly. 1994. *Acceptability of First Trimester Abortion.* New York: The Population Council.

———— and Suzanne Wymelenberg. 1997. *The Whole Truth About Contraception: A Guide to Safe and Effective Choices.* Washington, DC: Joseph Henry Press (National Academy of Sciences).

Working Group on the Health Consequences of Contraceptive Use and Controlled Fertility. 1989. *Contraception and Reproduction: Health Consequences for Women and Children in the Developing World.* Washington, DC: National Academy Press.

World Health Organization, Division of Reproductive Health.

1998. *Emergency Contraception: A Guide for Service Delivery.* Geneva: World Health Organization.

———. 1998. *Unsafe Abortion: Global and Regional Estimates of Incidence of and Mortality Due to Unsafe Abortion, With a Listing of Available Country Data.* 3rd ed. Geneva: World Health Organization.

World Health Organization Task Force on Post-ovulatory Methods of Fertility Regulation. 2000. "Comparison of two doses of mifepristone in combination with misoprostol for early medical abortion: a randomised trial." *British Journal of Obstetrics and Gynaecology* 107 (April), 524-530.

World Health Organization Task Force on Psychosocial Research in Family Planning. 1981. "A cross-cultural study of menstruation: implications for contraceptive development and use." *Studies in Family Planning* 12 (1), 3-16.

Wu, Z. C. and others. 1992. "Induced abortion among unmarried women in Shanghai, China." *International Family Planning Perspectives* 18 (2), 51-53; 65.

Wyatt, Lewis and others. 1995. "Office abortion services for women: private physician providers." *Women and Health* 23 (2), 47-65.

Zeidenstein, Sondra, and Kirsten Moore (eds.). 1996. *Learning About Sexuality: A Practical Beginning.* New York: The Population Council.

Zhou, Wei-jin, Gao Er-shen, Yang Yao-ying, Quin Fei, and Tang Wei. 1999. "Induced abortion and the outcome of subsequent pregnancy in China: client and provider perspectives." In Axel I. Mundigo and Cynthia Indriso (eds.), *Abortion in the Developing World.* New Delhi: Vistaar Publications, 228-244.

Zimmerman, Mary Kay. 1977. *Passage Through Abortion: The Personal and Social Reality of Women's Experiences.* New York: Praeger.

Printed in the United States
1307200001B/336